AMERICA
at MID-CENTURY

The Truman Administration
The Eisenhower Administration

by

WILLIAM FRANK ZORNOW

The Kent State University

HOWARD ALLEN, Inc. Publishers

AMERICA at MID-CENTURY
The Truman Administration
The Eisenhower Administration

Copyright © 1959 by William Frank Zornow
Library of Congress Card Catalog No: 59-12822
FIRST PRINTING

Manufactured in the United States of America

Note on the production of this book:
Designed and composed by Jackson Typesetting Company of Jackson, Michigan, the text type is 10 point Old Style as are also the heads and subheads. The chapter heads are 24 point Coronet and the title page is set in Goudy Handtooled Open and Old Style. The presswork, by Hollerith-Whitelock, Inc., also of Jackson, Michigan, is offset lithography.

IN MEMORIAM

William Fred Zornow

Theodore H. A. Schroeder

P R E F A C E

This volume is offered to my colleagues on the assumption that many of them share one of my objections to history textbooks—they become outdated too soon. Recent and current events are of considerable interest to students because they are remembered and personal; but they are not covered in most textbooks because of infrequent revisions. In this volume I have confined myself to a brief summary of the leading developments in recent American foreign policy, politics, and domestic legislation. I have written it as a supplement to the larger textbooks in the introductory American history course, the advanced twentieth century American history course, and as background reading for the special type of current history course offered by many technical, professional, and non-liberal arts colleges. Future additions and revisions are planned in order to assure contemporary coverage.

I am indebted to Miss Margaret Waterman for her suggestions and editorial assistance. A brief bibliography does not pretend to be a complete list of the many excellent books in the field. Its purpose is to suggest supplementary reading for the student as well as acknowledge my indebtedness to those authors whose works I have read and whose ideas and materials I have utilized in the preparation of this book.

William Frank Zornow

April, 1959
Mentor, Ohio

CONTENTS

The Truman Administration

*The Contents and the Index for the second section of this book, *The Eisenhower Administration,* follow page 134. Note that instead of continuing with page number 135, this second section is renumbered starting with page 1. This device permits separate publication of the second section for use with the larger survey textbooks that carry through the Truman Administration but do not have a concluding chapter on the Eisenhower Administration. (See inside of the front cover for publication notice.)

I THE TRUMAN ADMINISTRATION

Mr. Truman of Missouri

Who was this man?

JOHNATHAN DANIELS later recalled that on April 13, 1945 Harry Truman entered the President's office, glanced about like a minute-sized, myopic owl, and gradually eased himself behind the large desk upon which only a few hours earlier the profuse collection of toys and trinkets assembled by Franklin D. Roosevelt had reposed. It seemed as if both the chair and the job ill-befitted the new incumbent.

Harry S. Truman had on April 12 been elevated to the presidency by the sudden but not unexpected death of President Roosevelt. Who was this man? Truman of Independence, Missouri, had entered both politics and matrimony at middle-age. He was born on May 8, 1884 at Lamar, Missouri. His formal education had been limited but despite the faulty vision which had forced him to wear heavy lenses since childhood he had read widely with a particular penchant for American history.

A veteran of the first World War, a farmer, a clerk, and an unsuccessful business man, Truman faced an uncertain future at a time in the early twenties when he was prevailed upon to stand for election as a Missouri county judge, a curiously misnamed, nonjudicial position. His election in 1922 began an active political career that has continued without interruption. He later claimed he never actually sought any political office to which he was elected. This seems true enough. He first appeared on the Washington scene in 1934 when he was elected to the United States Senate although, before the campaign, he had given serious thought to running for the House of Representatives. In spite of his consistent support of the administration's policies, Truman labored under a stigma. Kansas City politics were dominated by Boss

1

Tom Pendergast, and Truman, as a Missouri politician, was suspected of being the machine's Washington tool. Roosevelt paid little attention to him and on one occasion even angered the Senator by having James Farley call Pendergast to ask that he instruct Truman how to vote on an appointment. Although Pendergast's friend (a relationship which existed even when that political boss later faced indictment), Truman was not the mouthpiece of any machine. He voted his own way. He was never known for any lack of courage, independence, or strength of conviction. Senator Truman was re-elected in 1940 and following the fateful December 7, 1941, he offered his services to the Army. Chief of Staff General George C. Marshall put a high value on Truman's services in the Senate and dissuaded him from exercising his service option as a colonel in the National Guard. As the war effort gained momentum, Truman became alarmed at the waste and inefficiency generated by the billions being poured out for armaments. His honest, thrifty nature rebelled at such waste and the abuse and corruption that followed in its wake. From his knowledge of past history he knew that the Civil War Congress had created a Committee on the Conduct of the War. Although this group became a cross that Lincoln had to bear and, according to Lee, was worth several divisions to the Confederate cause, Truman believed that a new watchdog committee might be useful providing it avoided the mistakes of its predecessor. This was the origin of the Committee for the Investigation of the Defense Program, popularly known as the "Truman Committee." As one of the most effective organizations in Washington during the war, it saved the taxpayers millions of dollars. Truman's reputation as a useful legislator began to grow.

It would be a mistake to assume that by 1944 Truman came out of nowhere. He was a well-known and respected figure on the Washington scene by the time the Democrats made preparations for Roosevelt's fourth-term bid. When *Look Magazine* conducted a poll of Washington correspondents for the purpose of selecting the ten most valuable men in the capital, the only member of either house to make the list was Senator Truman of Missouri. The campaign to nominate an acceptable Vice President preceded the 1944 Democratic convention by several months. Truman, as usual, was destined to be chosen for a job for which he was not a candidate. He went to the Democratic Convention in Chicago with the expectation of supporting James F. Byrnes and then learned through conversations with the labor leaders—Sidney Hillman, Alexander F. Whitney, George Harrison, and Philip Murray—that he was also

2

being given serious consideration. In a meeting with Robert E. Hannegan and other party leaders, Truman was informed that he was Roosevelt's choice. Hannegan produced a letter written and signed by Roosevelt, which read, "Bob, it's Truman." Although the President had written letters which could be construed as endorsements of Henry A. Wallace and William O. Douglas, as well as encouraged Byrnes' expectations, later evidence suggests that Truman was his first choice. Roosevelt's aide, Harry Hopkins, told the President's biographer, Robert E. Sherwood, that the decision had been made long before the convention.

Many observers might have seconded Admiral William Leahy's cryptic comment when he learned of Roosevelt's decision, "Who the hell is Harry Truman?" but there were good reasons why Truman's nomination made sense. His consistent support of Roosevelt's program was proof that the President would have a friend in command of the Senate. With the end of the war in sight the problems of peace and reconstruction would again enhance the importance of the Senate when it would be advisable to have a Vice President with ten years' experience in dealing with that body. Furthermore, Truman—from a border state—had no known enemies nor had he alienated any significant group of voters.

. . . successful administration is . . . strong Presidential leadership.

After the election Roosevelt left the capital. He was in Washington less than one month out of the three that Truman served as Vice President. When Roosevelt died suddenly the new President was insufficiently briefed on the duties of his office. Fortunately, Truman was an avid reader and had acquired the skills that permitted him to assimilate the multitude of reports and digests that were suddenly thrust upon him by his new aides at the same time, he carried on with the responsibilities of office. He told reporters that he felt the stars, moon, and planets had all fallen on him at once. And although he greatly admired Roosevelt and considered himself an heir entrusted with the task of carrying out his predecessor's policies, he was not wholly in accord with all that Roosevelt had done. Roosevelt had not taken his aides into his confidence and for long periods of time he seemed actually to be functioning as his own Secretary of State and Secretary of the Treasury. Truman, unlike Roosevelt, did not propose to juggle half a dozen cabinet portfolios himself nor carry all the details of office in his own

3

head. He picked able administrators, showed them his confidence by placing them in complete charge, and let them do the work. He explained to members of his Cabinet that they were free to differ with him on matters of policy but would be expected to follow an official line once a policy had been established. He did make it plain that ultimate decisions were to be his and his alone.

In April 1945 the Cabinet consisted of: Edward R. Stettinius, Jr., Secretary of State; Henry Morgenthau, Jr., Secretary of the Treasury; Henry L. Stimson, Secretary of War; James Forrestal, Secretary of the Navy; and Attorney General Francis Biddle. Harold L. Ickes, Claude R. Wickard, Henry L. Wallace, and Frances Perkins headed the departments of the Interior, Agriculture, Commerce, and Labor respectively. Frank C. Walker was Postmaster General. Changes were made almost immediately. Walker left on July 30 to be replaced by Robert Hannegan, the chairman of the Democratic National Committee. Before Independence Day, Thomas Clark had replaced Biddle, and Clinton Anderson moved into the agriculture post. Frances Perkins was about ready to leave her job. Truman had already indicated his conviction to Budget Director Harold D. Smith that postwar labor-management problems would require a new Secretary of Labor acceptable not only to both sides but to Congress as well. Federal Judge Lewis B. Schwellenbach was his choice. With Wallace, these four new appointments made five men in the Cabinet from states west of the Mississippi.

Another important cabinet change occurred early in July. Truman wanted James F. Byrnes as Secretary of State, as soon as Secretary Stettinius could complete his work at the San Francisco Conference on the United Nations. Since there was no Vice President, Truman was concerned because his successor, in the event of his own death, would be Stettinius, a man who had never held an elective office. The President intended to recommend a new order of presidential succession, but meanwhile wished to be sure that the Secretary of State, his next in line, would be a man with administrative experience as well as one who had held elective office. Byrnes was appointed in July, as was Fred M. Vinson, who replaced Morgenthau. Vinson had succeded Byrnes sometime earlier in the influential position of Director of the Office of War Mobilization and Reconversion. John Snyder moved into this post when Vinson departed.

By August Truman retained only four of Roosevelt's Cabinet: Wallace, Stimson, Ickes, and Forrestal. "I don't know how I ever got

4

out of that mudhole," Truman later remarked in speaking of his Cabinet, but even at that time he was by no means "out of it." Many chief executives have had men in their Cabinets who were also rivals for the presidency. Lincoln had Salmon Chase and William Seward; Truman had Byrnes and Wallace, either of whom could have been Vice President in 1944. There was bound to be some friction and resentment. The break with Byrnes began in 1945, although he did not agree to resign until 1946. The Wallace crisis and the showdown came later, but when it did come, it was more dramatic and serious.

Truman, who knew Congress better than any other President of this century, was, at the same time just as much an advocate of party government as any one of the legislators. Many pundits were sure that Truman's elevation to the presidency would mean the beginning of a new era in which Congress would overshadow the chief executive as was the case after Lincoln's death and Wilson's departure from office. But this was not the case. Truman believed in teamwork, but he believed that each branch of the government had its specific responsibilities as well as powers. It was his responsibility as chief executive to prevent Congress, or his own subordinates, from encroaching on his duties and powers. To Truman the President was five men in one: executive officer of the government, party leader, commander of the armed forces, social head of the state, and performer of certain limited legislative duties.

Truman's first-term occupancy of the White House was marked by a growing estrangement between the President and the leaders of both parties in and out of Congress. This was inevitable, although Truman's decision to support certain policies undoubtedly widened the rift. From 1933 to 1945 Roosevelt had held together a heterogeneous party composed of groups representing every shade of political, economic, and social thinking. Perhaps the depression and the war were largely responsible for his success, since such crises compelled everyone to cooperate for survival. And it is undoubtedly true that even had Roosevelt lived, he would have been unable to secure the continued support of such diverse elements. The end of the war was to release forces that would have been beyond the skill of even that adroit politician to control.

Truman was heir to these problems and faced the dissolution of the party. His position was not unlike Andrew Johnson's. Truman had to conclude a war successfully, negotiate an acceptable peace settlement, demobilize and reconvert the greatest military and industrial machine in the nation's history, as well as try to continue the social,

5

economic, and political gains of the New Deal years. All this had to be done by working with a Congress bent upon reversing the fifteen-year trend toward strengthening the excutive branch of government at the expense of the legislative branch. It had to be done at a time when the new President was being compared unfavorably with the old; Johnson had likewise seemed a poor copy of Lincoln. Truman's problems were even more serious, since he was the only President to be in office during two wars. He came to power in the midst of war, passed through a period of reconstruction and left in the midst of another "police action." A modern Tolstoi, writing the history of Truman's era, might have used the title, *War and Peace and War.* Louis Koenig, in his volume *The Truman Administration,* said that Truman's greatest gifts were courage, the ability to see issues clearly, and the skill to explain the issues in succinct and uncomplicated language.

Americans have always tried to reduce personalities and issues to too simple terms. After all, every American is, at heart, something of a Manichean heretic. Men, problems, and solutions are either, good or bad, right or wrong, white or black. It is evident, however, that a President cannot make a selection from among correct or completely good choices. The selection is only from among choices more or less evil, incorrect, and discolored. From 1945 to 1952 Truman chose repeatedly from the available courses of action the one which, although not perfect, seemed most acceptable and workable. Having made the choice, he worked to implement it without public deception, without confession of misgiving, and without periodic, confidence-shattering assertions that he was drastically altering his course. He set a course, plodded inflexibly toward it without worrying about the reaction of others. "A successful administration is one of strong presidential leadership. Weak leadership —or no leadership—produces failure and often disaster." This was Truman speaking on the occasion of his seventieth birthday.

A New Course for American Foreign Policy

. . . the required instrumentalities.

NOT SINCE Peter the Hermit roused the West in the eleventh century to save the Holy Land from the infidel has there been a people so responsive to the crusading spirit as Americans. All our wars, in our eyes, have been crusades to gain lofty objectives. Like Peter's crusaders, too many Americans thought that a better world could be achieved through good will, prayer, hope, and faith; but these, after 1945, proved to be insufficient weapons against intransigent and unresponsive dictatorships. In 1945 many Americans accepted the optimistic premise that all men by nature wish to be free, at peace, and comfortable; and that these universal goals could be realized if people would cooperate. They had failed to read history. Few realized that countless alliances, born of wartime necessity, were moribund before the ink had dried on the treaties. The friend of one war was as likely as not to be the enemy of the next. There was a general but erroneous assumption that the wartime allies could establish a permanent system of international cooperation which would bring freedom, peace, and the full dinner pail to all men.

We had tried to formalize our postwar dream of international security in the Atlantic Charter of 1941 and the United Nations Declaration of January 1, 1942. But before this could be accomplished there were enemy states to be disposed of and liberated countries to be reconstructed. Moreover, there was a growing suspicion that another *bête noire* had risen to replace Hitler and Mussolini. Our confident expectation that we could draw the Russians into a permanent system of international cooperation was already in question before Truman took office. Despite the warnings early in 1945 that the Soviet would not fit into our plans for a postwar world, the suspicion had not become general. We were still talking about the magnificent achievements of the Red Army and toasting our great and good friends—the Russians. The horrible caricature of the bearded anarchist of the twenties and thirties had disappeared from the public press.

Whatever America's objectives might have been for the postwar world, it should have been evident that certain instrumentalities were necessary to effect them. In April, 1945, America possessed the military, economic, and political power (the required instrumentalities) to bring its plans to fruition. However, as events developed during that year, America dissipated its strength rapidly. At the height of its military power, even before the Japanese surrendered, the United States began to reduce its armed forces unwisely. When the Japs collapsed unexpectedly any plan for a gradual demobilization soon evaporated before the inexorable pressure of the voters. Within twelve months the United States did not have the military power to initiate, let alone implement, its policies.

Our economy and industrial production suffered a similar fate. Although industrial production continued at high rates during the war, its postwar direction changed rapidly. There was a demand for consumer goods, and without a system of government controls it was impossible to keep industry geared to the production of war materiel needed to enforce American policies abroad. The demands of the "free" economy group plus the demands of those who wanted balanced budgets, tax cuts, and less spending were too much to offset the warnings of those who maintained that we could not initiate our foreign policies without the economic power to support them.

A political element is also necessary if military and economic power are to be used to enforce foreign policy. During the war the allies operated through a host of committees, agencies, and organizations, but many of them were speedily disbanded after the war or allowed to lapse through lack of use. Some survived, but the trend was unmistakably toward the termination of cooperative wartime agencies. And key personnel drifted away from Washington into private pursuits with the consequent loss of guidance and experience in national affairs. Despite the decline of our military, economic, and political structure after the war, it could be argued that the potential remained. But as events transpired it was soon shown that this potential was not enough to assure the success of policies.

America's goals for the reestablishment of international society were theoretically achievable and our resources sufficient for their realization. The implementation of American foreign policy broke down on the specific level, even though it appeared achievable on the general level. The general inevitably must be reduced to the specific. But, those whose responsibility it was to put our policies into operation in concrete instances had to call on actual forces in being—not simply military potential. The memory of the Marines' glory at Guadalcanal was no help to men confronted with a difficult situation in Poland or the Balkans. They could only use the resources at hand, not those which might be produced in a year if an assembly line could be retooled for war production. They had to make use of administrative agencies staffed by actual people, not agencies that existed on paper only. Thus the disparity between goals and means, between the actual and the potential, became glaringly apparent. The goals of 1945 were unattainable. It is only against this background that Soviet expansion can be explained. Truman was blamed for failure to impede that expansion but he and his policy planners were often powerless to act in the face of popular demands to demobilize, to buy new homes and cars, and to return to the more lucrative pursuits of private life.

> . . . . *a mockery of democratic procedure.*

Roosevelt died in the midst of preparation for a world conference at San Francisco to frame a United Nations Charter. Truman announced that he would not attend the meeting or make any change in the delegation his predecessor had chosen. One of the delegates was Arthur H. Vandenberg, Republican Senator from Michigan, who was to become one of the staunchest supporters of the new administration's foreign policy. During his earlier career Vandenberg had been an ardent isolationist but after Pearl Harbor he became a champion of internationalism. By now there was much concern over Russia's actions even though the Yalta conference in February 1945 had marked the high point of allied cooperation. At this meeting Roosevelt, Churchill, and Stalin had agreed that democratic regimes were to be established in Europe. However, the conference had scarcely adjourned when the Russians installed Communist-dominated regimes in Hungary, Bulgaria, Rumania, and Poland. They proceeded at once to make a mockery of democratic procedure with their one-party, bayonet-point rule.

The principal problem of 1945 was Poland. The war began in 1939 ostensibly to save Polish independence and now that unhappy land had fallen under another dictatorship presumably imposed against the will of the majority. During the war there had been a Polish government in exile in London and the Russians sponsored another one at Lublin. At Yalta it had been decided to broaden the Lublin government by the inclusion of Polish democratic elements living abroad as well as in Poland. This new government was to arrange for free elections. The Russians later insisted they dared not weaken the Lublin government by an indiscriminate inclusion of non-Communist leaders in Poland; that they could not permit genuinely free elections since Russian security required a friendly government in adjacent Poland.

Because the Russians violated their agreement, Churchill urged that Truman join him in a statement publicly setting forth the reasons for the Big-Three estrangement. Truman could not draw his big gun on Russia since his advisers stressed the growing need for her assistance against Japan. They also feared that news of a breakdown in negotiations with Russia would demoralize the Polish people. However, a note was dispatched to Stalin restating Anglo-American concepts of the Yalta agreement concerning Poland. When, on April 20, 1945, Truman met W. Averell Harriman—then ambassador to Russia—Stettinius, Under-Secretary of State Joseph C. Grew, and Russian expert Charles E. Bohlen, Harriman warned Truman that the Russians gave evidence of having become expansionist-minded. Truman promised to be firm in dealing with them.

A few days later Molotov stopped off in Washington enroute to San Francisco. He cleverly avoided direct answers to Truman's insistent interrogation about Poland and about Russia's interpretation of Yalta. The President pledged that America would abide faithfully by all its promises but warned the Soviet emissary that cooperation was a two-way street. Only once did Molotov's irritation come to the surface. "I have never been talked to like that in my life," he told Truman. "Carry out your agreement and you won't get talked to like that," snapped the President, as the brief conference terminated.

From Washington Molotov moved to the Golden Gate with an attaché case filled with monkey wrenches of assorted sizes. At several points he succeeded neatly in jeopardizing the success of the conference but the main crisis arose over the veto. It had been agreed at Yalta that the permanent members of the Security Council of the proposed United Nations could not exercise the veto if a member state brought up for discussion a complaint against one of them. Molotov now insisted that even a proposed discussion could be vetoed.

It was fortunate that, as the conference tottered on the brink of dissolution, Harry Hopkins was in Moscow to interview Stalin. The dictator agreed that the American position was correct and Molotov discontinued his attempts to alter the Yalta agreement on the veto. The United Nations Charter was drafted and ratified by the United States Senate by an impressive vote of eighty-nine to two. The completion of the charter in June 1945 left the way clear for the last great wartime meeting of the heads of state. The Potsdam conference was convened under trying circumstances. Roosevelt had died, Stalin's arrival was delayed by a minor heart attack, and in the midst of the conference Churchill had to return to England for the national election only to be defeated by the Labor Party. The new Prime Minister, Clement Atlee, replaced Churchill during the last stages of the conference.

Potsdam . . . with trump cards already played.

After a brief delay, the Potsdam conference met on July 17, 1945. This was Truman's first assay into world politics but he faced his new assignment with bumptious confidence. In his opinion the handling of foreign affairs was based on a thorough knowledge of local affairs. To him, people were the same everywhere and the difference between human problems in Jackson County, Missouri and the human problems of the world was one merely of degree, not kind. It was this interpretation of foreign problems which induced Truman to liken Stalin to Tom Pendergast (and this was meant as a compliment), and also prompted his remark that Russian affairs were similar to those in Jackson County. "But," added the President, "you have to recognize that the people of Jackson County came out of the dark ages in 900 A.D., while Moscow emerged from the dark ages only in 1917."

The Russians were confident and suspicious. They were confident because they had proved themselves. Their system, lampooned and ridiculed by the West for a generation, had stood up under the bludgeoning of one of the most formidable war machines in history. Russia was now sitting down as an equal at the same table with the haughty capitalists and imperialists of the West, and she could not help but gloat a little. The Russians were suspicious because they remembered the British had openly expressed their hopes that Germany would attack Russia, that the West had always opposed the Communist system, and that America had rapidly cancelled Russian lend-lease after the fall of Germany in May.

The Russians were also thinking solely in terms of power. Stalin talked as if the little states did not exist at all and opined that the Big Three should handle everything themselves. When the question of Catholic rights in Poland was brought up, Stalin uttered a now-famous cynical remark, "How many divisions has the Pope?" To the Russians actual power was all that counted.

The two main points of discussion were Germany and Poland. Germany had capitulated before the Yalta agreements had been put into effect. She was without a government, so a workable arrangement had to be made immediately. At Potsdam it was decided to disarm and demilitarize the country completely as well as root out all remnants of Naziism. Germany was to be divided into four zones of military occupation, but it was understood that the Control Council in Berlin (the city was also divided into four separate zones of administration) would operate the country as an economic unit. Although no central government would exist, it was assumed that the four allies would work together harmoniously. Special secretaries were to be established for such economic activities as communication, industry, trade, transport, and finance. Efforts were to be made to establish a democratic regime in Germany.

At Yalta the biggest stumbling block had been Poland and it continued to be a major issue at Potsdam. The Russians had still taken no steps toward the free elections decided upon in February, although they offered reassurances that they would take place soon. Much German territory had been added to Poland but neither Britain nor the United States would accept as final any Polish occupation of German territory as far west as the Oder and Neisse Rivers. It had been agreed that Poland was to receive some German territory to compensate for lands lost east of the Curzon line to Russia but this was too much! However, the fact remained that Poland occupied this area and to dislodge her would take more than pleas and cajoling, particularly when big-brother Moscow was arguing the case for her.

The conference also created a Council of Foreign Ministers entrusted with the tasks of drafting peace treaties, reaching decisions concerning reparations, and arranging the settlement of less important matters. The session ended with many serious problems still unsolved although it was felt that definite strides had been made toward dealing with Germany.

There was still the matter of Japan. At Yalta and Potsdam Russia had agreed to intervene in the Asiatic war but only on condition that she be restored to a position on the Asian continent similar to the one she had occupied before the Russo-Japanese War. Both Britain and America agreed to Soviet demands and also induced China to sign a treaty with Russia acceding to this settlement.

On the first day of the Potsdam conference, President Truman received secret news that an atomic weapon had been successfully tested in New Mexico. This momentous project, undertaken at Roosevelt's orders, was one of the most closely guarded secrets of the war. Truman had encountered it briefly during his senatorial investigation days but had shied away when requested to do so. He had scarcely taken office when Stimson informed him about the project. Truman ordered it continued until satisfactory results had been achieved.

The news of the bomb was relayed to Churchill immediately but it was not until July 24 that Stalin was told of the new development. He seemed rather unimpressed and simply said that he hoped good use would be made of it against the Japanese. At Potsdam Truman consulted with his advisers about the bomb and it was at this time that a decision was made to use it against the Japanese. Actually, his military advisers were not too certain that the bomb would be decisive; they still thought that the Japanese home islands would have to be invaded by the American army and they did not look for Japanese collapse much before the end of 1946. They were worried about the concentration of Japanese troops in Manchuria. This great independent force was still intact and were it to be moved to the home islands, American losses during the invasion would be tremendous. Consequently, Russian entry into the war was sought as a means of neutralizing the Japanese Manchurian army.

In retrospect it would seem that the United States gained little from the Potsdam conference. Eastern Europe was still under Communist control, and the four-power administration in Germany was bound to produce problems. When Russo-American relations deteriorated so rapidly after 1946 Truman was criticized for not having allowed the American Army to penetrate farther into eastern Europe. The suggestion was made during the war that the American Army hold a line from Berlin, through Prague, to Vienna, but it was overruled. The Russians were allowed to enter these cities first. A proposal to send our columns into Berlin ahead of the Russians was rejected by General Eisenhower, who explained that the German capital had no strategic value and would not be worth the effort. No one in 1945 had yet come to think in terms of propaganda, of ideological and psychological advantages in the coming struggle for power. Actually, the American Army did advance beyond the original point agreed upon and when Germany surrendered on May 7 American troops held territory that was to have been liberated by Russia. The British urged the Americans to sit tight and use their position for bargaining with Russia. But Truman overruled their suggestion and in June our troops began to withdraw from this area. This was on the eve of Potsdam. The decision left Truman with all his trump cards already played. He had nothing with which to oppose Stalin except the ineffective but satisfying knowledge that we had behaved as men of good conscience.

After Potsdam—atoms and economics.

Truman was still on his way home aboard the cruiser *USS Augusta* when word was flashed on August 6 that the atomic bomb had been dropped on Hiroshima. Within a few days he learned that the Japanese were ready to surrender. On August 14, 1945 the second World War ended.

With the war behind it the United States turned to remodeling the world in its own image. But, for the first time, our planners were brought to grips with short-term goals and specific instances. The first hope was to transform the enemy states into peaceful democratic countries. For the two principal enemies the plans were decidedly different. In the United States there was much hatred for Germany. She was held responsible for the holocaust of World War II and the revelations of Nazi brutality had sickened the public against all things Teutonic. Germany, according to what came to be known as the Morgenthau Plan, was to be disarmed, denazified, and reduced to an agrarian society. Her central government was to be obliterated and she was to be stripped of her industries for reparations. Russia was to be permitted to take capital goods from the other three German zones, as well as her own, to compensate for the extensive damage done to the homeland by the German invasion. The aim was to punish and weaken Germany so that she would neither wish nor be able to wage aggressive war again but it was soon recognized that she could not be destroyed without creating a power vacuum in central Europe as well as a weak link in Europe's economic structure.

As for Japan, militarism was to be rooted out and her capacity for aggressive war reduced. Her entire culture pattern was to be altered to prepare the ground for the seeds of democracy. However, there were also significant differences. The central government was not destroyed, as it had been in Germany, and because of our growing suspicion of Russia, we

14

refused to assent to any type of zonal administration of the home islands.

In the Moscow Declaration of 1943 the powers proclaimed that Austria was to be freed, but the Soviet position in Bulgaria, Hungary, Rumania, and Poland seemed unassailable. Tito was busy building a Soviet-like state in Yugoslavia. Any notion of free elections and democratic regimes in these countries had gone down the drain. The Russians were allowed to do as they pleased in eastern Europe, primarily because we lacked the power to do anything about it. It had been argued during the war that pro-Soviet regimes in eastern Europe were necessary to assure the Russian line of communication to the German front. By 1945 they could not be dislodged. Only Czechoslovakia seemed to have escaped from the Soviet orbit. For the other European states—France, Greece, Belgium, Italy, and the Netherlands—American ambitions were about the same. We hoped to strengthen their economies, reestablish democratic regimes, and help them regain the prestige and position they had lost during the war. The position of Italy, a former enemy, was unique, and plans to rebuild that country met with strong opposition from the Soviets as well as from France and Yugoslavia, both of whom had suffered severely at Italy's hands. The most serious problem arose over France, since it was the only one of this group which had previously enjoyed major power status. France's drop had been deeper, and so it was proportionately more difficult to restore her to her former state. Much effort was expended by the United States to underwrite France's restoration to the status of world power; a restoration that proved to be largely fictitious.

The position of China was most important to the United States in 1945. With Japan eliminated as a power in the Orient, a vacuum had been created. The United States, hoping to substitute China for Japan, exerted much effort to prove that China was also a world power. As in the case of France, this led to disillusionment and pathetic failure. Nevertheless, America continued in its determination to restore China's lost territory, strengthen the government of Chiang Kai-shek, and infuse new life into the country's economy.

This, briefly, was the situation after Potsdam and the Japanese armistice in August 1945. Between the formal surrender of Japan on September 2, 1945 and the announcement of the Truman Doctrine on March 12, 1947, some significant changes occurred in our concept of foreign policy. When Truman spoke on Navy Day in October 1945 he outlined a policy, which, with the exception of its internationalism, might have been endorsed by any of his predecessors. America, he said, sought no territory, believed in self-government for all men, would approve no territorial changes unless they represented the wishes of the people concerned, would recognize no government imposed against popular will, endorsed freedom of the seas, opposed militarism, favored easy access to raw materials for all, re-emphasized "good neighborliness" for the states of the western hemisphere, favored full economic cooperation of all nations to improve the standard of living, endorsed freedom of religion and the United Nations. It was our inability to achieve these aims that forced a re-evaluation of our policies.

The many international conferences held late in 1945 and early in 1946 emphasized the growing differences between the United States and Russia. Our specific indictments against Russia included the failure to treat Germany as a single economic unit as opposed to merely a zone of another satellite. It included the disruption of the free flow of agricultural goods and raw materials to Western Germany in return for manufactured products. This paralyzed the entire German economy. Russia delayed the elections in Poland until, in January 1947, she was certain that the Lublin government was in control. The proposed peace treaties for Germany's five European allies—Italy, Hungary, Rumania, Bulgaria, and Finland— were also delayed. With the latter four countries the Russians were ultimately able to secure treaties which protected their interests and assured their economic and political control in these areas. In Finland's case the Russians were content, not to occupy the country, but to lop off some small strategic provinces and shackle the Finnish economy by heavy reparations settlements. Despite American and British willingness to give Italy special consideration for having joined us against Germany, the Russians insisted upon, and to a measure achieved, a harsher treaty than originally planned. With Austria the Russians were more tractable, and although the country was divided into four zones, they did not attempt to operate their own as an independent entity. Elections in Austria were decidedly anti-Communist.

New points of friction developed on the European periphery. In 1942 the Russians and British had agreed that all foreign troops would be withdrawn from Persia (Iran) within six months after the end of hostilities. Both countries had specific zones of administration and, as in Germany, the Russians gave every evidence of regarding their zone as little more than an enclave of the homeland. American and British troops left before the deadline of March 2 but the Russians lingered to enjoy the salubrious climate of Iran while a movement was generated by self-determinationists

16

who petitioned for annexation by the Soviet Constituent Republic of
Azerbaijan. Iran brought an indictment against the Soviets before the
ations. Suddenly, in May 1946, the Russians reversed themselves
drew voluntarily. In Turkey the Russians wanted adjacent ter-
d a new agreement on the use of the Straits. In Greece the Soviets
d the Communist rebels along the northern border. Through the
adjacent to Greece, Russia was able to support Greek rebels
plies of arms, leaders, and advice.

all the issues between Russia and the United States in 1945-1946
s more significant than that of atomic energy and its control. On
3 the President went before Congress and requested special
n so that some kind of national policy governing atomic energy
e formulated. He proposed the creation of an Atomic Energy
sion and indicated his desire to initiate talks with England and
Canada since, at Quebec in August 1943, Roosevelt and Churchill had
agreed to share atomic information. The new prime minister, Clement
Atlee, was due to arrive in Washington to discuss atomic energy as well
as a contemplated loan of five billion dollars. Before Atlee arrived in
Washington the President delivered his Navy Day foreign policy speech
on October 27. This was soon followed by a conference of Truman, Atlee,
and Canadian Premier MacKenzie King in November to reach an agreement on the use and control of atomic energy. All seemed to agree that
the United Nations should exercise the control over its more destructive
forms.

Actually, the national and international control of atomic energy was,
by 1945, an international question, and had to be treated accordingly.
Truman's proposal to Congress had been followed promptly by the introduction of the May-Johnson bill on atomic energy. This rapidly became
the most controversial bill of the session. A special committee on atomic
energy was created in the Senate under Brien McMahon of Connecticut to
consider the question. The issue at stake was whether atomic energy
should be under military or civilian control and both Truman and Mc-
Mahon were inclined toward the latter. On March 12, 1946, McMahon's
committee approved an amendment, introduced by Senator Vandenberg,
which would have virtually assured military control over atomic energy
in America. Both Truman and Byrnes were afraid that the Senate move
would jeopardize plans for international control.

The question of international control had also been referred to a
special committee appointed by Secretary of State Byrnes and headed by

his subsequent successor Dean Acheson. Acheson's committee report on international control of atomic energy became known as the Acheson-Lilienthal Report. It was decided to appoint Bernard M. Baruch as the American representative to the United Nations Commission on Atomic Energy and it was his job to present the Acheson proposals to the UN. Baruch brought the American plan before the UN which promptly revealed the sharp division between the Russian and the American viewpoints. The United States proposed the creation of an international commission with full power to license and inspect all activities in this field throughout the world. Once this agency was established, the United States promised to destroy its existing bomb supply and surrender its secrets to the commission. The Russians urged us, in effect, to reveal our secrets and destroy our bombs first. Only after this was done would they join us in the creation of a world commission with very limited powers.

Although the UN deadlocked and was unable to solve the question of international control, Congress finally arrived at a suitable settlement of the domestic side of the problem. The congressional bill was amended to restore civilian control and was approved August 1, 1946. The Atomic Energy Commission, created by this act, went into operation on January 1, 1947, with David E. Lilienthal, former head of TVA, as its chairman.

All of these issues between America and Russia brought about a change in our foreign policy. In 1946 we tried to bolster a faltering Britain through a $3,750,000,000 loan and a $650,000,000 settlement under the terms of the Lend-Lease Act. There was a growing conviction that only by firmness could we induce the Soviets to cooperate in the achievement of universal peace, democracy, and economic revival.

During 1946 the American people were confronted with a serious foreign policy debate. At that time Harry Vaughan, Truman's Washington aide, and Franc L. McCluer, president of Westminster College, had prevailed upon the President to ask Winston Churchill, who was then vacationing in Florida, to speak before the college in Fulton, Missouri. The British leader said nothing new at Fulton. He had expressed such views to a limited circle of acquaintances for a long time but for the first time they were given wide reportorial coverage. This was his famous "Iron Curtain" speech. Although the term had already appeared in his private correspondence in 1945, it was not until the Fulton speech that it became popular. He cautioned the American public that the only thing the Russians understood was strength, particularly military strength, and he proposed that his country and the United States should join in an alliance to achieve peace. He rejected completely the prevailing American concept that peace would be realized and the United Nations made to function on the basis of big power solidarity. Such harmony did not and could not exist, he said, but an Anglo-American alliance would bring Russia to terms by confronting it with a power bloc that it would respect. This view was not too well received at the time in the United States.

Six months later, on September 12, 1946, a second possible approach was suggested by Henry Wallace. He went before a New York audience and scored the United States for having frightened the Russians by belligerent talk. He called upon America to substitute softness for harshness and to utilize every possible means of building confidence and relieving suspicion. The Wallace message produced a serious crisis for the administration. Secretary Wallace later claimed that he and the President had gone over the speech page by page; Truman was just as emphatic in his insistence that he had not read any part of it. At the time of the speech it was widely assumed that what Wallace said in New York represented official administration policy.

Byrnes, who was in Europe at that moment trying to stiffen resistance to the Russians, suddenly found the ground cut from under him by a fellow cabinet officer, apparently with Presidential sanction. Byrnes and Truman held a teletype conversation in which the President assured his Secretary of State that Wallace did not have his official blessing and that he would not speak again. Senator Vandenberg announced that, although the Senate was eager to support administration policy, it could follow only one Secretary of State at a time. It was clearly evident that Wallace had outlived his usefulness in the Cabinet and he was ousted. W. Averell Harriman took his place. The Wallace debacle placed another roadblock between Truman and Byrnes. Earlier in 1946 the President criticized his Secretary for not keeping him fully informed on developments during a European conference and also accused him of having been too soft toward Russia on the matter of the eastern European states. In April 1946 Byrnes suggested that his resignation might be in order. However, he continued in the Cabinet throughout the year in order to negotiate treaties with Italy, Hungary, Rumania, and Bulgaria. By December 1946 the treaties were completed and signed at Paris on February 10, 1947. Byrnes had left the Cabinet in January, and Truman immediately summoned General George C. Marshall to assume his place.

As far as the country was concerned, neither the Churchill nor the Wallace views were acceptable. Some kind of middle-road policy was necessary in the fall of 1946, particularly in view of our declining armed forces, approaching congressional elections, popular concern over taxes, unbalanced budgets, and the size of the national debt. A growing restiveness in the Senate hampered the President in dealing with foreign problems.

By January 1947, in his State of the Union message, Truman emphasized the close relationship between goals and means and a difference between actual and potential power. Either our goals in foreign policy had to be reduced in accordance with the limited means available or we had to increase our means to support our world-wide goals. Potential power had to be converted into actual power.

By this time the public's attitude had also changed. We had come to regard the Soviet in a new light. We began to face the fact that it was no longer a nation of backward, taciturn people fearful of their security and suspicious of foreign influence who conceivably might, in time, grow more sophisticated, confident, and gregarious. They were now looked upon as a nation which—because of its peculiar, aberrant philosophy—regarded itself as waging a kind of perpetual holy war against western capitalism. Under these circumstances all hope of agreement, all hope of eventual change, all hope of regeneration would be as vain as the notion that the Devil could be brought to baptism. Our experts in 1946 concluded that the Soviet forces could overrun most of Europe in a few months, although we might save England from disaster and also hold our position in Japan. Even though Russia had the power, it was also assumed that she would restrain herself from using it. It was reasoned that she was too badly shaken by the war to undertake new conquests and would direct her main attention toward consolidating her position. The atomic bomb was also looked upon as a Russian deterrent although it would seem that we reached this conclusion in retrospect.

American experts, in 1946, were gradually coming to see Soviet objectives in a new light and no longer believing that she could be brought into a world society as a cooperative member. They were also conceiving a different structure of international power. With our American gift for over-simplification and tendency to reduce all issues to two sides, the popular concept of a "bipolar" world was inevitable. Hope that four powers working together could run the world was fading and the obvious conclusion was that concentration of power in two places reduced other states to the status of satellites or pensioners.

In 1946 it was evident that the Soviet had to be restrained by means of economic, political, and military pressures with one, two, or all three used to fit the individual circumstance. However, since 1945 the United States had been committed irrevocably to the United Nations, which Americans regarded as the ultimate hope of world security. It was true, by 1946, that Russian attitudes had made the United Nations a mockery but did we dare bypass it ourselves? By 1947 the role of the United States in foreign affairs was one based on an economic policy rather than political or military policies. Our first significant postwar change in foreign policy did not operate through the United Nations, but neither was the UN bypassed entirely. This policy, associated with President Truman, was the doctrine which bore his name.

. . . imminent danger . . . and the Marshall Plan.

February 21, 1947, marked the beginning of the period that Joseph M. Jones, in his *The Fifteen Weeks,* called, "a major turning point in American history." On that day the British Embassy delivered to Loy Henderson, Director of the Office of Near Eastern and African Affairs, two notes concerning Greece and Turkey. The British, who had been bolstering Greece with economic and military aid, announced that they could no longer continue in that capacity after March 31, 1947. A Russian victory in the eastern Mediterranean seemed inevitable unless the United States reassessed its position and agreed to assume the burdens which were becoming too great for the weakened British Empire.

Many leaders in Washington, in February 1947, were not aware of a European crisis or, if they were, chose to ignore it. By that time Truman's honeymoon with Congress, the press, and the public was about over. Up to that date his administration had seemed one succession of blunders on both the domestic and foreign fronts. Communist gains had been impressive everywhere and the national situation certainly was not promising, what with shortages, labor disputes, high taxes, unbalanced budgets, and inflation. Wiseacres were already making Truman the butt of their jokes and predicting that in November 1948 the voters would retire him to Independence, Missouri, where he belonged. The Republicans had scored impressive victories in the congressional elections in 1946. The ill-starred Eightieth Congress was destined to be both a joy and a thorn to Truman, but by the early part of 1947 it seemed to be merely another of those innumerable instances in American history when a President of one party and a Congress of the other would spend two years glowering at each other.

On February 24, 1947 the British notified Marshall of the same distressing news that they had given Loy Henderson on the twenty-first. Work had already begun in Washington on the formulation of a new policy. There were continuous conferences involving high level representatives from the Cabinet and the State Department. On February 27 the President and his advisers from the State Department met with congressional leaders from both parties.

Marshall and Acheson drove home to them the full implication of the British announcement and the imminent danger of a Russian victory. America would have to assume a new role in world affairs if this tragedy was to be avoided. This was their repetitive theme. Other conferences were held, and it was finally decided that Truman should go before a joint session of Congress to, as Senator Vandenberg put it, "scare the hell out of the country." The message that Truman delivered to Congress on March 12, 1947 described graphically the situation in Greece and Turkey and pointed out that after March 31 the British could not continue their assistance. "Greece must have assistance if it is to become a self-respecting democracy," and, he warned that her continued independence was vital to western Europe's security. Truman asked for $400,000,000 by June 1948 to aid the two countries. He recognized that this was a revolutionary doctrine. "I am fully aware," he said, "of the broad implications involved if the United States extends assistance to Greece and Turkey." But such a step was imperative. The main objective of American policy, he reminded Congress, was to "insure the peaceful development of nations, free from coercion," but this was not always possible because of hostile pressure. "I believe," he added, "that it must be the policy of the United States to support free peoples who are resisting attempted subjugation by armed minorities or by outside pressures." This support should take the form of economic and financial assistance.

The cost worried many while others predicted that it would provoke Russia to war. Some, like Henry Wallace, said it would merely keep rotten, corrupt, reactionary regimes in power. Others objected to the speed with which the administration seemed to be moving but despite these critics the new doctrine had wide support and there was little doubt that it would be approved. The main issue came from the fact that the United States seemed to be by-passing the UN which, up to that moment, the administration had upheld as the only hope for world concord. Truman was aware of this possible criticism, but he explained that the urgency of the situation compelled the United States to take action where the UN could not. Senators Arthur Vandenberg and Tom Connally helped draft resolutions which proclaimed that our aid was within the spirit of the UN charter; that by aiding Greece and Turkey we were assisting all states which stood for freedom and supported the UN. Warren R. Austin, our UN representative, presented these to the Security Council. The final link was forged by Vandenberg's amendment of March 31 in which the President was instructed to withdraw aid if the people of Greece or Turkey requested it, if the Security Council or the Assembly said our aid was no longer needed, or if the President felt that the purposes of the act were achieved.

In the public hearings Acheson made it clear that the program was designed to aid the free nations; that it was not a gigantic scheme to roll back the Iron Curtain. The Senate Committee on Foreign Relations approved unanimously and on April 22, the Senate voted affirmatively sixty-seven to twenty-three. On May 8 the House concurred 287 to 107, and on May 22 the President signed the bill. The vote was impressive and truly bipartisan.

It was recognized that aid under the Truman Doctrine would plug no more than a small hole in the dike and could not save the entire economy of Europe. Many felt that Truman's plan was too ideological and that as an aid program it could degenerate and become merely a military assistance program. These critics envisaged something less improvisational in character, something broader and more comprehensive in scope. What was not generally known was that the administration already had groups of experts evaluating plans for a more effective program of foreign aid.

At Cleveland, Mississippi on May 8, 1947, Acheson gave a speech on foreign affairs in which he stressed the need for a comprehensive American aid program.

The stage was now set for Secretary Marshall's Harvard speech. The Secretary had returned shortly before from Moscow much disillusioned over Russia's refusal to agree on a settlement of the German question. He had turned to George Kennan who headed the new Policy Planning Staff of the State Department and instructed him to make a study and submit recommendations on the European economic situation. Kennan and his experts had before them some intensive studies that had been made by several agencies and such experts as William Clayton and Charles E. Bohlen. Kennan was firmly convinced that Western Europe's salvation was of vital necessity to the United States. He wanted America to initiate a program of economic assistance to encourage general recovery. He worked intermittently with Carlton Savage, Joseph E. Johnson, and Jacques Reinstein who assisted the committee in preparing a memorandum for Marshall's study. After several conferences with his aides Marshall was ready with a policy statement.

Charles E. Bohlen, one of the State Department's Russian experts, was asked to draft a speech based on the Kennan report and a memorandum on European economic conditions prepared by William Clayton. Marshall delivered the speech on June 5, 1947 as a commencement address at Harvard University. He stressed that Europe's economic requirements from other countries, particularly America, exceeded her capacity for payment. To prevent complete economic collapse, the United States, as the world's richest and soundest country, should assume much of this burden. However, "The initiative . . . , " Marshall said, "must come from Europe. The role of this country should consist of friendly aid in the drafting of a European program and of later support of such a program as far as it may be practicable for us to do so. The program should be a joint one, agreed to by a number of, if not all, European nations." Before the month was out the British and French had invited the Russians to join them in Paris to discuss the situation.

. . . that history would vindicate his action.

What made this new foreign policy possible? Of course, conditions of the times accounted for much: the adverse European balance of payments, low coal production, a famine induced by unusual weather conditions in 1946-47, the political instability of France and Italy, and the dangers in the Mediterranean and Near East. On the other hand the political warning flags were flying after the election of 1946. Had Truman been an individual of less courage he would have paused and considered the hostility of Congress, the press, and the public and tried to buy their friendship by speaking softly, discarding the big stick, and limiting his support to tax cuts, balanced budgets, and reduced expenditures. But he saw that the national security could be maintained only by pursuing policies which made these things impossible. In his previously mentioned *The Fifteen Weeks*, Joseph M. Jones paid tribute to Truman's "courage, decisiveness, clear-thinking, and informed judgment." It was Truman's contention that history would vindicate his action. Without detracting from his excellent advisers, Truman deserves the credit for what was done between February and June 1947.

24

III THE TRUMAN ADMINISTRATION

Postwar Reconversion and the Eightieth Congress

A twenty-one point program for domestic security.

ON FOREIGN POLICY Truman's relations with Congress were most successful, but he had been in office only a few months when serious opposition developed against his domestic policies. Although at that time his party had majorities in both houses the situation was deceptive. Because of their unusually long tenure in office many Southern congressmen had risen to key positions as committee chairmen. They were able to control much of the legislation in Congress and they were hostile to many of Truman's domestic policies. They found willing allies among the Republicans and this coalition time and time again blocked Truman's domestic program. A situation had arisen in American politics in which the divisions were not necessarily along party lines. Right-wing members in the two parties were closer together ideologically than were the right and left extremes within either party. This Southern Democrat-Republican coalition became more sharply drawn after 1945, although it certainly existed in Roosevelt's administration.

The liberals at first thought that Truman was a conservative and that, as a former senator, he would be subservient to Congress. Actually, many conservatives were of the same opinion, and since Truman was so occupied with foreign problems during the early weeks of his administration, there was no opportunity for them to learn otherwise. The notion was rudely shattered when Truman presented a message to Congress on September 6, 1945. In it he left no doubt about his stand on domestic legislation. He threw down a New Deal gauntlet to the conservatives. Truman told Jonathan Daniels that the reason he delivered his "declaration of independence" was that he "wanted to let the Hearsts and McCormicks know they were not going to take me into camp." He later said that this speech marked his accession to the Presidency "in his own right" although many of the proposals he enunciated were Roosevelt's.

Woodrow Wilson startled the world with his fourteen-point program for international security; Truman startled the country with a twenty-one point program for domestic security. He said the freedoms of religion, press, speech, and assembly, even though important and precious, were not enough unless they were sustained by other security guarantees. Our citizens are "not interested in boom prosperity—for that only too often leads to panic and depression," he warned. "But they are interested in providing opportunity for work and for ultimate security." He called for a "national reassertion of the right to work for every American citizen able and willing to work . . . [which] will help to avert fear and establish full employment." He was determined that each citizen should be free from fear of unemployment, inadequate education, disabling sickness, and the infirmities of age; businessmen should be free from fear of unfair competition; and labor and agriculture should not fear being denied the full reward of their toil. Adequate food, clothing, housing, education, medical care, and protection against unemployment, illness, accident, and age should be offered everyone. Truman asserted that the responsibility for providing these belonged to private enterprise in normal times but on occasion the responsibility was beyond the capacities of private enterprise. Then the federal government had a duty and right to step into the breach.

Truman's definite proposals were an increase in the minimum wage, a national housing and slum clearance program, broadened social security, health insurance, the creation of a permanent Fair Employment Practice Commission (FEPC), and federal aid for scientific research. In addition, the President requested a national program for resource development, assistance for farmers and small businessmen, and a public works program. For the postwar transitional period he also requested that selective service, certain wartime powers, and various controls be continued. Truman dropped this tidy bundle into the lap of Congress and awaited developments.

. . . "disintegrate" and reconversion.

Two of the most pressing problems, after 1945, were demobilization and reconversion. As early as May 1945 a point system was devised to speed service discharges. Meanwhile, Secretary Stimson, General Marshall, and Admiral Ernest J. King had recommended to Congress that a system of universal military training (UMT) should be adopted for the country. Whatever sentiments might have existed in favor of this step were dissipated quickly by the Jap surrender. The clamor to demobilize ("disintegrate" Truman called it) became irresistible and Congress speeded up the discharge rate.

Truman presented a military security program which included UMT, to his Cabinet on August 31, and on October 22 he brought his views before Congress. "The day of the Minute Man who sprang to the flintlock hanging on his wall is over," he solemnly warned the legislators as he recommended the creation of a military organization based on a small regular Army, Navy, and Marine Corps, a stronger National Guard, an organized reserve for each of these services, and a general reserve for all young men who had received one year of training at the age of eighteen or upon high school graduation. There would be no exemption except for physical disabilities. This proposal met with lukewarm support in Congress. The armed forces declined so rapidly in 1945 that by the end of the year it became necessary to decelerate the rate of discharge to maintain our garrisons. A storm of protest throughout the country was barely calmed by Chief of Staff Dwight Eisenhower. Still the discharge rate was too high, and it was shown that by the end of 1946 our army, which was supposed to stabilize at 1,550,000, would drop to about a million. Under the circumstances Truman's only recourse was an appeal to continue the draft act. Congress approved its continuation to March 31, 1947, when selective service finally lapsed.

With so many facets to the problem of reconversion it was inevitable that the President and Congress should find some points of agreement. One was reward to the veteran. Actually, Roosevelt had signed the Servicemen's Readjustment Act ("G. I. Bill of Rights") on June 22, 1944 so, during the Truman administration, the main provisions of this act needed but slight modification to meet new situations.

Tax reduction was another question of reconversion upon which there was widespread agreement. In November 1945 Congress permitted reductions of more than six billion dollars. Excess profit taxes were terminated; surtaxes, corporation taxes, and regular levies were reduced while various exemptions were increased.

The main work of reconversion fell upon John Snyder's Office of War Mobilization and Reconversion (OWMR). Contract cancellations proceeded at a rapid rate and the controls exercised by the War Production Board (WPB) were relaxed rapidly. Government-owned factories as well as surplus goods were placed on the market at a fraction of their original cost and provided astute businessmen with a windfall of bargains.

The depression and the war had so curtailed home construction that by 1945 the housing shortage was serious. Many veterans, now assured of financial support from the government, were determined to own their own homes. Earlier marriages and an all-time high in savings were also instrumental in creating a heavy demand for more homes. On October 1, 1945, Truman ordered the Federal Public Housing Authority to arrange the sale of temporary homes and trailers which had been provided near defense plants. Snyder's OWMR prepared a study of housing construction late in 1945; and Wilson Wyatt, former Louisville mayor, became Housing Expediter to speed construction. Wyatt called for 2,700,000 homes in two years. Seven months later the Veterans' Emergency Housing Bill was enacted to provide emergency assistance and a subsidy—which Congress cut drastically—to speed the manufacture of needed housing materials. The bill failed in Congress. The cut in the subsidy, the failure to enact the comprehensive, low-cost home construction plan—as envisioned in the Wagner-Ellender-Taft Bill—and the curtailment of OPA worked against Wyatt who reported in October 1946 that only 350,000 homes had been completed rather than the 1,200,000 he had estimated for the year.

The nation's labor cup was still not filled.

It was on the issues of full employment, price-wage controls, and labor that Truman encountered the most serious opposition from Congress. On the first issue he achieved a partial victory but lost on the other two and was severely criticized from all quarters for failure and shortcomings. His inability to deal effectively with these problems paved the way for a Republican victory in 1946. Many economists—and they were not all Russians—predicted that within a few months after the war millions of Americans would be unemployed and a major depression would be the reward for military victory. The possibility that an abrupt transition from chow, draft, and ration lines would lead to unemployment compensation and bread lines was a catastrophe that had to be averted at all costs.

In 1944 the Democrat's platform called for full employment after the war and Truman, in September 1945, repeated this promise. The Republicans sided with the Democrats in principle but maintained that less government control and interference, not more, could effect full employment.

The liberal Democrats' views were embodied in Montana's Senator James E. Murray's full employment bill presented to Congress in 1945. It provided that the President and his aides were to prepare a production budget each year, and with this to guide it, a Joint Congressional Committee on the National Budget was to decide how much federal spending would be required annually to maintain full employment. The Republicans disliked this measure because it smacked of Roosevelt's two New Deal bogies, deficit financing and economic planning. However, they did agree with the basic principle that *some* federal assistance was in order. The compromise was the Employment Act of 1946 which accepted the principle of federal responsibility but was less inclusive than the original proposals.

A significant distinction was made between "full" and "maximum" employment. A three-man Council of Economic Advisers was created to prepare an economic report which was also to be less inclusive than the production budget of the original bill. And though the original bill specifically called for federal funds to insure employment, the act reduced the federal government to a coordinating activity.

The compromise on the full employment act, which Truman signed, was generally acceptable, but on the labor issue Truman was unable to arrange an equally acceptable compromise. Between 1939 and 1945 the average factory worker's pay had risen from $23.19 to $47.16 weekly. Naturally, the workers hoped to carry these gains into the postwar period, but the obstacles were the decline in working hours, the disappearance of fat overtime checks, and the shelving of the generous "cost-plus" principle. With competition restored it was argued that employers could not continue the high scale of wages unless there was a corresponding increase in productivity or prices.

By the spring it was evident the "little steel" formula, which during the war had held wages to a fifteen per cent rise over the 1941 levels, was no longer workable. The battle began when John L. Lewis of the United Mine Workers ordered the anthracite miners to strike. On May 3 Truman placed the mines temporarily under the Department of the Interior. However, the strikes eventually brought the miners raises of $1.25 and $1.37½ in the soft and hard coal fields respectively. But, work stoppages continued during the fall and labor difficulties increased. Truman was reluctant to invoke the provisions of the Smith-Connally Act of 1943 since he felt it really offered no solution, and he chose instead to call a labor-management meeting in Washington, which made no tangible suggestions. So the President asked Congress to create fact-finding boards.

By this time the 250,000 United Oil Workers struck at eleven oil companies and demanded a thirty per cent increase in wages. On October 4 Truman ordered the Navy to seize the plants. Strikes now spread to the packing and auto industries, so Truman established his fact-finding boards by executive order rather than await authorization by Congress.

On November 21, 1945 nearly 180,000 members of the United Automobile Workers Union went on strike at eighty General Motors plants and they were soon joined by another million workers from the electrical and steel unions. The auto workers, too, demanded a thirty per cent wage increase, and their vice president, Walter Reuther, captured public attention by insisting that GM could easily meet these demands while holding price lines. He challenged them to make their books public to prove him wrong but the company refused to open its books to Lloyd K. Garrison's fact-finding committee which finally negotiated an 18½ cent increase. Ford and Chrysler had previously accepted the 18½ cent figure without strikes and this raise now became a yardstick for labor demands and many settlements during 1946.

Meanwhile, an even more serious crisis had arisen in the steel industry. Work stoppage here was threatening the entire reconversion and national defense programs. Philip Murray of the CIO asked for a 25-cent raise but Benjamin F. Fairless of United States Steel would listen to no demands until the government agreed to a steel price increase of seven dollars per ton. Truman was willing to compromise at four dollars per ton and 18½ cents. The basic issue was whether wage increases could be made without price increases. Chester Bowles of the OPA argued that because of tax reductions, industry could absorb the increased production costs. John Snyder insisted that by stimulating production, increased prices would alleviate the current steel shortages. On February 14, 1946, Truman yielded at five dollars per ton and 18½ cents.

The Supreme Court added to the labor tension when it ruled, in the decision of *Anderson v. Mt. Clemens Pottery Co.*, that workers were to be given back pay for "on the premise" activities not actually performed "at the bench." This "portal-to-portal" pay concept opened the field for much litigation to claim back pay.

Labor crises seemed about over but they weren't. John L. Lewis, disturbed over the gains made by Murray, decided that the time was ripe to strike a decisive blow for the miners. Lewis was disturbed over the heavy accident and high disability rates with the attendant, prohibitive insurance costs. Lewis was determined to obtain sizeable wage increases and health and accident protection as well. The most controversial of the demanded "fringe benefits" was the creation of a welfare fund to be replenished with a royalty paid by the operators. This fund was to be administered solely by the union. When the operators refused to consider these demands, Lewis ordered his 400,000 miners to leave their pits on April 1. In the next six weeks it was necessary to curtail industrial output and restrict heat consumption to husband the meagre stock of coal. Just before a complete economic breakdown, Lewis, highly aware of growing public disapproval, magnanimously permitted his miners to resume their jobs on May 13. He made it clear that the strike was not being called off, that this was merely a twelve-day truce to find a basis for negotiation.

The nation's labor cup was still not filled. In July 1945 twenty railway brotherhoods had asked for wage increases averaging $2.50 a day and forty-five changes in the working rules. Negotiations dragged on for months. Eighteen unions had indicated their willingness to continue but two refused. Under the Railroad Labor Act of 1926 Truman appointed a fact-finding board and finally, on April 18, the board recommended a 16-cent hourly raise and seven rule changes. Alvanley Johnston of the Brotherhood of Locomotive Engineers and Alexander F. Whitney of the Brotherhood of Railway Trainmen ordered a strike for May 18. The President met this with an order to seize the lines on May 17, and by phone, induced Johnston and Whitney to accept a five-day truce so that further negotiations could be conducted at the White House. The President offered 18½-cent hourly increases and asked the unions to accept the existing rules for one year. Eighteen of the twenty brotherhoods assented to these terms, but Whitney and Johnston refused to yield. At the expiration of the deadline the strike began.

Truman felt certain that the strike was the work of a few willful men and after two cabinet meetings on the question he decided to go before Congress and the nation. To a national radio audience on May 24 he identified this as the greatest crisis since Pearl Harbor and placed the entire blame squarely upon the shoulders of the two recalcitrant labor leaders. "It was inconceivable," he said, "that in our democracy any two men should be placed in a position where they can completely stifle our economy and ultimately destroy our country." He promised, if necessary, to use the army to assist the Office of Defense Transportation. He then addressed a joint session of Congress and asked for a comprehensive emergency labor act which among other things would give him power to draft strikers in those industries managed by the government. Actually, John Steelman, Johnston, and Whitney had reached an agreement a few moments before Truman spoke. So, at the conclusion of his message he was able to delight the legislators with a dramatic announcement that peace again reigned on the labor front.

Meanwhile, John L. Lewis had come to terms when the government seized the mines on May 22. Within a few days Lewis and Secretary of the Interior Julius Krug had compromised on the 18½-cent raise, better safety rules, and vacation pay. It was arranged that the medical fund would be administered solely by the union, but management would join it in handling the welfare and retirement funds.

Truman had gone unsuccessfully to Congress in December, 1945 and May, 1946 with requests for labor legislation. However, in the latter instance the House rushed through a draft-striker bill by an impressive 306 to thirteen vote. Ohio's Senator Robert Taft, who branded it a call for "involuntary servitude," and Claude Pepper of Florida led the counterattack which sent the amended bill back to the House to die in committee. On May 29 Congress finally passed a bill of its own to control labor (the Case Federal Mediation Bill), but it was vetoed June 11 by Truman who, in a lengthy message, said it would encourage rather than discourage labor strife.

The third issue . . . of controls.

The third issue to divide Truman and Congress was that of controls. An executive order of August 18, 1945 prescribed Truman's policies to avert inflation. The Office of Price Administration (OPA), the Secretary of Agriculture and the Director of Economic Stabilization were to cooperate in holding down living costs. Gradually the OPA ended rationing on most items and through its systems of priorities and controls held the rise in living costs to about three per cent. Chester Bowles of OPA insisted that only price controls could avert an inflation like the one that followed World War I, but his arguments were systematically demolished by the well-financed campaigns of many lobbies. Public pressure became irresistible and black marketing increased enormously. By executive order, on February 14, 1946, Truman had granted some price adjustments to prevent hardships. Actually, those congressmen who wanted to end controls completely and those who wanted to continue them were outnumbered by those who wanted merely to modify them. This majority finally enacted a drastically amended Price Control Bill on June 27, 1946. It extended OPA for another year.

Bowles resigned in protest and Truman pondered the question of "inflation with a statute and inflation without one." On June 29 he sent a veto message to Congress criticizing the "bonanza formulas" of the bill's authors, Robert Taft and Kenneth Wherry. The veto took Congress by surprise and for three weeks the hiatus in control legislation saw price rises of nearly twenty-five per cent. On July 1 Truman tried to continue some functions of OPA by executive order until Congress could act again.

On July 25 Truman signed the second Price Control Act, which in many respects was no better than the first. It continued OPA until June 30, 1947 and restored most controls, but it also specified that ceilings were to be raised to give manufacturers the same profits made in 1940. Many products were not to pass under controls until August 20 and a special board was created to alter ceilings, remove, and restore certain items from the control list when advisable.

The stage was now set for the political drama of 1946.

The "beefsteak election" of 1946.

A congressional election was approaching in November 1946. Truman had not made much of a record; most of his twenty-one points had been ingloriously shelved by Congress. He had lost support on every hand. Labor was up in arms because of his handling of the railroad and coal strikes, but he had made an equally bad impression on businessmen who were suspicious of his New Deal tendencies and his support of controls. Conservatives in both parties had been frightened by his liberalism.

Truman had alienated the liberals, too. The extreme left wingers were angered by his dismissal of Henry Wallace and by the appearance in Washington of a number of former Missouri cronies who came to bask in Truman's glory. Many of the "Missouri Gang" were regarded as conservative, colorless mediocrities of questionable honesty.

None of Truman's appointments aroused more controversy than his attempt to make Edwin Pauley Undersecretary of the Navy in January 1946. While this appointment was under scrutiny, Ickes told a senate naval affairs committee that Pauley had promised to deliver some campaign funds in California if the Justice Department dropped its tidelands oil cases. When Truman defended Pauley, Ickes, long admired by the New

Deal liberals, resigned as Secretary of the Interior. Since Stimson had given way to Robert Patterson in 1945, this left Forrestal as the only hold-over from the Roosevelt Cabinet. Previously, Snyder had taken over in the Treasury from Vinson who had been elevated to the Supreme Court.

The final straw that turned the electorate against Truman in 1946 was the price control situation. Sam Rayburn predicted that it would be a "beefsteak election," and he was right. Meat was one item scheduled to pass under controls on August 20 but before that date prices had risen rapidly and there was plenty of meat on the counters. When controls were re-imposed on August 21 suppliers and farmers hoarded meat and house-wives were left without. The Republicans quickly capitalized on the situa-tion with the slogan "Had enough?" and the voters answered by giving the Republicans control of both houses for the first time since 1930. In the Senate they gained twelve seats, increasing their strength to fifty-one, and in the House they gained fifty-four for a total of 246 seats. Except for the South the Republicans cut heavily into machine-controlled states and major cities. Twenty-five northern governors were Republican. The defeat was so pervasive that Democratic Senator J. William Fulbright suggested that the sensible and patriotic thing for Truman to do was to resign in favor of a Republican.

The wage-price spiral.

Truman's program to restrain inflation had been defeated in the election. There was nothing to do but give in, so at once all controls were removed except those on rent, sugar, and rice. The emergency housing program was also scrapped when Truman refused to follow Wyatt's advice to keep building materials under control. Both Wyatt and Paul Porter, head of OPA, resigned and the latter agency began to suspend its opera-tions. Gradually the few remaining controls were dropped, although Con-gress continued rent controls until March 1, 1948.

The inflationary spiral began immediately. Bureau of Labor Statistics showed that prices rose more in 1946 than at any time since the first World War. Retail prices advanced eighteen per cent in all, fifteen per cent during the last six months of the year when controls were being relaxed. The rise continued into 1947 and set the stage for another round of wage hikes.

The country was becoming alarmed at labor's aggressivness and in many quarters the election was considered a labor rebuke. Nevertheless,

John L. Lewis announced he would call out his union in the bituminous mines. The bituminous mines were still partially controlled by the government and he gave it until November 20 to capitulate or face a strike. On November 18 an injunction was obtained from the federal district court of the District of Columbia, an injunction which Lewis ignored completely with an order to strike on November 21. This was too much. Judge T. Alan Goldsborough held both Lewis and the United Mine Workers guilty of contempt and fined them $10,000 and $3,500,000 respectively. Lewis was not cowed and persisted until December 7 despite severe coal shortages, industrial brown-outs, slow-downs, and the suspension of transportation. On the anniversary of Pearl Harbor he relented and sent the miners back to the pits until March 31, 1947, and the case was carried to the Supreme Court. Lewis was confident of his position but the Court surprised him by sustaining the Goldsborough verdict, although it cut the union's fine to $700,000. The Court added, however, that if the strike was resumed on March 31 the fine would revert to the original figure.

Just as it looked as if Lewis were beaten, Fate dealt one of those tragic blows that can be turned to good advantage by a clever opportunist. On March 25 a terrible mine disaster occurred in Centralia, Illinois. This gave Lewis the opportunity to underscore graphically the lack of safety regulation; the very point he had been trying to make without success for more than a year. Four days later, at Lewis' order, the miners left their pits for a protracted period of mourning. On March 31 the miners were actually on strike in violation of the Supreme Court's order, but nothing could be done about it. The mourning went on while Lewis wrangled with Krug and the operators; in June he secured a new contract which was a decided victory for the UMW.

Although Lewis scored a victory for his miners, his actions made labor regulations inevitable. Critics of organized labor, unable to make any headway for many years, now had two things they formerly lacked—a sympathetic public and a Republican Congress.

The spiral, plus budget vs. taxes.

Although in time Truman came to regard the Republican Eightieth Congress as the "luckiest thing that ever happened to me," he undoubtedly did not feel this way before November, 1948. He was in constant disagreement with the Congress and used his veto power freely. When Congress overrode six vetoes (three in one week) it set a record unmatched since the days of Andrew Johnson.

The Republicans had promised the voters they would cut taxes, remove controls, and discipline labor. Taft claimed the Wagner Act of 1935 was loaded against management, and that a new law was needed to restore a balance between labor and management. Labor, its critics argued, had outgrown the necessity of protection, which logic, ironically enough, the Republicans never applied to the field of tariff legislation.

Taft wanted a strong labor regulatory act and as a result of the elections anticipated no serious trouble with the Democratic party for many years to come. He was able to win most of his points and although the original labor bill was introduced by Fred A. Hartley, Jr. of New Jersey, the Taft-Hartley Labor-Management Relations Act of 1947 was largely Taft's brainchild. It passed both houses by impressive votes, 308 to 107 and sixty-eight to twenty-four. When Truman vetoed the bill on June 20, the House repassed it the same day by equally impressive votes, 331 to eighty-three and sixty-eight to twenty-five. When the Senate passed it on June 25 it was another example of the southern Democrat-conservative Republican coalition at work.

Union leaders were unanimously opposed. They called it the "slave-labor" act. No provision was more severely criticized than Section 9h, which denied labor leaders access to the National Labor Relations Board unless they signed affidavits that they were not Communists. In 1946 Lewis had brought the UMW into the AFL, but when the president, William Green, approved Section 9h, Lewis withdraw his union again with one of the most laconic announcements on record: "We disaffiliate."

The Taft-Hartley Act was to become one of the most controversial measures since 1947, but like Mark Twain's weather everyone talked about it but did nothing. Its basic outlines remained unchanged. The dire predictions that labor would be stifled did not come true. Management showed little desire to rob labor of its basic rights and the harsher aspects of the act were used circumspectly. Rather than growing weaker, unions have become stronger, richer, and larger. Although labor leaders denounced the act, there was no disobedience.

The Eightieth Congress was also moved in 1947 to control the flood of portal pay suits (totalling more than five billion dollars) which had been released following the Supreme Court decision in the Mt. Clemens case. A law, reluctantly approved by Truman, outlawed such suits unless permitted by labor contracts.

The years 1947 and 1948 were relatively quiet on the labor front. There were fewer man-days lost in 1947 than in 1946, and the record was bettered in 1948. Increasing living costs necessitated wage increases in both 1947 and 1948, but the latter barely kept pace with the former. In 1948 Truman invoked the Taft-Hartley law to halt a railroad strike and a telephone strike. The miners, packing-house workers, auto-workers, and railroad brotherhoods were militant in 1948, but the violent strikes of the year were those of the longshoremen. They struck on both coasts and for several weeks they tied up more than five hundred ships, many of which were loaded with badly needed foreign aid. The final settlement gave the longshoremen better wage increases, paid vacations, and a welfare fund. That year also saw the history-making labor contract concluded between General Motors and the UAW, a contract which set the pattern for many others. Its unprecedented features provided that wages were to be tied to the consumers' price index and that annual raises were to be given as productivity increased.

The President appealed to the public to cut prices voluntarily. He also asked that food consumption be limited so that more would be available for foreign shipment. People were asked to give up eggs, poultry, and meat on certain days of the week, but the appeal was ineffective as such appeals usually are. One example of an attempt to comply was a plan inaugurated by the citizens of Newburyport, Massachusetts to cut prices arbitrarily by ten per cent. They hoped the plan would be emulated elsewhere. Despite much fanfare and expectation that the movement would snowball, it expired ingloriously within a month.

On November 17, 1947, Truman called Congress into special session to tackle the problem of inflation. He outlined a ten-point program of controls, credit restrictions, and rationing. "When so many people are not sharing fairly in prosperity the road is being paved for a recession or a depression," he noted in justification of his request. Although he regarded it as a weak measure, Truman signed the bill once it was passed. It provided no effective curbs to inflation, but it did permit agreements on allocating scarce materials by setting aside anti-trust laws, continued export and transport controls until February 28, 1949, permitted the restriction of the use of grain by distillers until February 1, 1948, and appropriated a small fund to aid food-conservation study.

Congress slashed the 1947-1948 budget, largely at the expense of the federal power and reclamation projects. The controlling Republicans also favored more tax cuts. Truman and Secretary of the Treasury Snyder were unalterably opposed. With heavy national defense commitments as well as a new policy of foreign aid in the making, Truman insisted that reductions in revenue would be unwise. Furthermore, he argued, tax cuts should not be made during prosperous times but held in abeyance for a slump when the economy might need a stimulant. With the national debt at an astronomical $269,400,000,000 in June 1946—but going down—Truman proposed that any prospective surplus should be applied to the reduction of the debt. The final argument was that tax reductions were inflationary. The Republicans countered by insisting that tax cuts would stimulate productivity and release investment capital.

So eager were the Republicans to cut taxes that the first order of Congressional business was Harold Knutson's bill to reduce income tax levies ten to thirty per cent as well as to increase the number of exemptions. The bill passed the House 220 to ninety-nine and the Senate forty-eight to twenty-eight but on June 16, 1947 Truman sent it back with a caustic veto message. Considering the infrequent times that Presidents have dared to oppose tax reductions, this was a brave step. An identical measure was re-submitted in July except that the cuts were postponed until January 1, 1948. Once again Truman sent it back. Not enough votes could be mustered to override the vetoes.

By mid-August 1947 the budget went into the black for the first time in seventeen years. This merely sharpened the Republicans' demand for reductions and by April, 1948 a third version of the Knutson bill was sent to Truman. This one removed 7,400,000 persons from the tax rolls and reduced federal income by five billion dollars. Truman vetoed the bill again, but this time the coalition of southern Democrats and conservative Republicans overrode Truman's veto. The final act increased exemptions from $500 to $600, applied the community-property principle by permitting husbands and wives to pool their returns, and reduced rates.

Reforms: welfare, military, political

Truman did not let Republican control of Congress deter him from renewing his requests for the reforms outlined in his message of September 6, 1945. On most issues he was completely unsuccessful. His requests for new social security coverage, federal assistance to education, and increases in minimum wages from forty to seventy-five cents an hour were lost before they could be brought up for serious discussion.

One matter dear to Truman's heart was health insurance. He was dismayed at the poor national health so graphically illustrated by the high rejection rate in the Army. Shelving the proposals of the Murray-Wagner-Dingell Bill, Truman introduced his own plan in a message to Congress on November 19, 1945. This was a national compulsory health insurance program to be financed through payroll deductions. It provided for individual selection of physician, paid medical expenses, and protection against work-loss through illness. It called for more federal aid for maternal and child care and other public health programs as well as construction and support of medical schools and hospitals. It was promptly opposed as "socialistic" and was rejected by both the Seventy-ninth and Eightieth Congresses. Nevertheless, Truman stubbornly reopened the fight for it before the Eighty-first Congress, but was no more successful than before.

On national defense policy Truman and Congress were also in serious disagreement. Congress did not renew selective service when it ended on March 31, 1947, and for more than a year the armed forces depended upon voluntary enlistments to maintain their strength. The Army and the Navy could not recruit enough men for their monthly needs of thirty thousand and 12,500 respectively. In 1947 the Army proposed Universal Military Training for men between eighteen and twenty based on six months of school and six months in camp. It was received with apathy. In 1948 Truman renewed his request for both UMT and selective service. Although the former was ignored, Congress did enact a new Selective Service Act providing for the registration of men between eighteen and twenty-five. No one under nineteen would be drafted but those younger were at liberty to enlist for one year. Under this act the service period was to be twenty-one months.

Congress also stressed the need for a powerful Air Force but here again a serious argument arose between the administration—favoring a fifty-five group Air Force—and the legislators—who wanted a seventy-group Air Force. Victory in this instance went to the Air Force clique in Congress, largely at the expense of the Army and the Navy.

One of the bitterest controversies in the Eightieth Congress arose over the unification of the armed forces. As early as 1945 the Army and the Navy had discussed unification or at least closer cooperation. The admirals feared that unification would de-emphasize seapower; that the Marine Corps would lose its identity; and that too much emphasis would be placed on land-based planes. Truman, with the advice of his Secretaries, Forrestal and Patterson, favored a single national defense department. Inter-service negotiation continued and on January 16,

1947 Forrestal and Patterson informed him that a compromise had been reached. On February 26 Truman sent a bill to Congress which was passed July 25. It provided for the National Military Establishment headed by a Secretary of Defense—Forrestal was named—with cabinet rank. There were departments for the Army, Navy, and Air Force, each of which was presided over by a secretary. For the first time the Joint Chiefs of Staff were given legal recognition. It also provided for a Munitions Board, a Research and Development Board, a National Security Resources Board, and a National Security Council composed of the heads of these three boards in addition to the President, and the Secretaries of State, Defense, Army, Navy, and Air Force. The act also provided for a Central Intelligence Agency charged with the responsibility of providing the National Security Council with information upon which policy could be based. Services unification was one of the most significant achievements of the Truman administration. Although James Forrestal and Louis Johnson, Forrestal's successor after March 1949, found that the mere signing of an act did not bring cooperation and end inter-service jealousy and rivalry, they realized that a long stride had been made toward counterbalancing the Communist military threat.

In a few areas of political reform Truman actually was successful. In 1947, with congressional approval, he appointed a committee to be headed by elder statesman and ex-President Herbert Hoover to study methods for reorganizing the executive branch of the government. On the basis of extensive and thoughtful reports submitted by this committee many changes were made in the executive departments for greater efficiency and economy.

Truman was very much concerned over the order of presidential succssion, possibly because he had come into office by this route. Out of his interest came the Presidential Succession Act of 1947. Under the old system the Vice President was to be succeeded by the Secretary of State and on down the line of cabinet officers. Truman's objection was that the presidency would devolve upon men who had not been elected to office. Under the new act the succession passed from the Vice President to the Speaker of the House, the president *pro-tempore* of the Senate, and then to the cabinet officers. In 1947 Congress also approved the Twenty-second Amendment (ratified by the thirty-sixth state on February 26, 1951) which limited any President to two terms, or to one term if that person had served more than two years of his predecessor's term.

It was inevitable that Truman, who for years had championed minorities, would be interested in civil rights. Given the conservative temper of Congress, it was also inevitable that a controversy would develop. Within a month after he assumed office Truman urged, unsuccessfully, the creation of a permanent Fair Employment Practice Commission (FEPC). By 1948 Truman proposed a ten-point program to Congress. He asked again in 1948 for a permanent commission on civil rights, a joint congressional committee for civil rights, and a stronger civil-rights divison within the Department of Justice, a permanent FEPC, and new civil-rights statutes. The federal government was to protect voting rights; prohibit discrimination in interstate transportation; prevent lynching; grant an independent government to the District of Columbia, statehood to Alaska and Hawaii; settle the claims arising from those Japanese-Americans who had been evacuated on the west coast during the war; and give every alien resident of the United States an equal opportunity to become naturalized. Truman's firm stand on civil rights not only angered Congress but threw the conservative Democrats into confusion and sent them off in all directions seeking a replacement candidate for 1948.

Throughout 1948 Congress toyed with an anti-lynch and anti-poll tax measure without success, but it did reach a suitable settlement concerning Japanese-Americans. Despite opposition from Generals Bradley and Eisenhower, Truman ordered equal status of all races in the armed forces.

Truman and Congress also squared off over the issues of housing and rent control. The President's request for a continuation of rent controls until June 30, 1948 was partially accepted when, in 1947, Congress permitted a continuation of greatly modified controls until February 29, 1948. However, this concession was virtually valueless since no real measure of regulation could be expected in this one small area when the rest of the economy had been decontrolled. And as for housing; it was estimated that more than twenty million Americans lived in substandard dwellings. The Wagner-Ellender-Taft plan of 1945 for the construction of a maximum of fifteen million homes in ten years looked like a godsend to the twenty million Americans who lived in substandard dwellings. Nevertheless, by 1947, Congress had failed to consider housing legislation.

During 1948 Truman repeated his requests for low-cost housing, slum clearance projects, rent control, assistance for the construction of

41

rental property for moderate income groups, housing research, and a Federal Housing Commission. Modified rent controls were continued, in both 1947 and 1948. Congress amended the 1944 "G.I. Bill of Rights" to extend its guarantees for veterans' housing mortgages. The government could also insure up to ninety per cent of loans to apartment-house builders for low-cost units, but the inadequacy was attested by the fact that only 800,000 units were under construction that year.

Congress did not act to admit unfortunate displaced persons from Europe until 1948 when a measure was passed, objected to by Truman because it discriminated against Jews and Catholics, that charged the 205,000 displaced persons admitted against future immigration quotas from their respective countries.

Agriculture was the last significant domestic issue. The parity formula, based on the years 1909 to 1914, no longer seemed workable in 1948. In that year Congress passed an agriculture act which continued the ninety per cent of parity price formula on many items, but also replaced this by a flexible support price ranging from sixty to ninety per cent on other commodities at the discretion of the Secretary of Agriculture.

Although, during the Presidential campaign of 1948, Truman continually characterized the Eightieth Congress the "second worst in history"—sometimes he gave it top billing—there was no doubt that such a judgment only partially balanced its failures with tangible achievements. Its record in the field of foreign affairs, which included the ratification of treaties with Bulgaria, Rumania, Italy, and Hungary, approval of the Truman Doctrine, approval of the Marshall Plan, military aid to China, and the continuation of the Reciprocal Trade Agreements Act, was notably brilliant.

The pollsters had stopped counting noses . . . .

Those few persons who bet against the Republicans in the 1948 elections were considered downright foolhardy. Truman was being ignored completely as Congress went its own way. With victory in sight, the Republicans were overstaffed with candidates for the presidency. The ideal one was, of course, General Dwight D. Eisenhower, and although he could have easily secured support for the nomination, he chose to refrain from running. Gradually, however, the Republican leaders were brought back to Thomas E. Dewey, the unsuccessful candidate in 1944. He was a powerful voice for internationalism and mild progressivism. At the Republican convention in Philadelphia in June, Dewey captured most of the seventy-three man delegation from the key state of Pennsylvania, and rode to victory on the third ballot. Governor Earl Warren of California was then chosen as his running mate. The Republicans accepted much of the New Deal, endorsed the ECA, the UN, and promised to reduce taxes, increase governmental efficiency, and combat domestic Communism. They then closed ranks and prepared to storm Capitol Hill. Truman read of Dewey's nomination and remarked, "The nomination of Dewey last night I think will make the campaign easier—all he can do is to make a 'warmed-over' approach to the situation with which the country is faced and I don't think the country is going to take a 'warmed-over' approach." Such optimism seemed out of place in a man whose chances seemed so small that some observers predicted he would not even win renomination.

Truman not only had little hope of support from the extreme left or the conservative Southern element of the Democratic party, but he was also having trouble with the progressive wing and the center. These dissident Democrats tried to bury their difference by turning to Eisenhower. The practical city bosses; Frank Hague of New Jersey, Edward Flynn of New York, and Jacob Arvey of Chicago, openly hoped the General could be induced to stand for election as a Democrat. The Roosevelt boys—James and Elliott—Leon Henderson, James F. Byrnes, Harold Ickes, and Senator Claude Pepper denounced Truman for not having followed FDR's policies, but despite this opposition Truman remained calm. As a student of history he knew that "presidential control of the convention is a political principle which has not been violated in political history." The President was right because he was nominated on the first ballot. Senator Alben W. Barkley of Kentucky was chosen as his running mate. The nominations were without incident but the drafting of the platform precipitated a split. Truman was committed to a vigorous civil-rights program, but the platform committee submitted a milder version for its civil rights plank. This was denounced by Hubert H. Humphrey and the Americans for Democratic Action (ADA). Finally a stronger civil-rights plank won by a small majority. The plank called for anti-lynch and anti-poll tax laws as well as a permanent FEPC. Southern delegates were adamant in their opposition and thirty-five of them bolted the Convention. Governor J. Strom Thurmond of South Carolina was asked why they felt so strongly when actually the civil-rights plank was no stronger than those advocated by Roosevelt at previous conventions. "I agree," replied the Governor, "but Truman really means it."

With the regular conventions out of the way the malcontents held their own sessions. On July 17 the "Dixiecrats" met in Birmingham, Alabama, and nominated Thurmond and his fellow-governor Fielding Wright of Mississippi. They hoped to win control of the Southern Democratic party (which they did not do) and thus force the election into the House of Representatives where they could bargain for their votes.

On July 22 the left-wing Democrats held their meeting in Philadelphia. A group known as the "Progressive Citizens of America" helped form the Progressive Party which nominated Henry Wallace and Senator Glen Taylor of Idaho. Their platform called for friendship with Russia and a highly socialistic form of New Dealism. Actually the old-line progressives were shocked by the extremity to which Wallace's party had been driven by the fellow-travelers and Communists who had infiltrated its ranks. An appeal for Russian friendship seemed absurd in view of the Soviets' new foreign policy after 1945, and the plank calling for nationalization of industry was too extreme for the traditional American liberal who had never been willing to abandon free enterprise.

Truman, jauntier and cockier than ever, arrived in Philadelphia to accept the nomination. The gloomy party leaders on the convention hall stage were in violent contrast to Truman who literally bounced as he poured forth his unbridled optimism, "Senator Barkley and I will win this election and make these Republicans like it—don't you forget that." Then, during his speech, he hurled his bombshell. He called Congress into special session for July 26, known as "Turnip Day" in Truman's home state. With studied irony he said he was giving the Republicans a chance to enact the housing legislation and the price restrictions they were promising in their campaign platform. Truman contended that these and many other platform promises could be translated into legislation in fifteen days if the Republicans really meant what they said. The net results of this short special session—from July 26 to August 7—were modest measures to limit bank and consumer credit and to stimulate home construction, but they fell far short of fulfilling the Republican campaign pledges.

While Dewey acted as if the presidency was an overripe plum about to drop into his lap, Truman toured the country with the vigor of a much younger man. "I'm going to give them hell," he told Barkley in speaking of his opponents, and he did. Confronted early in the campaign by a near-empty auditorium in Omaha, Truman decided then and there that he would avoid major speeches in larger cities and take his case instead to the grassroots by means of a "whistle-stop" campaign. In a whirlwind effort he logged 31,700 miles and delivered 356 speeches in thirty-five days. He estimated that he must have talked to fifteen million voters.

The election was a simple case of "the Democratic party and the people against the special interests of the privileged few," Truman told an audience in Akron, Ohio, on October 11, and he sounded the same battle cry everywhere. He bombarded the "do-nothing" Eightieth Congress and called for the speedy enactment of his September 6 New Deal program.

Dewey was confident of victory. The pollsters had stopped counting noses a few weeks before the election because they could see no possible way for Truman to save himself from a crushing defeat. Then, as the results rolled in, the unexpected began to happen: Truman was carrying states that were supposedly solid Republican. Wisconsin, Illinois, Ohio, Minnesota, Iowa, Colorado, and California began to edge into the Democratic column, although New York, New Jersey, Pennsylvania, Maryland, Connecticut, and Michigan went Republican. Finally at 11:14 a.m. on November 3, Dewey conceded the election when it became apparent that Ohio, Illinois, and Iowa had gone Democratic.

When the final results were in, Truman had polled 24,105,695 popular and 304 electoral votes to Dewey's 21,969,170 and 189. Truman had taken twenty-eight states and Dewey, sixteen. Thurmond captured four states for a total popular vote of 1,169,021 and thirty-eight electoral votes. Wallace ran a poor fourth, 1,156,103 popular and no electoral votes. The Eighty-first Congress would again be Democratic. There would be fifty-four Democratic senators to forty-two Republicans. In the House the Democrats had 262 seats to the Republicans' 171. One seat went to the American Labor Party.

Dewey's explanation of his defeat was that at least three million Republicans, too confident of victory, had neglected to go to the polls. This was probably very true but it is also true that over-confidence worked against the Republicans in other ways. Many people were alienated by Dewey's smug, patronizing attitude that seemed to say that the election had been assured as early as July and that counting the vote would be a mere formality. There can be no doubt that Truman's personality was by far the more engaging and appealing.

Another important factor in the Democratic victory was the old adage that the people never vote a party out of power during prosperous times. The nation had seldom enjoyed a wave of prosperity comparable to this one and with money in the bank, plenty of jobs, and an increasing supply of consumer goods, there were few arguments anyone could advance to discredit the administration. The dismal failure of the Wallace movement was also a contributing factor. Wallace was expected to lure away the progressive wing of the Democratic party but he captured only 20 per cent of the five million votes conceded to him before November 2. The record of the Eightieth Congress was also a factor. Truman relentlessly drove home the idea that the Republican Congress was the creature of a privileged minority: that only by a return to the Democratic party could the people hope to hold the gains of the New Deal. Undoubtedly the biggest single factor was the agricultural situation. Farmers had not shared in the general prosperity of 1948 and when the Republicans insisted upon deserting parity and supporting a new system of flexible crop supports they sealed their doom. The midwest farm belt went over to Truman.

Throughout the summer of 1948, when the political cause seemed hopeless, Truman radiated confidence, never doubting that he would win. Undoubtedly many voted for him in tribute to his stubbornness in refusing to admit that he was beaten. Better than anyone he had his finger on the pulse of the times. Progressivism was the American way. The war and the Eightieth Congress had caused a temporary deviation from this general course and Truman seemed to know this. He was also sure that the nation was ready to accept its international responsibilities and make them a part of our future policies. In retrospect, the reasons for Truman's confidence seem plain enough. That he was sure of winning seems to have been his opinion alone.

IV THE TRUMAN ADMINISTRATION

The Years of Containment

The UN, economic recovery, military assistance, and Point Four.

During the "Fifteen Weeks" a new course was charted for American foreign policy. It was set to resist further Soviet expansion and to assist other countries of the world who might join in the same task. The old line of thought of world union of states functioning through the United Nations on the basis of universally respected principles had been temporarily abandoned in favor of building new alliances to oppose Soviet designs. Actually, the UN was reduced to the role of a tool for achieving this objective.

The Marshall Plan was designed as a comprehensive policy, based on American and European cooperative effort, to replace the patchwork aid program previously employed. American loans, even as extensive as they were by 1947, had produced few lasting benefits. International economic recovery required an all-out, comprehensive, cooperative effort. The Marshall Plan was such an effort. The Paris conference of England, France, and Russia concerning the Marshall proposals fell as flat as one might have expected. The Russians were as intransigent as ever. The British and French, however, extended a second invitation on July 3, 1947 to various countries to attend another conference; fourteen accepted. The Soviet satellites, restrained by their masters, failed to attend. The Europeans estimated their need; the Americans their resources. As the conference opened on July 12 a Committee of European Economic Cooperation (CEEC) was organized for the purpose of investigation. Its report, issued in August, proposed a multi-billion dollar American aid program for a four-year period.

While the Europeans were preparing a statement of what they thought they might require, the Americans were estimating what they thought

47

they could afford. From the defeat of Germany to the announcement of Truman's doctrine, the United States had already made eleven billion dollars in aid available to the Europeans. Three American committees reported that our resources were still sufficient to support an even more elaborate program of assistance.

In a speech to Congress on December 17, 1947 Truman made use of the sixteen-nation report which stressed the urgent need for food, fuel, raw materials, capital equipment, and money to rebuild the continent. The United States was the only nation with the capacity to close the gap between supply and need in Europe. Truman called upon Congress to provide seventeen billion dollars between April 1, 1948 and June 30, 1952 with an appropriation of $6,800,000,000 to cover the first fifteen months. The President said, in explaining the purposes of the program:

> In proposing that the Congress enact a program of aid to Europe I am proposing that this nation contribute to world peace and to its own security by assisting in the recovery of sixteen countries which, like the United States, are devoted to the preservation of free institutions and enduring peace among nations. It is my belief that United States' support of the European Recovery Program will enable the free nations of Europe to devote their great energies to the reconstruction of their economies. On this depends the restoration of a decent standard of living for their peoples, the development of a sound world economy, and continued support for the ideals of individual liberty and justice.

The program encountered some opposition, but powerful lobbies were at work to assure its passage. Such incongruous bedfellows as the CIO, AFL, and the National Association of Manufacturers were among those who gave support. In Congress, however, there were opponents, including the influential Senator Robert Taft, who branded the program as nothing more than "global New Dealism"; outside of Washington, Henry Wallace still warned that the measure's enactment would provoke Russia to war. Once again it was up to Senator Vandenberg to pilot the proposals over dangerous Congressional shoals. In this capacity he proved to be one of the greatest compromisers since Henry Clay.

Truman had asked for seventeen billions over a period of four years but Vandenberg, reluctant to tie the hands of Congress for so long a time, proposed annual appropriations and recommended that five billions be made available for the first year. Thus, the House was not asked to surrender its control over the purse strings. Vandenberg placated Senate opposition by providing that the appointment of a program director was to be confirmed by that body. And he pacified the "China Lobby" by including a $463,000,000 appropriation to aid that country even in the face of reasonable doubt that Chiang's government could survive. After preliminary hearings Vandenberg opened the Senate debate with a masterful speech in support of the program. The Foreign Assistance Act was signed by Truman on April 3, 1948, making $5,300,000,000 in aid available for the first year to Austria, Belgium, Great Britain, Nationalist China, Denmark, France, Greece, Iceland, Ireland, Italy, Luxembourg, the Netherlands, Norway, Portugal, Sweden, Switzerland, and Turkey.

The European Recovery Program (ERP) was created under the guidance of the Economic Cooperation Administration (ECA) directed by Paul G. Hoffman, president of the Studebaker Corporation. In time, the Office of Special Representative was established in Paris as well as missions in the participating states which in turn were represented in the Organization of European Economic Cooperation (OEEC). Until the ECA was replaced in December 1951 by the Mutual Security Agency, more than twelve billion dollars was distributed to aid world recovery. The European states assumed the responsibility of administering the system and the results were impressive.

Events of the times undoubtedly influenced final congressional support for the measure. The Communist coup in Czechoslovakia saw the disappearance of the last eastern European state behind the Iron Curtain. Germany was in the throes of an economic crisis and the Communists seemed certain victors in the approaching Italian elections.

While ERP was being debated in Congress early in 1948, the European states took action of their own which was impelled to a considerable degree by the distressing news from Czechoslovakia. In January, 1948 the British proposed that France and the Benelux states (Belgium, the Netherlands, and Luxembourg) should join with her in making the Anglo-French Treaty of Dunkirk of 1947 the nucleus of a comprehensive system. The Dunkirk treaty was designed specifically to guard against a resurgent Germany, but by March these five states had concluded a fifty-year treaty of collaboration at Brussels which was aimed at aggressors in general. A Western Union Organization was also created to insure military cooperation. American observers attended the Brussels meeting to give moral support to an alliance designed to check Communism.

The containment policy, originated in 1946, was fully elaborated in

1947, and George F. Kennan, who had helped draft the Marshall Plan and directed the work of the State Department's Policy Planning Staff, explained it clearly in an article in the July 1947 issue of *Foreign Affairs*. He developed the thesis that peace could be attained only if the United States were willing to use its power to check Communism throughout the world. America would have to be firm, patient, and optimistic as it exerted continuous pressure on the Soviet sphere from every angle. Such pressure, if religiously maintained, would in time bring about the destruction of the Russian empire. Just as rock is imperceptibly worn away by dripping water, so the Russians would ultimately break if pressure were maintained constantly. The policy of containment involved reaction rather than action and its success depended upon patience. These were hard choices for a nation of impatient, action-loving people—almost "un-American" because they were so alien to the national characteristics of speed and decision.

The Brussels Pact provided a foundation upon which to erect an anti-Communist bloc to contain Russia's further expansion in Europe. It remained only for the United States to become a participant. In May, 1948 Senator Vandenberg introduced a resolution, which was ultimately accepted, urging the President to associate the United States with other powers in regional and collective pacts. Between July and December the representatives of the United States and European countries completed the draft of a treaty.

On April 4, 1949 a treaty, creating an anti-Communist bloc in Europe, was signed in Washington by the United States, Britain, Canada, Denmark, France, Iceland, Italy, Norway, Portugal, and the Benelux states. The senatorial debate on ratification and newspaper editorial comment revealed some stout opposition to the treaty. To those who criticized the Truman Doctrine because it bypassed the UN, the treaty seemed another—even bigger—stride in the wrong direction. They were dismayed at the thought that instead of daring the "brave new world" of collective security the United States had fallen back on the old alliance system—time-honored though often impractical and unworkable. Article 3 and Article 5 were the most controversial and significant. The first pledged the signatories to use mutual aid and self-help to build their capacity to resist attack while the second was a solemn pledge among the contracting parties that an attack on one would be considered an attack on all. In the event that such an attack occurred, each and all, under the rights given by Article 51 of the UN charter for individual and collective defense, would assist the victim by "taking forthwith, individually and in concert with the other Parties, such action as it deems necessary, including the use of armed force." To many the last clause had an ominous ring. They said it would deprive Congress of its constitutional right to declare war. Nevertheless, on July 21, 1949 the treaty was approved by the impressive vote of eighty-two to thirteen.

By August the powers were ready to begin the creation of the North Atlantic Treaty Organization (NATO). The North Atlantic Council and other subordinate agencies were organized to administer the alliance and to plan for integrated defense of the community. A Supreme Head-quarters of Allied Powers in Europe (SHAPE) was established in Paris. Immediately Truman asked Congress for $1,450,000,000 to arm NATO and other countries. This request was based on a 1948 recommendation of the National Security Council. This Mutual Defense Assistance Program substituted an integrated program for a patchwork program. It was the military counterpart of the Marshall Plan. And just as the Prague coup in February, 1948 had dissolved congressional resistance to the Marshall Plan, so the news on September 23, 1949 that Russia had exploded an atomic bomb dissipated all resistance, and on September 27, 1949 Congress made $1,314,000,000 available for military aid under the Mutual Defense Assistance Act.

As a result, America had now lost some of the detachment with which it had previously conducted its foreign affairs. No longer did we possess power divorced from responsibility, nor did we behave like a married man who reserves, for himself, the free-wheeling days of bach-elorhood. Under NATO the United States was a co-partner with other states in planning defense. Nevertheless, under the defense act of 1949, we defined the conditions for assistance and thereby retained the power to determine the uses to which the alliance was to be put.

In 1947 the critics of the Truman Doctrine warned of an inherent danger; that eventually military aid might be substituted for economic aid. They were more prophetic than they knew. By 1949 the United States was offering guns instead of butter. Originally Truman had offered his doctrine as an ideological clash to win the allegiance of the world's peoples. A Communist victory could be prevented and Communist ideology contained, he said, by aiding the economic recovery of the Greeks and the Turks. The aid was offered, not to human beings in need, but to stop the spread of Communism. The test for granting aid was always—will it stop Communism? Consequently, it was an easy

51

step from economic to military aid. All that was necessary was for someone to demonstrate that the latter would check Communism more effectively than the former. Had the program been designed merely to help people in distress there would have been less, if any, justification for shifting from economic to military aid. The President undoubtedly saw that America was moving gradually away from the concept of economic to military aid and so, in his inaugural address of January 20, 1949, even before the mutual defense act was discussed, he sought to return to the concept of aid to needy peoples. Actually, as Truman later told the press, aid to underdeveloped nations had been under discussion since the first days of the Truman Doctrine and the Marshall Plan. The latter was primarily designed to aid postwar rehabilitation and reconstruction in Europe but more aid was needed for under-developed countries elsewhere.

In his inaugural address Truman pointed to three main lines of foreign policy; support for the UN and its related agencies, a program of world economic recovery, and military assistance to those countries threatened by aggression. Truman proposed to add a fourth, which he described as a "bold new program for making the benefits of our scientific advances and industrial progress available for the improvement and growth of underdeveloped areas." This was the famous Point Four Program which, on the one hand, was hailed as a brilliant, and inspired plan to bring the "backward" peoples of the world a better life and, on the other hand, ridiculed as a wild, far-fetched New Deal scheme to bring the blessings of modern plumbing to every Hottentot. Although Point Four was designed to help people in need, it was also a means of combating the strong appeal of Communism to downtrodden and exploited peoples. Frequently they were located in key raw-material-producing areas. It was necessary to keep their allegiance if NATO was to be armed.

On June 24, 1949, Truman sent a special message to Congress recommending an appropriation of not more than forty-five million dollars to begin the Point Four program. Congress adjourned the next month without taking action, so he repeated his request six months later. The Point Four Program became a reality a year after the first request for funds when a modest $34,500,000 was finally made available. The act had encountered much opposition in Congress. The plan aroused the old anti-New Deal sentiment of the Republicans. The long debate took the edge off Truman's announcement in 1949, and the spirit of altruism, which might have turned the program into a glorious experiment, was stifled by congressional modifications. The recipient states were expected to pay part of the cost and their full cooperation was made a prerequisite for receiving aid. They were also expected to give full credit to the United States for its assistance. This seemed an absurd requirement, for there is nothing better calculated to destroy good will than to force a beneficiary to testify publicly to his gratitude and indebtedness.

By executive order on September 8, 1950 Truman established the International Development Advisory Board and made the Secretary of State responsible for carrying out the program. Nelson Rockefeller, the Board's first chairman, was later replaced by Eric A. Johnston. The Technical Cooperation Administration was also created, and in November 1950 Truman appointed Henry Garland Bennett its administrator. After his death in a plane crash in Iran, the President appointed Stanley Andrews.

In two years, more than two hundred projects were undertaken in thirty-three countries under the Point Four Program. These were teaching and demonstration programs designed to impart superior technical and scientific knowledge and implant new skills. The various aid programs were consolidated in 1952, technical and economic assistance in southeastern Asia and the Pacific was placed under Harriman's Mutual Security Agency, while the TCA continued to be responsible for the program in the Middle East, Africa, southern Asia, and the American republics.

American-Russian conflict; direct and indirect.

In order to see the practical application of the Truman foreign policies it is necessary to examine the specific issues between the United States and Russia from 1946 to 1950. The two giant adversaries came to grips directly in some instances but in most others their contact was indirect as each maneuvered for influence in some intermediate country.

One area in which the two Leviathans faced each other was Germany. The four-power administration of that country proved unworkable. Through its agency, the Office of Military Government, the United States established an administration in its control zone and encouraged the formation of democratic parties. The United States now favored the economic revival of Germany based on a fusion of the four zones. Henry Morgenthau's proposals that Germany be reduced to an agrarian state were discarded and by 1946 Secretary of State Byrnes spoke of Germany's revival and supported ultimate reunion.

By the following year, while the Truman and Marshall Plans were being framed, a Council of Foreign Ministers was in session in Moscow trying to solve the German question. The Russian Foreign Minister Molotov contended that his country was entitled to reparations out of current production as well as capital equipment. The United States and England, through their representatives George Marshall and Ernest Bevin, argued that this was contrary to the Potsdam agreement. This was not the only bone of contention at the Moscow meeting. The Russians also insisted that the Oder-Neisse boundary had to be recognized. In 1946 the British and Americans had reached agreement on the economic union of their zones. The French were concerned over the creation of this "Bizonia," and at the Moscow conference they created an impasse by insisting on the internationalization of the Ruhr Valley and the separation of the Rhineland from Germany.

Friction also arose over the type of government to be installed in Germany. The Americans preferred a federal type but the Russians wanted a highly centralized government over which the occupying powers would have much control. Since agreement was impossible, the ministers adjourned until November, when they resumed their wrangle unsuccessfully for another two months in London. By the end of the year the Allied Control Council in Germany was completely disrupted. Early in 1948 France began to move closer to the British and Americans on the German question. In February the United States, Britain, France, and the Benelux states met in London to consider German affairs and in March they announced they had agreed on a form of government as well as tri-zonal cooperation. The Soviets watched these developments with alarm and their seizure of Czechoslovakia in February was partly a countermove to the German situation. The Cominform (the international Communist organization), which had been reactivated in October 1947, began an extensive propaganda campaign against the West and a meeting of Communist satellites was called in Prague to denounce the London decisions.

French opposition gradually abated and plans for a German state, with or without Russian participation, went forward. Between September 1948 and May 1949 American, British, and French delegates labored at Bonn to draft a constitution for Western Germany. The new federal government was to be composed of the eleven German states within the three zones. The door was left open for the eventual inclusion of the five German states within the Soviet zone. The new German government strongly resembled the French system. There were to be two houses in the legislative body, as well as a president and a responsible chancellor. The Allied High Commission, a civilian body, replaced the military government, although occupation troops remained on duty. The commission had wide powers over foreign relations, armament, trade, and reparations. Gradually more power was transferred to the Germans. To appease the French the Ruhr Valley was placed under an International Authority.

During the revolution of 1848 the German and Prussian constitutions were hammered out respectively at Frankfort and Berlin in the midst of violence and bloodshed. The German constitution of 1949 was shaped under similar trying circumstances. Before it was completed the Russians, always bent on obstructionism, played a trump card. On April 1, 1948 they announced they were restricting traffic from the west into Berlin. This was possible since all passengers and freight traffic moving to Berlin from the French, British and American zones had to cross Russian territory. Almost two months later the Russians slammed the gates shut on all entrances to Berlin. This happened at the moment when the Allies introduced a new currency common to all three of their zones. The Allied Kommandatura—the four-power agency set up to administer the city—was unable to find a solution, and on July 1, the Russians walked out of the meetings.

It was evident that the Russians were trying to force the western powers out of Berlin and thereby score a brilliant propaganda victory. President Truman was just as insistent that we would remain and he approved the plan to supply Berlin's western zones by air. Available American and British planes were rushed into service and supplies were taken in on a twenty-four hour schedule.

In June 1948 there was no way to judge the length of the blockade or its consequences. Hotheads were advising Truman to send an armed convoy through the Russian zone with orders to shoot if stopped. Truman wisely ignored this advice as well as the suggestion that the American Air Force be given atomic weapons to use in case the Russians refused to lift the blockade. When Russian fighters buzzed cargo planes bringing in supplies, the American and British pilots followed instructions and withheld their fire. As the days lengthened into months and the airlift continued to function without any apparent end in sight, the people grew more restive and demanded action. Time seemed to be on the Russians' side for, as Churchill commented, they were sitting in a chair while we were standing on our heads. Industry in Berlin was slowing down for lack of fuel and, as the long winter months approached, the Berliners faced the bleak prospect of neither fuel nor work.

No wonder the Russians were smug. They stood firm on the currency question and in their opposition to the plans to administer the allied zones of Germany without them. We, on the other hand, would discuss no settlement while the blockade was operating. While diplomats labored the drone of planes continued monotonously over Berlin day and night as the Americans and British brought in 2,343,315 tons of supplies in 277,264 flights. Somehow the pilots continued to fly through the winter of 1948-1949. Despite fog, snow, rain and Russians, the twenty-four hour schedule was maintained so there was enough food and fuel to carry Berlin through.

Suddenly the Russians eased their demands. In January 1949 Stalin answered some questions submitted to him by an American newsman and Dean Acheson, who had just replaced the ailing Marshall as Secretary of State, was quick to note that Stalin no longer coupled the lifting of the blockade with the currency question. Was this just coincidence or was it design? Philip Jessup, American representative to the UN, asked Soviet UN delegate Jacob Malik if this omission was deliberate. Malik replied that his country no longer considered the two issues inseparably linked and negotiations proceeded.

On May 12, 1949, the Russians lifted the blockade. In return for this the western powers, with their work completed on the German constitution, agreed to another foreign ministers' meeting in Paris on May 23. This conference was also a failure and when it dissolved in June the West continued with its plans for the creation of a Federal Republic of Germany. The Russians, in the meantime, were at work organizing a German Democratic Republic in their own zone.

By the end of 1949 two German states confronted each other. Behind each stood one of the bipolar powers. Konrad Adenauer's Western German state was larger, more populous, and possessed more of the industrial complexes than the Russian-sponsored state. But the Soviet's state had many of the raw materials, most of the food-producing lands, and the psychological advantage of Berlin as its capital. The western capital city of Bonn had no historical significance to the German people. The Russians, in their zone, began building military power by coddling ex-Nazi officers and recruiting a special "police" force. Any thought of German unification was now impossible since America and Russia could accept unification only on their own terms. Each feared that a united

Germany would gravitate into one of the armed camps with disastrous results for the other.

The United States had supported a federal government for Germany from the start. This would mean free elections and democracy. With the promise of American aid it was easy to see how the Germans would have voted. The Russians could not accept this possibility, and America would not accept the Russian proposal of a centralized state with the occupying powers in dominant roles. Because we had already had too much experience with Soviet obstructionism in the UN and the German Control Council, we did not want Soviet interference with our recovery plans for Germany. West German industry was vital to the United States and its territory was necessary to give NATO forces some maneuverability.

After the passage of the Mutual Defense Assistance Act the first arms shipment to Europe was not made until 1950. While Communist sympathizers threatened to interfere with the unloading, *agents provacateurs* encouraged strikes and "peace" rallies denounced the United States as a warmonger; the North Atlantic Council went ahead with NATO plans, and finally on September 18, 1950, it announced that an integrated military force for the defense of Europe was to be assembled as rapidly as possible. Dwight D. Eisenhower was appointed the supreme commander. The decision to build an integrated military force made Germany even more important to the United States. German manpower had to be included, but the United States and France differed on how these forces were to be included in the NATO army. Realizing their importance in American planning, the Germans were able to drive hard bargains. During the closing days of Truman's administration the United States tried to find some suitable military setup to appease German nationalism, allay French fears, and quiet American anxiety over adequate defense.

The European and Near East complexes

The United States and Russia did not meet face-to-face in Britain, France and Italy, but the existence of strong Communist parties in France and Italy produced much indirect maneuvering. The United States recognized the need to stabilize the political, social, and economic structure of all three states if they were to pull their weight in the alliance.

After the war France was economically weak, without military power, and its people were divided. Collaborators and traitors were everywhere when the Resistance assumed control after the liberation. In the first election, in October 1945, three powerful parties emerged: the Socialists, the Communists, and the M.R.P. The coalition government of these three parties was already falling apart when the constitution of the Fourth Republic was approved in 1946. The fragmentation of parties, which had been the bane of French politics for years, began again in 1946; only the Communists retained their strength—a result of their wide appeal to the newly enfranchised classes following the war. The political situation was complicated by the country's financial plight and many loans had to be made to France well before Marshall Plan funds became available.

To combat Communism Charles de Gaulle organized, in April 1947, the R.P.F., an amalgamation of right wing parties. Another coalition of parties sought to provide a fulcrum between the extremists of both right and left, but this "Third Force" achieved nothing since its component parties differed as vehemently as the various political parties. The result was a French political system in which the cabinet posts were shuffled incessantly and ministries rose and fell with monotonous regularity.

Although the Communists were dismissed from the cabinet in May 1947, they continued to make it difficult to gain support for American policies. Since the Communists polled about one-fourth of the votes, it was impossible to ignore them completely. The judicious use of economic pressure and financial aid often proved effective in forcing the ever-changing French governments to adopt domestic policies that Americans could approve. But foreign policy was another matter. Here the French were less inclined to follow America's lead, since nationalistic aspirations and fear of Germany were forces no ministry could ignore. The French eagerly supported such alliances as those consummated at Dunkirk, Brussels, and Washington, since these offered security against both Germany *and* Russia; but they differed widely with the Americans on the question of how Germany was to be treated. France's foreign policy was more consistent than her domestic policy. Unlike many ministries, the portfolio did not change hands often; Georges Bidault and Robert Schuman were Ministers of Foreign Affairs during most of the Truman era. But even so, the French situation was complicated by its colonial problem. Syria and Lebanon were lost to native nationalism by the end of the war, while French possessions in North Africa and the Far East on the verge of momentary independence. French military and economic resources were drained off to defend the empire and it was therefore difficult for her to meet her commitments under NATO.

In Italy, too, there were three important parties. In June 1946 the Italians rejected the monarchy and moved to establish a new government. The Christian Democrats were the strongest party, but the Socialists and the Communists possessed a good deal of strength. It was to America's advantage to keep Alcide de Gasperi's Christian Democrats in power and to this end our operations and administration in Washington contributed a great deal. Through the use of aid, judiciously offered or withheld, the United States played the old game of carrot and stick to make the Italian donkey go. A peace treaty was imposed on Italy in February 1947 and occupation troops were withdrawn by the end of the year. The treaty was a harsh one. Italy lost all of her empire, Venezia Guila was ceded to Yugoslavia, and Trieste became a free territory. The Italians were also required to pay heavy reparations to Yugoslavia, Albania, Ethiopia, Greece, and Russia.

For a century Great Britain had played a key role throughout the world and she was still a power in some areas. American success was only possible in many areas because of a strong Britain, willing and able to fulfill her commitments. Britain had to be rebuilt in order to assume these responsibilities or the United States would have to assume them for her.

The victory of the Labor Party under Clement Atlee in 1945 brought to power a party committed to economic and social justice for the British people. The Laborites' answer was a welfare state. Basic industries were nationalized and such important statutes as the Children's Act, the National Assistance Act, the National Insurance Act, and the National Health Service Act were designed to give people a cradle-to-the-grave protection. But Britain was unfortunately embarking upon these elaborate programs at a time when the Exchequer's cupboard was nearly as bare as Mother Hubbard's. The United States feared these domestic expenditures would make it difficult for Britain to meet her international commitments. Heavy overseas debts and unfavorable trade balances drained Britain of her available credit and by 1948 she faced a serious fiscal crisis. That Britain had faced a financial crisis from 1945 to 1950 was additional incentive to implement America's promises of aid, as evidenced by Ernest Bevin's instantaneous response to Marshall's famous Harvard speech.

Many significant changes took place in Britain after 1945. A difficult psychological problem for the British was the realization that their country had ceased to be the Britain of Queen Victoria's day. England no longer enjoyed equal status with Russia and the United States, but was now reduced to joining a permanent alliance and to maintaining a large standing army in peacetime. The most significant changes occurred in her relations with the colonial world. India, Pakistan, Ceylon, and Burma left the British fold, and the Commonwealth, for the first time, became a colored man's world. It was a difficult task to fit the incongruous republics of India and Pakistan into a Commonwealth presided over by George VI or Elizabeth II. India persisted in pursuing an independent foreign policy, while Nehru cuddled closer to the Soviets. India and Pakistan quarreled over Kashmir and Daniel Malan in South Africa upset the delicate balance by denying colored men their rights.

By 1945, the entire Moslem world was seething with unrest. In that area the Italians had been driven from Libya, France had lost Syria and Lebanon, and the British were forced to recognize Jordan's independence. But still the stakes were unlimited, chiefly because of the great oil fields of the Persian Gulf and Arabia. The Moslem world furnished western Europe with nearly eighty per cent of its oil. True, sufficient oil could be obtained from America if eastern supplies were cut off but, because of unfavorable trade balances, Europeans were unable to pay for American oil. Since Europe depended on oil the Moslems used it as a bargaining wedge to gain concessions.

The whole Moslem complex was further complicated by the rising spirit of nationalism. This was not nationalism in a western sense because the loyalty was, more often, to a tribe or a family rather than to an area. Nevertheless it was a force so great that much of the controversy in this area grew out of the rivalry between the sons of Ibn Saud of Saudi Arabia and the grandsons of Emir Hussein in Iraq and Jordan. Such rivalries made Moslem unity impossible. The United States was concerned and often angered because the Moslem world was not sufficiently aware of a Communist menace and often persisted in cooperating with the Russians.

The Moslems were impressionable, quixotic, and lacking in the political experience to produce a stable government. At a time when Britain and France had lost face and power the United States was unable to take their place, due partly to natural reluctance, but largely because Americans had little of interest to offer these people. The Moslem world was

60

us of the West. The Marshall Plan might rehabilitate the com-
lustrial societies of the West but it was useless in an Arab world
he economic system had not changed since antiquity. Point Four
better approach but the Moslems suspected this as a clever ruse to
Western colonialism. The military assistance program, which
d so effectively in the West, again offered little to the East. The
Moslems often feared that our requests for bases and offers of arms
were concealed attempts to re-occupy their countries; we feared that
those who accepted arms might use them against our friends. And just
to complicate the situation even more, the Americans and the British
often worked at cross purposes. The British felt that we did not assume
enough responsibility in the East and that Point Four aid merely undermined their interests by encouraging nationalism and independence.
Americans, on the other hand, were not only unprepared to assume
responsibility in this area but were also afraid that support of British
colonialism would only encourage the spread of Communism.

During the Truman era there was one important Near Eastern crisis.
At the end of the war the British had military pacts with Egypt, Iran,
Iraq, Turkey and Jordan. In 1945 the Arab League was formed and
received American blessings in the interests of possible Near East stability. However, the Moslem rivalries continued and the power of the
League was directed toward driving the Jews from Palestine or freeing
other Arabs from foreign control.

In Palestine the British were trying to carry on with their mandate
from the old League of Nations. Jewish refugees who had flocked to
Palestine during Hitler's pogroms were badly received by the Arabs.
Armed clashes between Jews and Arabs placed the British in a difficult
position because they were no longer strong enough to police the whole
Near East. When Truman suggested that a hundred thousand Jewish
refugees should be admitted to Palestine, the British tried to involve
the United States by proposing the creation of a joint Anglo-American
Commission. When this failed, the British referred the whole matter to
the UN and withdrew their troops. The UN proposed that the land
should be divided between the Arabs and the Jews. President Truman
supported this suggestion and when the Jews proclaimed the state of
Israel on May 14, 1948, America granted recognition at once. Arabian
troops from Egypt, Iraq, Jordan, Syria, and Lebanon attacked the tiny
Jewish state, which, contrary to expectations, drove the invaders out
and seized more territory. According to the truce arrangements of 1949,

Israel emerged with more territory than it had originally been offered by the UN, but its existence was precarious indeed in view of the announced Arab intention to extinguish the state at some future time.

Meanwhile, British prestige had dropped to an all-time low. Great Britain was blamed for the whole mess by both sides and, as losers, the Arabs were bitter about the poor showing of their armies, the seizure of additional territory by the Israeli, and the latter's expulsion of more than a million Arab refugees.

In 1945 the Egyptians demanded that the British alter the condominium (joint dominion) over Anglo-Egyptian Sudan and begin the evacuation of the Suez Canal zone. Since this would leave no security guarantee for this vital area, American diplomats considered and then dropped a plan for building Turkey into a Near Eastern power. Near East problems continued to mount but it was only by 1950 that the Truman administration came to grips with this extremely difficult situation.

Although America and Britain differed over the conduct of affairs in the Near East, they nevertheless managed to pull together in Europe where an effort was made to form a union of states. At Churchill's suggestion a conference was held at The Hague in May 1948 to discuss European union. In November the Brussels states began discussions which resulted in the creation of the Council of Europe with headquarters in Strasbourg. The treaty was signed May 5, 1949, and went into force August 3, 1949. This Council of Europe included the Brussels powers, Denmark, Ireland, Norway, Sweden, and Italy, originally, but Iceland, Greece and Turkey joined later in 1949, and Western Germany joined in 1951. Although a Council of Ministers, Consultative Assembly, and permanent secretariat came into existence, the Council of Europe failed to achieve unity. In their zeal to prevent a German revival the French were among the strongest advocates of this union and it was also encouraged by the United States. In May 1950 Robert Schuman suggested the establishment of a European organization to control the iron and steel industries, and during the same year Premier René Pleven proposed the creation of the European Defense Community in which a common army would be created. On May 27, 1952 France, Germany, Italy, and the Benelux states signed the agreement to establish a new grouping to be known as the European Defense Community (EDC), which was to be closely linked with the new European Coal and Steel Community, NATO, and the proposed European Political

Community. Before any steps could be taken there had to be ratification by the signatories. The smaller states—Belgium, the Netherlands, and the Scandinavian states—readily supported American policy since their only hope for the future was to become part of a greater European family. Sweden's refusal to join NATO was badly received in America, but the Swedes placed confidence in their traditional neutrality which had seen them safety through two wars. They also realized that in the event of Soviet aggression the West would come to their aid, treaty or not, and there was more to lose than gain by joining NATO since such a move might provoke a Russian attack.

In eastern Europe Poland, Rumania, Hungary, Yugoslavia, Albania, and, in 1948, even Czechoslovakia were lost to democracy and freedom. This loss was partially counterbalanced by Yugoslavia's break with the Soviets. Although Tito remained a Communist and spoke an anti-western line, it was hoped that Tito's defection from Moscow might, in time, stimulate further examples of "Titoism." The Yugoslav-Russian rift also helped since the Greek Communist rebels could no longer obtain supplies from across the border. Greek Communist resistance ended by 1949, Turkey was saved, and Russian designs on Iran were foiled. The spread of Communism into the strategic Dardanelles area had been checked, due largely to American effort and aid.

Complications in the West: South America and the UN

There were American-Soviet clashes close to home as well as far away on the Rhine-Danube border. During World War II the Latin American states, with the exception of Chile and Argentina, severed diplomatic relations with the Axis before or shortly after the Inter-American Conference at Rio de Janeiro in January 1942. Chile followed a year later. Argentina was the last to sever relations. Many of Argentina's leading citizens were pro-Fascist and also there was a strong nationalistic resentment against the power of the United States, enhanced by Argentina's and America's rivalry in the production of wheat and beef.

In February 1945 the United States was instrumental in calling a conference against fascism in Mexico City. Argentina was invited to join. The conference promulgated the Act of Chapultepec which declared that an attack on the territory or an infringement upon the sovereignty of any of the signatories would be regarded as an attack upon all. Thus, the Monroe Doctrine, which had been a cornerstone of American foreign policy for generations, ceased to be unilateral. However, the

Monroe Doctrine referred only to foreign intervention, but this 1945 declaration covered internal and inter-American aggression too. Many felt that this was directed primarily at Argentina. At the last moment Argentina realized that it was better to keep on friendly terms with her neighbors, so she also joined in declaring war on the Axis. As a reward the United States, despite Soviet objections, secured a seat for her at the San Francisco conference and admission to the UN.

Since February, 1944 Argentina had really been dominated by the military clique under Colonel Juan Domingo Perón. This was ample reason to be suspicious of the puppet government. Despite our Good Neighbor policy the State Department began to interfere in Argentine domestic affairs and through our ambassador, Spruille Braden, called upon the people to overthrow their government. On the eve of the national elections the United States issued a *Blue Book* which exposed Perón's pro-Axis sympathies and accused him of plotting against the United States. On February 24, 1946, in a free election, the people triumphantly elected Perón as President and thereby registered their resentment against attempted American dictation in domestic affairs. Perón was strongly anti-American. The estrangement between the two countries continued to grow. Other states were drawn in unwillingly and although most of them seemed to dislike Perón, they frequently took his side because they resented the heavy-handed maneuvering of the American State Department.

In such an atmosphere it became obvious that the Act of Chapultepec was nothing more than a piece of paper. Truman and Secretary Marshall realized they would have to come to terms with Argentina if hemisphere defense was to be more than a dream, so, in August, 1947, the states of the Western Hemisphere met again, this time in Rio de Janeiro. The next month nineteen countries signed the Treaty of Rio de Janeiro or the Inter-American Treaty of Reciprocal Assistance, as it was known officially. A defense zone was established in the western hemisphere and all the countries pledged that an attack within this zone would be considered an attack upon all. Just as in the case of NATO this treaty was carefully related, through Article 51, to the UN Charter.

Between March and May 1948 the same countries met again at Bogotá, Colombia where they created an Organization of American States (OAS). The Council of the Organization, with one delegate from each of the twenty-one members, was to meet in Washington. There were to be meetings of a defense committee as well as the foreign ministers. A means was provided for the settlement of inter-American disputes. The Pan-American Union was made the permanent secretariat and the OAS was incorporated as a regional structure under the UN.

In spite of these elaborate inter-American gestures the Good Neighbor policy was of less importance to the United States in the fifties than it had been in the thirties. Like Europe, South America was the victim of an unfavorable trade balance. However, although the United States helped the Europeans restore the balance through heavy loans, no such assistance was offered to the South Americans. The result was economic crisis and violent disturbance. Although Communism reared its vicious head periodically from the various seed beds of illiteracy and low living standards, individual governments usually remained friendly toward the United States. With apparently so little to fear, our diplomats concentrated on the Near East, Europe, and the Far East; our own hemisphere was not watched too closely during the Truman era.

Within the borders of the United States we were face to face with the Communists on the floor of the United Nations. In this locale the conflict was a parliamentary one, at least on the surface. The UN Charter provided for a General Assembly in which each of the member-states was to have one vote. But most of the real strength of the UN was in the eleven-seat Security Council where five seats were permanently held by the United States, Russia, Britain, France, and China; the other six were elected for two-year terms by the General Assembly. Seven votes were needed to approve measures before the Security Council but on important issues the permanent five had to vote affirmatively. This was the celebrated veto power which the United States insisted upon at first and later accused the Russians of abusing. There was also a Military Staff Committee which was to direct the armed forces of the UN if such came into being. As might have been expected, Russia and the United States differed as to the type of UN military forces to be created. The Russians feared the use of American naval and air power with UN sanction; we were equally afraid of Russian ground power. Result: no UN army. Also the Charter provided for an Economic and Social Council, a Trusteeship Council, an International Court of Justice, and a permanent secretariat. There were many other subordinate agencies some of which were inherited from the defunct League of Nations.

One of the first problems to come before the new UN in 1946 was the Iranian dispute. By walking out during the proceedings, the Russian delegate, Andrei Gromyko, established a precedent that the Russians were to repeat constantly whenever events did not go their way. During the early days the UN scored successes in Iran, Indonesia, Trieste, and Palestine, but the overall picture was not encouraging. The bipolar powers used the UN to foster their own ambitions and as a means of embarrassing each other. The Russians, who up to 1950 had used the veto more than fifty times, protested that the United States was forcing showdown votes on matters they knew the Russians would veto; this they were doing simply to run up an impressive score for propaganda purposes. The UN had an impressive record on minor disputes, but on such things as control of atomic energy, disarmament, and the UN military force, it failed completely.

With Russian "nyets" coming too fast to count, and with Gromyko constantly stalking out of meetings and staying away for weeks at a time, the United States lost hope of any positive action in the Security Council. American strategy therefore was to depend more and more on the General Assembly and, in 1947, Secretary Marshall helped create the UN Interim Committee so that the General Assembly would be in permanent session and ready for business at all times. Then, if Russia blocked action in the Security Council by vetoes, Americans could muster comfortable majorities in the General Assembly. If the need were great then by pressure and manipulation of the American aid program it was possible to get even more votes. Although the vote of the General Assembly was looked upon as a moral voice of the globe speaking against Communism, Americans gradually lost confidence in the UN. Alliances were being created, presumably within the framework of the UN. Actually, nothing could have been farther from the purpose and spirit of the UN since that body was created to reduce international rivalry and friction. The UN became a sounding board for the free world's public opinion. Against this the Russians' only defense was the veto.

. . . had containment faced a major test?

As 1950 began, the Truman foreign policy, particularly Kennan's doctrine of containment, seemed to have been successful. Our own hemisphere stood united in opposition to Communism, and we had bolstered both western Europe and the Near East through economic and military aid. On these fronts Communism seemed to have been contained. But, had the containment policy really faced a major test? To counteract containment the Russians had replied in kind. To the Marshall Plan they retaliated by creating the Council for Mutual Economic Assistance. When we created a Western German State, they organized one in the east. The Russians had made a nuisance of themselves during the Berlin blockade. We countered them with firmness but this was scarcely a test of major importance. It was not of vital interest to the Russians to get us out of Berlin. They could, and did, in time, back down without losing face. By January 1950 the containment policy had yet to meet a major test.

Suddenly the situation changed. On February 14, 1950, the Chinese Communists signed a treaty with the Russian Communists pledging friendship and mutual assistance. More than six hundred million of the world's people were joined under one banner. This suggested to the discerning that Truman's foreign policy was in for its first real trial.

The China Crisis and the Search for Traitors

. . . hunting a culprit

In *The Price of Power* by Herbert Agar, one chapter is entitled "Hiss, Chiang, Fuchs, and the Bomb." As Mr. Agar has arranged them, these four words are fissionable material and once the chain reaction started they cost enough public support to defeat the Democrats in 1952, rendered the Truman administration powerless to carry on its foreign policy, undermined public confidence in the government at a time when confidence was urgently needed, and set in motion forces which were to culminate in one of the most remarkable outbursts of demagoguery in our history.

Events in the Far East were so closely associated with those in America that it is impossible to disassociate them. Truman's surprise victory in November 1948 was speedily followed in December by the news that Chiang Kai-shek had fled to Formosa. Nationalist China was reduced to a few square miles of real estate. Probably many people, particularly Republicans, were too stunned by the events of November to be aware of what had happened in Asia. Gradually, as they recovered their wits, the Republicans were horrified to discover that they had lost not only the United States but China too. The latter had succumbed to Communism, while the former had fallen to something worse—Truman-brand, creeping-socialism. The appalling thing about it was that a majority in each place seemed to be satisfied with the results.

By 1949-50 there was already dissatisfaction with the policy of containment. It seemed too slow; its results were not spectacularly evident, and there could be no assurance of ultimate success. People had questioned containment before; now, after the loss of China, their questioning became criticism. It was pointless to speak of efforts nullified by insuperable historical forces at work in China, because such a view was unacceptable to the critics. They reaffirmed the fact that China could have been saved if we had wanted to save it. Since China was lost, it must have been lost because we wanted to lose it. If we chose to lose it, that had to be the result of deliberate design. Therefore, there had to be villains; one or two men in key places must have sold out four hundred million Chinese and 150,000,000 Americans. Such an uncomplicated answer gave the public a simple, understandable solution.

Everyone rushed about hunting a culprit. The first villain suggested was Roosevelt—everything that had happened since 1933 had set the stage for this tragedy. In his *The Crucial Decade* Eric Goldman suggests the logic of the villain seekers was that Roosevelt had placed men in control who were Communists at heart. Using the depression as a shield, these appointees set about to destroy capitalism and to strengthen socialism. Socialism was equated with Communism. In foreign affairs the same pernicious conspiracy was evident. Roosevelt had recognized Russia, strengthened her through lend-lease aid, and betrayed our interests to her at Yalta. His State Department stooges tried to pass off the Chinese Communists as "agrarian reformers" and deceived Americans into believing that Russia, after 1936, had become more democratic. This sounded like conspiracy.

Unfortunately Roosevelt was dead. Accusers need living betrayers at whom they may point a finger and on whom responsibility can be fixed. Of course, Truman carried the ultimate responsibility, but his personal conduct was above reproach. The Secretary of State was more vulnerable, but again, he was personally unassailable. However, the accusation had to be directed at the State Department. If the accusation were pinned on an underling and could be made to stick, the discredit would reflect upon the Secretary, and soon thereafter on the President and his party.

Since January 21, 1949 the Secretary of State had been Dean Gooderham Acheson. He was listed in the social register; a graduate of Groton, Yale, and Harvard Law School; a remarkably successful attorney; always impeccably dressed; and a master of correct English. All of these qualifications angered his critics. "I watch his smart-aleck manner and his British clothes and that New Dealism, everlasting New

Dealism in everything he says and does, and I want to shout, 'Get out, Get out! You stand for everything that has been wrong with the United States for years!'" said Senator Hugh Butler of Nebraska as he echoed the common complaint against Acheson. Seldom was an *argumentum ad hominem* used more effectively than against the Secretary. Still, accusing Acheson of being a poor Secretary because he wore a Brooks Brothers suit did not produce the much sought living villain.

The chase became a rout when an accuser by the name of Whittaker Chambers pointed his finger at a State Department underling, Alger Hiss. Was there ever a more appropriate name for a villain than Hiss? Here was a tailor-made scapegoat. Not only did his name suggest villainy, but also he had been a young New Deal upstart long nurtured by the betrayers. Hiss had risen rapidly in government service to a position of some responsibility. When he left Washington in 1947 to assume the presidency of the Carnegie Endowment for International Peace, Hiss was considered one of the capital's brightest younger stars, liked and respected by everyone. It was then that Whittaker Chambers, a former Communist courier, testified before the Un-American Activities Committee that Hiss had been a fellow party member from 1934 to 1938. It was a shock that an American of Hiss' background and position could be seriously involved with Communists. It caused everyone to wonder just how many former radicals might have found similar safe haven in federal employment. Even worse, how many might still be Communists actively working for the Kremlin?

It was at this point that Truman entered the picture. In a press conference he branded the congressional investigation as "a red herring" offered to the public as hocus pocus to divert attention from congressional failure to check inflation.

Truman had reason to have confidence in what his administration was doing about Communism. Many Communist agents had been discovered in both America and Canada during the war and there was fear that some had infiltrated the government. On March 22, 1947, Truman issued an executive order providing for an investigation of all federal job holders by the FBI and the Civil Service Commission. Any person accused of membership in a subversive group was to have a hearing, counsel, a resumé of the charges, and the right of appeal. Permanent employees could appeal to the Loyalty Review Board headed by Seth Richardson, and temporary employees could seek redress before regional boards.

71

Despite criticism from both extremes that the rules of procedure were either too harsh or too lenient, the investigation went ahead without fanfare. More than three million workers were eventually screened. About two thousand resigned under pressure and 212 were dismissed because a "reasonable doubt" existed as to their loyalty. In August 1950 Congress later permitted the heads of "sensitive" departments to discharge "security risks." The important thing was that these investigations were conducted with precautions taken to protect the accused's rights. This system was more effective than the hit-or-miss approach of congressional committees which were often more interested in publicity and votes. But Truman's choice of the "red herring" phrase was unfortunate and it continued to dog him for the rest of his administration.

Developments in the Hiss case refuted Truman's red herring remarks. Hiss' decision to sue Chambers for libel produced an astonishing denouement. Chambers broadened his accusation by saying that Hiss had not only been a Communist party member but had also stolen secret government documents for transmission to him (Chambers) as a Communist courier. He took investigators to his Maryland farm where he produced a collection of documents theatrically hidden in a scooped-out pumpkin. They were said to have been typed on a machine owned by Hiss; others were in his handwriting. While Truman still spoke of red herrings, the New York grand jury indicted Hiss for perjury on December 15, 1948. He was not indictable for espionage because of the statute of limitations but, as his trial progressed, there was no doubt that, like Andrew Johnson, he was charged with one offense but actually prosecuted for another. In May 1949 his first trial began; it ended with a hung jury. Between November 1949 and January 1950 he was tried again and this time was sent to prison for perjury. The most significant bit of evidence was a Woodstock typewriter, which had belonged to Hiss. FBI experts testified that some of Chamber's pumpkin notes were written on this machine.

Both Agar and Goldman see in Hiss a symbol of the times. A scapegoat was needed upon whose shoulders could be cast the burden of losing China. Hiss had been in the Office of Far Eastern Affairs; his brother worked for Acheson's law firm; Hiss had accompanied Roosevelt to Yalta, and after his conviction, Acheson refused to turn his back upon an old friend. All these bits of information, each of which was true itself, could be fitted neatly together to produce, by inference and indirection, a fantastic story of betrayal and treason. The investigators had produced a minor villain, whose actual influence was negligible, and were able to blow him up on the political enlarger until he became one of the arch traitors of all times. That only one culprit was found was proof in itself of the loyalty of federal employees, but by clever manipulation, this one villain was made to serve a far-reaching purpose.

The United States, a comparative outsider in the Orient

It was in Asia that Truman's foreign policy faced its severest test. All Asia seethed with nationalism after 1945. Nationalism and anti-colonialism produced violent demonstrations and rebellions in Indochina, Burma, Malaya, and Indonesia, Thailand escaped from internal revolution possibly because it was the only state in southeastern Asia which had not been under foreign domination. Although the American press often blamed Communism for creating these disturbances, the Communists merely capitalized on sentiments and feelings which had deeper origins. The Dutch were forced to grant independence to Indonesia, and the British surrendered control in Burma. The French, on the other hand, resisted the nationalist demands of the Indochinese rebels.

The United States, a comparative outsider in the Orient, was not entirely immune from the virus of rebellion. The promise of independence to the Filipinos was delayed by World War II. Finally, the islands were granted independence on July 4, 1946. This was not an unmixed blessing. The economy had suffered because of wartime destruction, and the distress was intensified later because Congress decided to subject the islands to tariff restrictions. Although the Filipinos were angered by our insistence upon equal rights in the exploitation of natural resources, this was partially compensated by extensive American aid under the Philippine Rehabilitation Act. Early in 1947 the Filipinos granted the right to maintain American military bases on the islands and asked for a military advisory group to train native troops. Many nationalists resented this as too much American interference and a native insurrection of the Hukbalahaps attempted, and failed, to destroy the Filipino government as too pro-American.

Actually, in Southeast Asia, American policy was caught between the European Scylla and the Oriental Charybdis. If we were to encourage native nationalism and independence, we would seriously weaken the economic position of our European allies and therefore lose their friendship. If we favored our European allies, we risked driving the native nationalists into the Communists' open and waiting arms. Under the circumstances there was little to do but equivocate and await developments.

The United States was proud of its democratization of Japan. Although we insisted upon unconditional surrender, as we had in Germany, there were marked differences. The United States assumed sole responsibility for the occupation of Japan, and although Supreme Commander Douglas MacArthur sponsored a new constitution in 1947, revived political parties, enfranchised women, and drastically altered the administration of the country, the Japanese government, unlike the German government, was not destroyed. The emperor was permitted to remain in power. The reforms were not only political. The Supreme Command for the Allied Powers (SCAP) encouraged labor unions, broke up the industrial monopoly of the Zaibatsu, and tackled the difficult land problem by trying to reduce tenantry and absentee landlordism. All military forces were disbanded, the military clique was uprooted from office, and the educational system was revamped to de-emphasize nationalism. In Germany the war leaders were brought to trial at Nuremberg, charged with having violated the Kellogg-Briand Pact against war; in Japan the leaders were tried before the International War Crimes Tribunal in Tokyo.

Theoretically MacArthur's control was limited. There was an Allied Council in Tokyo to check on SCAP, but its powers were largely nonexistent. The foreign ministers' meeting in Moscow in 1945 had decided to establish an eleven-nation Far Eastern Commission, but it met in Washington and its recommendations had little effect upon MacArthur's actions. By 1947 the British, Australian, and New Zealand troops had left Japan, and only the Americans remained. MacArthur's power became almost absolute. He used his own initiative in bringing about reforms and far exceeded the specific instructions of his directives even though he often worked through the Japanese Diet. By 1948 the press was loud in its acclaim for MacArthur's achievements. The Japanese were busy playing at democracy and Emperor Hirohito publicly confessed that he was not a god and that Shintoism had been a false creed. He moved among his people with all the simplicity and bourgeois mannerism of Louis Philippe. But the democracy, as practiced in Japan during these years, always functioned under the shadow of American bayonets. There was some doubt that it would survive at all once the occupation terminated. MacArthur disclosed a mailed fist whenever the

Japanese leaned the wrong way. His encouragement of labor unions led to a general strike threat in 1947. It was met with repressive measures. But he tolerated a flourishing Communist party which polled over three million votes in the 1949 elections.

However, there was no real solution for Japan's basic problems. The war had stripped her of all her conquests since 1895; Japan was reduced in 1945 to the four home islands. As a result, seventy million people were crowded into an area scarcely larger than California—an explosive situation. The dissolution of the industrial monopoly of the Zaibatsu, the decentralization of industry, and the ban against trade with Communist-dominated countries seriously weakened Japan's recovery. By early 1948 the American representative on the Far Eastern Commission, despite objections, announced that we were changing our policies. We planned to rebuild the Japanese economy by prohibiting strikes, turning much of the industry back to the Zaibatsu monopolists, and ending various forms of American subsidies. Before the end of 1948 some economic recovery was noticeable but trade restrictions with prewar customers still hampered the Japanese.

This change in our Japanese policy was inspired by the situation in China. The economic weakening of Japan, as well as her disarmament, was poor policy in view of the Communist threat in Asia. When Nationalist China declined as a bastion of Far Eastern power, it became obvious Japan would have to be rebuilt. Japan, like Britain, had to be strengthened so she could pull her own weight; otherwise the United States would have had to asume too many of her responsibilities. America ignored Chinese and Russian opposition to these new plans for Japan and gradually SCAP's powers over non-military matters were relinquished. The Japanese resumed control over all affairs except those pertaining to defense and foreign policy.

The Korean war speeded the reversal of American policy. The 1947 constitution prohibited the Japanese from rearming, a limitation on their sovereignty which few Japanese resented. The bombing of the home islands and the devastation at Hiroshima and Nagasaki had demonstrated the futility and vanity of war, and the Japanese were only too glad to be relieved of the burden of armaments. Suddenly, the United States, which had fostered anti-war propaganda in the new democratic schools, called upon the Japanese to rearm. The result was bitter disappointment, and in many cases, it left the Japanese bewildered and uncertain. In July 1950 MacArthur authorized the formation of a National Police Reserve of 75,000 men to be trained by the Americans, but the Japanese supported this move reluctantly.

The matter of a peace treaty was still unsettled. Now that the United States was encouraging rearmament in Japan, it was evident that Russian, Chinese, and general Far Eastern opposition would increase. This impasse between the United States and other important world powers delayed the completion of the treaty. John Foster Dulles, as the principal American negotiator, presented a treaty to the world in 1951 which was roundly denounced. Signed in San Francisco in September 1951, it restored Japanese sovereignty and permitted her rearmament. This treaty was proclaimed as a settlement of Asian problems, despite its lukewarm support in Japan and vigorous opposition by Russia, Communist and Nationalist China, and India. On the same day, and independently of the other powers, the United States signed a separate agreement with Japan to permit American troops and bases on the home islands and, under certain conditions, to intervene in domestic affairs to prevent disturbances fomented by outside powers.

Although the United States maintained a friendly government in the Philippine Islands and established a hothouse democracy in Japan, the loss of China more than counterbalanced these achievements. It seems strange today that apparently neither the United States nor Russia anticipated a Communist victory in China in 1945. Both powers were willing to deal with Chiang, and the Russians even signed a treaty with him that year. However, the Russians obviously hoped for a Chinese Communist victory.

Why did the Kuomintang fail?

After the revolution of 1911 Sun Yat-sen attempted sweeping changes in China. The work of furthering his reforms was entrusted to the Kuomintang, eventually headed by Chiang Kai-shek. The Communist party, organized in 1921 by Ch'en Tu-hsiu, Mao Tse-tung, and Chou En-lai, at first cooperated and then split wth Chiang. The Communists wanted an immediate social revolution but Chiang preferred gradualism and was willing to keep the support of capitalistic elements both within and without China. He expelled the Communists from the Kuomintang and attempted to exterminate them but they were too well intrenched in their strongholds in northwestern China. The Japanese invasion of China in 1937 forced Chiang to slacken his campaign against the Communists. Theoretically, both sides combined against the Japanese but even during World War II the Kuomintang and the Communists were still fighting each other.

The Sino-Japanese war undermined the Kuomintang and strengthened the Communists. In 1937 the Nationalists (the Kuomintang) were the most important force in China. They were entrusted with the job of achieving Sut Yat-sen's three principles—nationalism, democracy and people's Livelihood. To a considerable degree they were successful. The economy was expanding, revenue was increasing, and administrative control was being extended gradually over the entire country. These changes were to guarantee greater peace and security. By 1945 the Kuomintang was a demoralized and conservative group, dominated for the most part by cynical, self-seeking men. Not only had its territorial control been weakened and reduced but also the economy of China was ruined. The Communists, weak in 1937, were now the stronger. They were the only dynamic force left in China, and although they controlled no more than three million people in 1937 they had extended their control to eighty million by 1945.

Why did the Kuomintang fail? The answer is complex and its general outlines can only be suggested. The Sino-Japanese War unleashed a tremendous force of nationalism and patriotism, just as the German invasion produced the same results in Russia. Most of the people rallied behind Chiang to drive out the invaders. He might have assured their continued support by offering moderate concessions by way of a popular government and a constitution. But Chiang ignored these popular pressures and the Communists exploited them. Part of their method of encouraging patriotism and nationalism was to build up the guerilla forces in North China. Every effort the Japanese made to extinguish the guerillas only aroused more patriotism upon which the Communists capitalized. Also, the Communists sympathized with the peasants' demands for land and local administrative reforms.

In defense of Chiang, it is true that he faced more serious problems than the Communists. While the Communists worked with local governments and guerillas, Chiang had the more difficult and expensive task of maintaining a central government and an army. When the Japanese seized the richer provinces of China, they destroyed Chiang's staunch supporters, the merchant classes. As the economy stagnated, the government inflated the currency by printing more paper money than its credit could stand. This ruined fixed-income groups such as the intellectuals and civil servants. Inflation encouraged speculation and manipulation.

77

Speculation encouraged corruption and cupidity, and these became the hallmarks of the Nationalist government. Cut off from foreign imports by the Japanese control of the seacoast and by enemy control of native industry, the Chinese suffered severe shortages. The loss of the coast also meant the loss of tariff revenue. Chiang had to depend on land taxes and was therefore obligated to the land-owning classes, who throughout history have been notoriously resistant to change or reform.

Hopelessly wedded to a cumbersome centralized government and an army which was far too big for its equipment, Chiang was no match for the Communists. They were efficient, successful, economy-minded; and they won the support of the progressive elements who favored reforms. Chiang and the Communists continued to feud. The Communists could not substantiate their claim that they were the only ones fighting the Japanese. They spent most of the time building up their forces in North China. Their resistance to the Japanese was negligible. By 1944 Chiang had diverted 400,000 picked troops to check the Communists.

In June of that year, Roosevelt sent Henry Wallace to China to appeal to Chiang for an agreement with the Communists so the two parties could join forces against Japan during the big offensives which were being planned. General Patrick J. Hurley also repeated the request the next year. Chiang's reply, in both cases, was that he could not cooperate with a group whose sole objective was the control of all China. He would admit them, he said, only when they surrendered completely to his government. To many Americans this demand sounded like Hitler's "peace" offers to the Poles and Czechs during the 1930's.

In *The China Tangle* Herbert Feis has analyzed the confusion that existed in American thinking at the end of the war. Both Ambassador Hurley and General Albert C. Wedemeyer, the commander of American troops in China, tried to work with Chiang to assure the continued success of his regime. But lesser officials representing America in China were convinced that the decay and corruption of Chiang's regime made its success unlikely. They urged Washington to force Chiang to cooperate with the Communists or to abandon him if he refused. Some even suggested we might do better to throw our support behind the Communists.

It could be argued that had the United States not kept a foot in both camps but thrown its full support to Chiang, his regime would have been saved. On the eve of his death Roosevelt offered only half-hearted support for Hurley. He agreed that we must continue to support Chiang, but he still hoped to find a *modus vivendi* for Nationalist-Communist cooperation. Americans still felt no appreciable fear of Chinese Communism. American agents had learned that the Russians did not favor the Chinese Communists and did not regard them as brothers. Russia promised that she would not intervene in the Chinese civil war but would support, in principle, the unification of China and her armed forces under Chiang. Ambassador Harriman warned from Moscow that Stalin was not sincere, and George F. Kennan, in a special memo, said the problem was essentially a matter of understanding what the Russians really meant. He warned that although Russia favored a unification of the Chinese armies in 1945 under Chiang, Stalin also knew this could be done only on terms acceptable to the Communists. Stalin would accept a united, free, and democratic China because this would permit Russian infiltration unhindered by foreign influences. A free China seemed a good way to eliminate America from Asia.

Truman inherited this uncertain China policy. He instructed Hurley to continue his quest for cooperation between the Communists and the Nationalists but he left no doubt that he favored the latter. When the war ended, the United States joined Chiang in accepting the surrender of Japanese troops. Our Navy and our Air Force were made available for transferring Nationalist troops to strategic areas, and our Marines even occupied key cities until they could be relieved by Chiang's men. Chiang seemed in control everywhere except in North China and Manchuria.

In 1945 Chiang still had an opportunity to win China. As head of a victorious government, now ranked among the great powers, he had gained much good will and prestige. The people might have flocked to his banner had he offered them hope, reform, peace, and some control over inflation. But, confronted by the Communists, Chiang had only two alternatives: cooperation or civil war. Either one had to be preceded by reforms to win popular support. Chiang decided to fight, but in so doing he made two serious errors. He did not offer the people the reforms which might have earned their support, and he moved into Manchuria and North China simultaneously. His armies were unprepared and the result was disastrous. The Communists, schooled in a decade of guerilla fighting, were more than a match for Chiang's overextended armies. The Russians conveniently supplied the Chinese Communists with captured Japanese equipment. In the end, the Nationalists' superiority in manpower was offset by the lack of a will to fight, corruption, inefficient command, inflation, disappointment over the failure to effect reforms, economic stagnation, and impossible logistics.

Truman still groped for a suitable policy in China. There were three choices. We could withdraw entirely from China and let the Nationalists and Communists fight it out. We could try to mediate and force Chiang's compliance to a settlement by threatening abandonment. Or, we could commit a small force to hold a buffer zone between the two. This third choice was not considered seriously. After four years of war, Americans were in no mood to send an expeditionary force to China. Besides, such a move could lead to a major war.

The first possibility received only token support; there was no thought that we should simply abandon China to her fate. Only the second was tried. Late in 1945 Wedemeyer and other observers reported on the grave situation in China, so there can be no doubt that Truman's subsequent decision was made with the full facts before him. Much thought went into the formulation of a policy in 1946. The military leaders, believing that a war with Russia would be largely fought in the air, relegated China to a minor strategic role and so resolved not to commit troops to Chiang's defense.

Since intervention was ruled out, the American influence in Chinese affairs was limited to economic or political action plus some military assistance. The experts were assuming by 1946 that the Communists would win a civil war. It followed that if Chiang were to be kept in power a civil war had to be avoided. Therefore, the decision was made to favor a coalition; a decision made in ignorance of Communist aspirations to rule only on their own terms. However, it must be remembered that the belief was widely held that cooperation with Russia was still possible, and so there was also reason to believe the same for China. The presumption was that China's Communists could be bought for our side just as other Oriental warlords had been bought in the past.

It was later argued that Truman was wrong when he accepted the argument that Chiang would be defeated in a civil war even if given extensive aid. At that time the experts were convinced that even with aid Chiang would not survive because of the corruption of his government. Moreover, Chiang consistently refused to accept aid contingent upon reforming his government. By mid-1946 American aid had virtually stopped.

If Chiang's government was corrupt why hadn't he been assisted in cleaning out the corruption? Chinese officials could not be replaced by more dependable Americans without arousing the hatred of the Chinese who would have interpreted this an American "imperialistic" scheme. Chiang could not clean his own house; he was only one man surrounded by a palace guard of corrupt and venal politicians. The job was hopeless.

In December, 1945 General George C. Marshall was sent to China to mediate between the Communists and the Nationalists; a hopeless task from the start. Marshall labored for a year to find a solution but neither side trusted the other sufficiently to yield on any major points. When Marshall left China in 1947 the war began in earnest. Within six months the initial Nationalist advantages were gone and the Communists had assumed the offensive. In July of that year General Wedemeyer was sent to check the situation again. In his report two months later Wedemeyer recommended that extensive aid be given to the Nationalists and that Chiang be urged to reform his government. He warned that a Communist victory, which appeared to be inevitable at the time, would plunge all Asia into enemy hands. He also recommended that a United Nations force should occupy portions of Manchuria as a buffer between the two factions. Wedemeyer was among the first to warn against a policy that assumed that China was not of vital concern to the United States. Later, General Wedemeyer elaborated on this point in his book, *Wedemeyer Reports*.

Despite Wedemeyer's appeal for more assistance, Truman's request to Congress for aid to China was only $570,000,000 and Congress pared that to four hundred million. The United States was washing its hand of Chiang's regime. Left to sink or swim, Chiang's government tottered on the verge of disintegration as the Communists moved onward. By the end of 1949 Chiang, in a dramatic retreat, abandoned the mainland and withdrew to the island of Formosa (Taiwan) with the broken remnants of his armies. The United States wrote *finis t*o the China debacle on August 5, 1949 when the State Department published a White Paper justifying the Truman, Marshall, Acheson program and placing the entire blame for failure on the Kuomintang regime. More than three billion dollars in aid had been made available to Chiang, but more than dollars were required to halt the Communist advance. By October, 1949 Mao Tse-tung proclaimed the Peoples Republic of China. It was recognized promptly by the Russians and the British.

The giants faced each other as equals.

As the China tragedy was being enacted the red scare mounted in the United States. Late in 1948 Truman's red Herring statement seemed justified. In November the public had demonstrated its confidence in Truman by re-electing him. J. Parnell Thomas, chairman of the House Committee to Investigate Un-American Activities and butter-tongued defender of sacred tradition, was indicted for irregularities in office, tried, and convicted. The accuser had become the accused. The one-man policeman, district attorney, judge, and jury wound up playing the role of the prisoner too. On July 8, 1949 Hiss' first trial ended without a verdict. As of July 1949 the only game the red hunters had bagged was a young girl, Judith Coplon, an employee of the Justice Department who had relayed information on American counter-intelligence to a Soviet agent. She had loved too well but most unwisely. Her confessions of romantic rendezvous with the Russian agent, Valentin Gubitchev, made spicy reading in the scandal sheets until her conviction in March 1950.

After July, 1949 things changed and the atmosphere was suddenly filled with the odor of many red herrings. In August the White Paper on the Chinese write-off was published. Less than two months later Truman shocked the public with a dramatic announcement that the Russians had exploded an atomic bomb. The balance of power changed over night. Churchill had warned—and many Americans had repeated the warning—that the only deterrent to Soviet aggression was our exclusive possession of the bomb. Now that advantage was gone. The giants faced each other as equals.

In July, 1948 twelve Communist leaders, including William Z. Foster and Eugene Dennis, were indicted by a federal grand jury for violation of the Smith Alien Registration Act of 1940. Under this act, to teach or to advocate the overthrow and the destruction of the United States government was an indictable offense. By January, 1949 eleven of these leaders (Foster was too ill) were being tried before Federal Judge Harold R. Medina. The Communists' lawyers turned the trial into a farce. They interrupted constantly, they insulted the bench, and they used every means, fair and foul, to obstruct the trial. To Judge Medina's credit, he was able to maintain court order and the court's dignity through it all. Finally, in October 1949 the eleven were sentenced to prison for periods from three to five years. The defense attorneys also drew stiff sentences for contempt of court. Three months later Hiss' second trial ended with conviction and he received a five-year sentence.

The country soon learned how the Russians were able to produce an atomic bomb two to five years ahead of predicted schedule. In February, 1950 the British arrested a young German-born physicist, Klaus Fuchs, who had become a naturalized British subject. During World War II he had worked in New Mexico on the atomic project. He now calmly confessed that from 1943 to 1947 he had systematically passed information to the Russians. This, he insisted, was not for personal gain but the result of his concern over the terrible danger of one power having such a destructive weapon to itself. He believed all should share it. The FBI speedily arrested his associates on this side of the ocean.

He . . . sowed dragon's teeth at every step.

"Hiss, Chiang, Fuchs, and the Bomb" were now blended to produce the inevitable result. Countless purge committees, often self-appointed, were busy checking the loyalty of persons employed by schools, colleges, universities, libraries, radio and television stations, newspapers, magazines, research laboratories, unions, foundations, co-operatives, and government agencies. All agencies or persons responsible for spreading information, for study and research, and for the performance of public services were also checked. Many state legislatures created miniature Un-American Activities Committees, especially since the parent committee in Congress was now back in public esteem. Americans were forced to subscribe to strange oaths. It was not enough to swear that you were loyal to your country; you were also required to swear that you were not disloyal.

This set the public stage for the emergence of one of the greatest demagogues in American history. Few men in public life have been the subject of as much controversy as Senator Joseph R. McCarthy of Wisconsin. Although he is often compared to the late Huey Long of Louisiana, McCarthy was a more significant figure because his influence was greater and the ill-effects of his brief day of glory were longer lasting. It was impossible not to have had an opinion about McCarthy and it was usually an extreme one. He was a man who sowed dragon's teeth at every step. His partisans, who were numbered in the millions, looked upon him as the champion of democracy against the clandestine, subversive, and decaying influence of New Dealism and its handmaiden, Communism. His critics, who were also numbered in the millions, regarded him as the greatest threat of all time to American democracy and civil liberties.

McCarthy's supporters explained their hero thus: Communism was a menace to America and evidence, although somewhat inadmissible, had been presented to show that its agents had infiltrated the government, betrayed its secrets, and subverted its policies. The traitor-ridden administration was too inept and incapable to take counter action. Into this confusion rode Senator McCarthy whose bright torch of truth instantly illuminated the labyrinthian tunnelings of the traitors. Whereas the administration was unable to act to preserve the country, McCarthy had seen the menace and proceeded to do something about it. It was true that he had behaved in a rough, high-handed manner, but the situation warranted such actions. There was no point in treating traitors with kid gloves. "You have to fight fire with fire," said his partisans. The Senator's opponents reminded his friends that fire was more effectively fought with water. McCarthy's roughshod tactics reminded them of the old man who burned down his barn to get rid of the rats. They agreed that Communism was a menace and that its proponents would have to be ferreted out for punishment and removal from responsible government posts. They were in complete harmony with McCarthy's objectives, but they insisted that means were just as important as ends.

The critics were shocked to find citizens proscribed before legislative investigating bodies, denied their civil rights, deprived of their livelihood because they might have some remote connection with Communist sympathizers. The term *guilt by association* became popular. It meant that a man was judged a Communist sympathizer or "fellow traveller" if he had once been associated with a subversive organization, or if he was known to have consistent social or business relations with persons suspected or known to be Communists. It mattered little that the organization was not considered subversive at the time the victim belonged, that it had been judged disloyal only at a later date. It mattered still less if the victim denied that he knew his associate was connected with Communism.

On the balance sheet of today, it is still impossible to assess McCarthyism. Despite the dire predictions that the Senator's methods would destroy civil liberty and undermine democracy, the country has survived and returned to sanity. McCarthy died in 1957 in relative obscurity; at least he no longer had the following he did from 1950 to 1953. It is impossible to tell how many individual careers were destroyed by his persecutions. Undoubtedly the total number would be small, but, on the other hand, the country's philosophy is based on the belief that each individual is important and that what happens to one reflects upon all. The system is designed to protect every man from injustice, and tampering with the system weakens the very foundations McCarthy claimed to be preserving.

There is no way to measure the effect of McCarthyism on our educational system and research. Any movement which forces a teacher to withhold information, give a bias to his discussions, distort the truth, and live in fear of losing his position, makes the pursuit of truth impossible. McCarthyism had that effect. The excessive secrecy forced upon our scientists through security restrictions was also injurious. Many competent men were discouraged from continuing their research, many who were needed refused to enter government service and it also became difficult to transmit new knowledge to teachers so they might train the next generation of scholars.

There is no doubt that McCarthyism demoralized government services. Many reliable public servants were driven from office and it became harder to recruit capable personnel while the investigations continued. The effect was deleterious on our foreign policy. The foreign countries we were trying to win as allies were amazed at the wild sideshow in Washington and the successful conduct of foreign affairs from 1950 to 1953 became impossible since the State Department was hamstrung by investigators at every turn. The most serious consequence of McCarthyism on foreign policy was that it encouraged the return of partisanship. By 1950 it was evident that the Truman foreign policy was to be a major issue in the congressional elections. Senator Vandenberg was already fatally ill, but sensing the incipient dangers in bipartisan foreign-policy split, he returned to the Senate floor in January 1950 to hold his party in line. However, the task was too great for him and even before he died in April 1951 the Republicans were already in strenuous opposition to Truman's foreign policy.

Since McCarthy insisted that ends rather than means were important, one may judge McCarthyism only in terms of what it accomplished. The final results of McCarthy's three-year reign of terror were discouraging. Not one single Communist was convicted as a result of evidence turned up by his investigation. Communists, of course, *were* convicted and security risks *were* discharged, but these actions came as a result of the patient and unobtrusive work of the FBI, the Central Intelligence Agency, and the administration's loyalty boards.

The only defense of McCarthy's conduct might be that he was

overzealous. An overzealous man may often be excused, although not justified, if he is convinced that his cause is righteous and that he is performing a necessary service. McCarthy's career leaves considerable doubt about his sincerity. He had a record of opportunism that was difficult to ignore. History may judge the senator as a callous, self-seeking demagogue who capitalized on his nation's crisis to enhance his power and prestige and to feed his monstrous ego.

McCarthy fired his opening gun on February 9, 1950 before the Women's Republican Club of Wheeling, West Virginia. There he denounced the State Department for its Asian failures and concluded by alluding to the existence of an active Communist cell within the department itself. The Senator claimed to possess inside information about its activities. Just what happened in Wheeling will never be known. The speech was not well covered by the press and those present are uncertain as to just what McCarthy said. He is supposed to have held aloft a piece of paper upon which he claimed to have the names of 205 State Department Communists, but this may not have been the case. However, the figure 205 became associated with McCarthy and presumably represented the sum-total of communist enemies. The next day he spoke in Salt Lake City, and later at Reno. By this time his remarks were receiving wide press and radio coverage, although, by this time, he had reduced his list of traitors to fifty-seven. He continued to drop the bar on his political high jump. His critics demanded that he stop talking and name some of these Communists. He dropped the bar again to an irreducible number; McCarthy promised to name *one* Communist but hastened to assure his critics that although he would not name the 204—or fifty-six—the one would be the "top Russian espionage agent" in America. The Senator said he would rest his case on this one man. There was much disappointment when he failed to mention a man who was active in the State Department. His ultimate villain was Professor Owen J. Lattimore of Johns Hopkins University, an occasional consultant for the department on Asian affairs. Despite intensive FBI investigation Professor Lattimore was cleared of the charges. Senator Millard Tydings headed a special senatorial investigation committee which also cleared Lattimore. The Wisconsin senator was not distressed by the inability to make his charges against Lattimore stick. On the premise that the best defense was a vigorous offense, McCarthy launched out in all directions with blanket accusations against everyone in sight. He never remained silent nor stood still long enough for his opponents to pin him down. The "Big

Lie" technique of Hitler and Goebbels was his strongest weapon in an arsenal which included every form of duplicity, evasion, villification, and innuendo.

. . . this basic attack on our freedom . . . .

While McCarthy blustered on into the next administration, saner heads tackled the Communists problem by effective legal means. With the eleven Communist chieftains behind bars, the Department of Justice speedily moved against lesser Communist leaders and in June twenty-one of them were indicted. The department was assisted by the Supreme Court which, on June 4, 1951, upheld the constitutionality of the Smith Act in the case of *Dennis* vs. *United States*. In April Julius and Ethel Rosenberg were convicted for espionage and condemned. Morton Sobell and David Greenglass, two more proven Communist agents, were also sent to prison for long terms for espionage. Late in 1950 the so-called "little Hiss case" involving William Walter Remington and Elizabeth Bentley began. Although Remington was convicted in February 1951, the courts later released him. (He was later convicted for perjury in 1953.)

The Communist party itself came in for serious attack. Many wanted it outlawed on the grounds that it was really not a party in the American sense of the word, but a well-conceived conspiracy taking orders from a foreign and enemy power. Others were opposed. Not only did they feel that it would violate our civil liberties to outlaw a "political" party, but it would also do no good. Communists would exist with or without a party, and the dissolution of the party would simply drive the movement underground where the FBI would only have more difficulty in coping with it. In 1948 the Mundt-Nixon bill, which had been introduced to control Communism, was opposed by Truman for precisely these reasons.

President Truman was brought into sharp controversy with Congress in 1950 over the McCarran Internal Security bill, which had been passed in September. This bill was prepared in haste and confusion under the pressure of McCarthyism. It sought to control Communism by denying its adherents passports, employment in defense industries, or admission to the United States if they were aliens. Naturalization laws were tightened and all Communist and Communist-front organizations were required to register with the attorney general's department and submit membership list. A Subversive Activities Control Board was also established to ferret out subversives, but this seemed hardly necessary inasmuch as all of them were supposed to be registered.

Truman thought the bill was a patchwork of contradictions incapable of enforcement. He said in summarizing his objections in a veto message it did not clearly define Communism or a Communist organization; that it made the work of the FBI and the CIA more difficult; and that it discouraged Communists abroad from breaking with the Kremlin because they were denied a haven in this country. But since Congress was in no mood to listen to any advice from a red herring expert, it promptly repassed the measure.

No one summarized the basic issues involved in McCarthyism better than Truman when he said, "If the government cannot produce witnesses in court, then it cannot prosecute. And if a man cannot be prosecuted in the courts then he should not be persecuted by a Senate or House committee." Regrettably, the heat of the moment impelled many Americans to forget a basic cornerstone upon which their nation is built. But so great was the fear of Communism that this basic attack on our freedom went almost unchallenged.

The War in Korea

A line had to be drawn in Korea.

TRUMAN WAS MORE DEPENDENT upon Congress than Roosevelt for the successful conduct of foreign relations because Congress had to appropriate the money for the various assistance programs. Congressional participation assured more public discussion and both parties were asked to endorse Truman's policies. It became fashionable to speak of bipartisanship in foreign policy but the term applied almost exclusively to foreign policy in Europe, an area about which the two parties were in substantial prior agreement. It was recognized from the start that bipartisanship did not apply to foreign policy in the Far East; consequently there was much maneuvering for political advantage. The Republicans, with a tradition of vigorous Asiatic foreign policy from the days of William Seward, when he arranged the purchase of Alaska, insisted that Truman was giving disastrous priority to Europe. In 1948 Senator Taft said, "I believe very strongly that the Far East is ultimately even more important to our future peace than is Europe." Whatever the comparative balance, it was certain that the Chinese debacle forced us to re-examine our Asian policy. Probably the United States would have recognized Mao Tse-tung's new government in 1949 had the Chinese not embarked on an anti-American campaign to discredit us in Asiatic eyes. We replied in kind, and by 1950 there was so much dislike of Red China that not only have we never recognized China but also we have consistently opposed her admission to the UN. In addition the powerful "China Lobby" in Congress pressed hard for more and more assistance to Chiang Kai-shek.

Early in 1950, instead of trying to formulate a new China policy, the main interest was in trying to fix responsibility for the failure of the old one. While the Republicans looked backward upon a situation they could no longer understand nor influence, the President could gain little support for trying anything new. The State Department, thanks to the McCarthyites, was regarded as little more than a minor appendage of the Politburo. The interest was in personalities rather than in policies.

A line had to be drawn in Asia, one that the United States felt competent to defend with its meager forces. Communist armies controlled most of continental Asia except for South Korea, Indochina, and a few pockets of resistance in China. In January 1950 Truman had made it clear that America would not be drawn into the Chinese situation even if Mao's armies attacked Formosa. We gave little encouragement to the resistance forces in China, because there was no assurance that they still favored Chiang. In a speech before the National Press Club of Washington on January 12, 1950, Acheson confirmed what Truman had said a week earlier. Acheson drew a "defense perimeter" beyond which American forces would not venture. The line passed from the Aleutian Islands through Japan, Okinawa, and the Philippines. Korea and Formosa lay beyond this line and apparently it was to be assumed that America accepted no responsibility for their defense. These remarks were to plague Acheson later when he was made the goat for telling the Communists that we would not defend South Korea and thus encourage them to attack. Actually Acheson was spelling out General MacArthur's remark, "Anyone who commits the American army on the mainland of Asia ought to have his head examined." The general substantially conformed with Acheson and the Defense Department also confirmed the Secretary's demarcation line. However, as the first to announce publicly that America would not defend continental Asia, Acheson had to bear the blame. There is certainly no evidence that the Communists would not have attacked had Acheson remained silent. Had the Communists feared American intervention it would not have been too late for them to withdraw after our ground forces were committed on June 30. At that moment the war was not a week old. The North Koreans could have dismissed the affair as an extensive raiding operation and thus saved face. That they continued to fight after American intervention clearly indicated their goal was to conquer Korea even if it meant war with the United States. No doubt the Chinese Communists took further courage from the knowledge that Russia also possessed the atom bomb; a fact that compelled the Truman administration to reconsider all American military strategy after September 1949.

. . . the unmistakable voice of history.

At Cairo in December 1943 the major powers, including Russia, had declared their support for an independent Korean state, and at Potsdam in 1945 it was agreed that both Russia and the United States would liberate the country. Soon after, it was further agreed that Russian troops would accept the surrender of Japanese troops north of the thirty-eighth parallel and that Americans would do the same south of that line. Russian troops had already entered the country on August 10, 1945, but the nearest American forces were far off in Okinawa. It was obvious that the Russians could overrun the entire peninsula without opposition so an agreement to stop at the thirty-eighth parallel made sense at the time. Some American forces arrived in South Korea on September 8, 1945, at which time the Russians apparently made no effort to go beyond the line agreed upon. The Koreans assumed that the Cairo Declaration would be implemented immediately and that freedom would be theirs within a few days after the final surrender of Japanese troops. They were sadly disappointed. By the end of 1945, when the foreign ministers met in Moscow, the country was still occupied. At Moscow the foreign ministers further angered the Koreans by proposing a joint commission and a provisional government to administer a four-power, five-year trusteeship.

The unification of Korea was impossible from the start. The Americans and the Russians could not come to terms over elections and the establishment of a single government. The Russians seemed intent upon a government of their own in North Korea. When all else failed, the United States presented the Korean problem to the United Nations. The UN set up a temporary commission in November 1947 to supervise country-wide elections with a view to creating unified government. The Russians barred the commissioners from North Korea and, when they appealed to the UN for further instructions, they were told to hold elections where they could with the result that on May 10, 1948 only the voters south of the thirty-eighth parallel went to the polls. A constitution was drafted, Syngman Rhee was elected president, and the Republic of Korea became an independent state in August 1948. The following month the Soviet's Democratic People's Republic of North Korea was also declared to be "sovereign."

The United States did not pay sufficient attention to the military need of this new child. Except for a small group of about four thousand men, the last American troops departed in June 1949. Mao Tse-tung had added five times that many trained men to the North Korean forces which now probably exceeded 200,000. Faced by this known northern superiority, the Americans should have bolstered the southern forces. The only possible excuse for failing to equip South Korea properly was a fear that Syngman Rhee would invade North Korea. Americans did build up the army—minus tanks, planes, and heavy weapons—but this was no more formidable than a large metropolitan police force. It was later demonstrated that the army of 100,000 South Koreans was as badly trained for the type of war they fought as were the British regulars at Bunker Hill or New Orleans. Schlesinger and Rovere in *The General and the President* claimed that the only man who was concerned about the inadequacies of the South Korean military forces was Dean Acheson. Most of our generals were confident that Rhee's men could give a good account of themselves.

On Saturday, June 24, 1950, President Truman received a hurried call from Secretary Acheson while he was visiting in Independence, Missouri: North Korean troops were reported to have crossed the thirty-eighth parallel. Truman wished to return to the capital immediately, but Acheson dissuaded him, saying that his hurried trip would create too much public alarm until the true situation could be ascertained. After all, Acheson contended, it might be merely a large-scale raiding party. The next day Acheson called again. There could be no doubt that North Koreans were across in force; it was an all-out invasion. Truman flew to Washington at once. The Security Council of the UN had been alerted for afternoon meeting. This left Truman three hours in which to consider his next course of action. Over the droning motors of his plane, the Sacred Cow, Truman could hear the unmistakable voice of history. He recalled that in the 1930's Britain and France stood by powerless and confused while Hitler and Mussolini compelled concession after concession by threats of force. Appeasement had ultimately failed, resulting in all the horror and heartbreak of World War II when that disaster might have been averted if the democracies had stood firm and defied the dictators. Truman resolved that the United States should not follow the same course now that it was threatened by naked, Soviet-inspired aggression. By Sunday evening he was joined by his aides in Blair House, the President's temporary residence. The Security Council had already met that afternoon and (thanks to the fact that Russia had been boycotting the meetings since January because of the failure to admit Red China to membership) approved a resolution describing the invasion as a "breach of the peace and an act of aggression." The North Koreans were asked to cease fire immediately and all UN members were asked to approve. This prior action of the Security Council enabled Truman to characterize American decisions as being wholly in line with UN recommendations.

At the Blair House meeting Secretary Acheson and the Defense Department recommended that General MacArthur proceed with the evacuation of American civilian personnel from Korea, and make supplies and ammunition available to the Republic of Korea forces. They also recommended that the Seventh Fleet sail from the Philippines to the Formosa Strait, and that a statement be issued to the effect that the fleet would prevent Chinese attacks on the Island of Taiwan as well as prevent Nationalist forays from Taiwan against the mainland. The President and his advisers agreed that although this invasion had to be met the United States should not be lured into fighting.

By Monday, June 26, the news from Korea was even more discouraging; the ROK forces were in retreat everywhere. That night Truman and his aides reached an important decision—there is no doubt that the final word was the President's. A statement—to be issued at noon the next day—declared that the gravity of the Korean situation required American air and sea forces to cover and support the ROK army. Word was flashed to MacArthur in Japan at 10:17 on the night of June 26; he immediately dispatched naval units as well as F-80's and F-82's to assist the embattled Koreans.

On the morning of June 27 Truman met with Congressional leaders and apprized them of what had been done to aid Korea. He indicated that every effort was being made to obtain UN support in Korea but, in Formosa, we were acting on our own initiative. That afternoon the Security Council ratified Truman's decision to send air and sea aid to Korea and called upon the members of the UN to "furnish such assistance to the Republic of Korea as may be necessary to restore peace and security in the area." A few planes, one light cruiser, and four destroyers were not enough aid to stave off a Communist victory; Seoul, the South Korean capital, fell on June 27. Most of Rhee's army was demoralized, decimated, and dispersed. When MacArthur flew to the battle front from Japan on Thursday, June 29, he saw a pitiful scene of inadequate preparation and disastrous defeat. The next day MacArthur made his report to Washington and confirmed what Truman and his advisers had suspected twenty-four hours earlier.

As they studied the periodic reports from Tokyo on Thursday, Truman and the members of the National Security Council realized the South Korean position was hopeless. The Seventh Fleet did not have sufficient ships to give effective aid and the Far East Air Force was pathetically unprepared for their part of the job. Only American ground forces could stave off disaster. Although they knew the decision was inevitable, Truman and his aides waited for a full report from Mac-Arthur. MacArthur's report confirmed the worst. He requested permission to commit one regimental combat team immediately and to build up to two divisions as quickly as possible. It was early in the morning when Secretary of the Army Frank Pace brought this request to Truman, who immediately accepted MacArthur's appraisal of the situation and ordered that troops be sent.

When Truman met with his aides again on June 30, the principal item on the agenda was Chiang's offer to supply 33,000 men in Korea. Truman was inclined to accept, but Secretary Acheson and the State Department experts as well as the Joint Chiefs of Staff were opposed. There was no point, Acheson argued, in sending the Seventh Fleet to defend Formosa if we were going to weaken the island's defense by 33,000 fighting men. The Chinese Nationalist troops were badly trained and inadequately supplied. To transport them from Formosa to Korea would take many ships urgently needed elsewhere. Truman declined Chiang's offer and apparently, at the time, MacArthur concurred in this judgment.

The United States was now at war. In a press conference on June 29, Truman explained that it was not really a war but merely an attempt to suppress a bandit raid. "Would it be correct to call this a police action under the United Nations?" inquired a reporter. The President nodded in approval. Hence a new phrase entered American vocabulary. Although men were killed and cities bombed; although refugees clogged the highways and civilians tightened their belts, this was not a war but a "police action." To the American public, however, it was a war and no amount of semantic juggling could convince them otherwise. As the war progressed, critics of "Mr. Truman's War" became more vocal—

94

their complaints would have sounded familiar to James Madison, who was taunted in 1812 with references to "Mr. Madison's War." At first, American response was favorable. There was a great sigh of relief. The containment policy was already partially discredited and George Kennan, one of its creators, had left his post in the State Department some months earlier. The popular reaction was that we were now meeting the Communists man to man in open battle and the decision would be made swiftly. This would teach them a lesson in the only language they understood.

It was not only the Americans who rallied to Korea's support; the UN did as well. Many free countries hastened to give assurances of assistance and by the end of August British and other troops were on the field. Obviously, throughout the war, the South Koreans contributed the largest numbers and suffered the heaviest casualties. Nevertheless, Americans shouldered an enormous burden in casualties, materiel, and committed equipment.

". . . what is happening [in Korea] is important to every American."

Although the Korean War was the greatest test of Truman foreign policy, there never was a master plan; decisions were made to meet new contingencies as they arose. They had to be made with full cognizance that a Russian-Chinese threat existed, that we were deeply committed to building up our European allies through NATO, that most of our military strength was locked up in Korea, and that we had pledged continuing support to the UN. Although the public and its leaders were at first bewildered by what had taken place, they soon recovered their equilibrium and began to see the Korean War in the light of our total relations with the Communists. The question was: should we fight in an area of limited strategic value and run the risk of being sucked into the "bottomless pit" of Asia, or withdraw and permit the Communists to get away with a flagrant act of aggression.

Truman tried to answer this question in a message on July 19. "Korea is a small country, thousands of miles away, but what is happening there is important to every American," he said. This attitude was quite different from that of Neville Chamberlain when Hitler overran Czechoslovakia in 1938. The Security Council had decided to punish the aggressors and, the President added, "these actions . . . are of great importance. The free nations have now made it clear that lawless aggression will be met with force. The free nations have learned the fateful lesson of the 1930's. That lesson is that aggression must be met firmly."

As Rovere and Schlesinger have pointed out in their study of Truman and MacArthur, *The General and the President,* the attack on South Korea threatened our security. Actually, we had no military stake in Asia, we were under no treaty obligation to defend Korea, and we had declared that country to be outside our defense perimeter. Why then was it of strategic value? It was of strategic value because the future military security of the United States was at stake. People all over the world were watching the rape of South Korea to see what the United States would do. The allegiance of millions of Asiatics hung in the balance, and those nations in Europe whom we had recently joined in NATO also awaited action by the United States. We had to show the world that we would back up our position by force, if necessary; and that having once done so, we would stand by our promises. We were also under obligation to defend Japan, to whom a Communist Korea would be more than a threat. These were the reasons America entered an Asiatic ground *war.*

But a second question arises: Why did the United States undertake this war in company with the UN? The UN was powerless for lack of an army of its own; we were restricting our freedom of action; and the presence of Russia within the group would undoubtedly be a disadvantage. It was the Americans' decision to fight and the UN had "just come along for the ride." Why did we need the UN at all? Part of the answer was that in trying to strengthen the UN, America could enhance the UN's prestige. Legally speaking, the UN was charged with maintaining world security and therefore needed as much support as possible. Also, diplomatically speaking, many countries could not or would not support American policies as such, but they would support the same policies identified as a UN effort to enforce its charter and secure world peace. Thus the legal and moral blessing of the UN was forthcoming for a policy which was essentially American in its inception.

Should the line be crossed into North Korea?

On July 7, 1950, the UN approved the creation of a unified command in Korea and the following day Truman announced that General MacArthur would assume the post. It was not an enviable position. The North Koreans continued to advance recklessly despite the presence of

American troops in the field. The public was assured that the defenders would not be driven into the sea. At last, on August 6, the UN retreat came to an end in a defense perimeter around Pusan Harbor. American, South Korean, British, French, Turkish, Dutch, and Australian troops now held less than four thousand square miles of Korean territory.

September 15, 1950, MacArthur counterattacked. His bold plan was reluctantly approved by the members of the Joint Chiefs of Staff; General Omar Bradley, General Lawton Collins, and Admiral Forrest Sherman. He executed a daring amphibious operation in which two divisions landed near Inchon, while a regimental combat team parachuted into the capital, Seoul. This operation was coordinated with an attack at the Pusan beachhead. The strategy worked magnificently and the North Koreans were hurled back on all fronts. Seoul was retaken as the North Koreans fled in panic. Most of their army was engulfed and systematically destroyed by MacArthur's pincers. The American Air Force strafed and bombed the retreating foe with murderous effect. By October 1 the UN forces were back at the thirty-eighth parallel.

Truman and his advisers were now called upon to make another momentous decision: Should the line be crossed into North Korea? The Russians had reappeared in the Security Council in August and were making every effort to hamper our plans. To complicate decision making even more, it was argued that the UN was under obligation to unify the entire country, and that because of Communist duplicity we could not permit continued Communist control in North Korea. Those who spoke of the danger of a Chinese or Russian intervention, or said we had no legal or moral right to go beyond the thirty-eighth parallel were dismissed as appeasers. MacArthur insisted that he could not guarantee the safety of his army unless he was permitted to enter North Korea. On September 29, 1950 a resolution was introduced in the UN to permit entry into North Korea. MacArthur had already crossed the line although he was cautioned not to provoke Chinese or Russian intervention. He was forbidden to violate the Manchurian border under any circumstance. The General Assembly approved the resolution on October 7 by a forty-seven to five vote and created a UN Commission for the Unification and Rehabilitation of Korea.

At the time MacArthur was directing his troops across the thirty-eighth parallel he was also in the midst of his celebrated quarrel with the administration. On July 31 MacArthur visited Formosa after which Chiang announced that he and MacArthur had agreed upon a basis for

Chinese-American military cooperation. The reaction was fear that Mac-Arthur might have overstepped his authority and encouraged Chiang to attack China. Truman sent Harriman to Tokyo for a five-day visit with MacArthur to brief him fully on government policy. MacArthur apparently ignored the briefing because he then prepared an address to be delivered to the Veterans of Foreign War convention on August 28, a speech that was not delivered because of action taken after copies, prematurly released to the press, had been read by the administration. In the prepared speech, MacArthur supported a vigorous policy in Formosa and branded as "threadbare" and "fallacious" the argument that "if we defend Formosa we alienate continental Asia." This was "appeasement and defeatism in the Pacific," he said. Although Truman was angry enough to remove him, he went no further than ordering Secretary of Defense Louis Johnson to have MacArthur withdraw the statement before it was presented to the convention officially. By then, however, the wide circulation of the document had ruined the efforts made to get the UN to assume more responsibility in settling the Formosa question.

Truman addressed a letter to MacArthur in which he again explained official Korean policies and, on October 18, he flew to Wake Island for a personal conference. Later reports indicated that MacArthur was told what policies he was expected to follow and that he apologized for any inconvenience he had caused. When the war was discussed, MacArthur dismissed any suggestion that China might intervene, saying that he expected to end the war by Thanksgiving. No more than fifty or sixty thousand Chinese could possibly intervene, he said, and these would be chewed to pieces in a few days. The conference ended on a high note of magnanimity. Truman returned to Washington and no further statements emanated from Tokyo for several weeks. Nevertheless, concern over Chinese intervention was well founded. On October 3 the State Department received the disquieting news that the Chinese were planning to enter the war. Foreign Minister Chou En-lai, in a conversation with Indian Ambassador K. M. Panikkar, had said that if non-South Korean troops crossed the thirty-eighth parallel, China would have no recourse but to fight. Despite the fact that similar warnings were received from other sources, the inclination was to discount Panikkar's word since he was considered to be pro-Communist.

On October 19 UN forces of seven American divisions, six South Korean divisions and smaller units from the UN countries, entered

Pyongyang, the North Korean capital. When MacArthur arrived in Pyongyang on October 20, it seemed as if everything was about over. However, within the next few days the North Korean resistance seemed to stiffen. The day after the fall of Pyongyang, Central Intelligence Agency reports indicated that Chinese forces were deploying in strength along the Yalu River, ostensibly to protect the bridges and power plants. It was not until October 26 that the first Chinese "volunteer" was captured deep within North Korean territory. Additional reconnaissance revealed the presence of an estimated 850,000 Chinese troops north of the Yalu. Interrogation of prisoners revealed the information that the first Chinese troops had entered Korea as early as October 16. Chinese intervention increased, and on November 6 MacArthur admitted that Chinese troops were coming into Korea in overwhelming numbers. "A new fresh army" was in action, MacArthur said.

MacArthur requested permission to destroy some Yalu bridges over which the Chinese were moving men and supplies. The President, supported by Secretary Marshall, General Bradley, and General Walter Bedell Smith of the CIA, did not consider this sound since it might broaden the war. Our allies were reassured on this point, more support was sought from the UN, and even more effort was made to obtain information about Chinese intentions.

It was not long before China showed her hand. On November 24, despite the existence of large-scale Chinese intervention, MacArthur launched a great offensive. The Eighth Army embarked upon the final drive, which the general assured the press would be over in time for the boys to "eat Christmas dinner at home." Two days later the Eighth Army was being swallowed in a China Sea. More than 200,000 Chinese struck the center of the line which was held by ROK units. The Koreans retreated in disorder and a Chinese breakthrough seemed imminent. The Tenth Corps, completely cut off, faced disaster; but in a brilliant maneuver, the First Marine Division, the Third and Seventh Infantry Divisions, and one division of Koreans extricated themselves from the trap and found a way through to the seacoast where they were evacuated in an operation similar to that at Dunkirk in World War II.

The war had entered a new and more dangerous phase. World War III loomed on the horizon. The entire army in Korea now faced disaster; it might be destroyed before supply and defense lines could be re-established. How to stop the Chinese without attacking their home bases? Would such an attack mean Soviet intervention?

Never had the country strayed so near to the brink of disaster as it did on December 1.

. . . debate . . . centered around MacArthur's removal.

All during the summer of 1950 the army was trying to fight a war while the public was preparing for its biennial pilgrimage to the polls. The Republicans persisted in their single-minded determination to call the Democrats to account for their Asian policies. Truman was subjected to acrimonious attacks and there were demands for "defense perimeter" Acheson's resignation.

Finally, when the voters registered their reaction, the Republicans gained five seats in the Senate and twenty-eight in the House. They now had forty-seven seats in the Senate and 199 in the House, but the Democrats were still in nominal control. Many of Truman's strongest adherents had gone down to defeat. Senators Claude Pepper of Florida and Frank P. Graham of North Carolina had not survived the primaries in their states; Senate majority leader Scott Lucas of Illinois and party-whip Francis J. Meyers of Pennsylvania were also defeated. The defeat of Tydings of Maryland, whose committee had exonerated Lattimore, was attributed to a doctored photograph showing the Senator listening in rapt attention to Communist chieftain Earl Browder. The Communist menace was most successfully exploited by a rising young Californian, Richard M. Nixon, who defeated Helen Gahagan Douglas in the Senate race. But the most significant results of the election were noticeable only in the statistical charts. The Republicans polled more popular votes than the Democrats and there was a swing back to Republicanism in the Middle West.

The re-election of Senator Robert A. Taft of Ohio was most important. Organized labor was out to defeat Taft because of his contribution to the Taft-Hartley Act. But, according to his biographer, William White, the very bitterness of the attack won Taft many supporters—even among union men, many of whom resented dictation by their own union leaders. White said that many Ohioans resented what they thought to be an out-of-state conspiracy to defeat the senator. The Democrats also wanted Taft's scalp but they bungled the job by nominating one Joseph Ferguson, a former state auditor, who conducted a shockingly inept campaign. At one critical point Democratic Governor Frank Lausche said he might vote for Taft and even Democratic Mayor Thomas

Burke of Cleveland was cool toward Ferguson. Taft carried Ohio by 430,000 votes. He, therefore, became one of the most powerful men on Capitol Hill and a leading candidate for the 1952 presidential nomination.

Fresh from his resounding victory, Taft rose in the Senate on November 10 and launched the "Great Debate" on American foreign policy. Implying that Truman's policies had failed, he demanded that all of them be carefully re-evaluated; he particularly objected to the President's requests that troops be sent to Europe. Ex-President Herbert Hoover followed this with a proposal that we withdraw our troops entirely from Europe and concentrate on defending this hemisphere. He maintained that only England and Japan should be considered within our defensive zone.

This debate continued throughout the early months of 1951. Senator Kenneth S. Wherry of Nebraska proposed a resolution that no American forces be sent to Europe until Congress had formulated a complete policy of European defense. Despite the fact that a majority of the Republican members of the House signed a resolution supporting Hoover's and Wherry's position, enough votes were finally found to endorse the President's policies. On April 4, 1951 the Senate approved Truman's request to send four divisions to Europe to serve under the NATO commander, General Dwight Eisenhower.

Most of the foreign policy debate in 1950-51 centered around MacArthur's removal. Although he had remained silent immediately after the Wake Island conference, the general became highly vocal again after the Chinese intervention. He now openly opposed the President's policies and recommended a course of action in the Pacific which his opponents predicted would simply lead to World War III.

The advance of Red China into Korea forced new considerations upon the United States. America was still operating through the UN, but many now wanted to bypass that organization and go it alone against the Chinese. Fortunately Truman never allowed the extremists to gain the upper hand. The stakes were too high to gamble with the West's future. War with China would mean full mobilization, make it impossible for us to continue assistance to Europe, split the alliance system we had worked so hard to build, drive the neutral states into Soviet arms, and possibly unleash the horror of atomic warfare. The decision was therefore to fight a limited war against China in the belief that a war of attrition would wear down the Chinese so that in time they would be willing to negotiate some settlement. Although both the UN and the U. S. were committed to a free Korea, they were not committed to assuring the freedom of the entire country. Moral obligations and national security could both be served if the situation could be restored to the status quo of June 1950.

General MacArthur was not willing to fight a war for such limited objectives. Although he was blamed for provoking China into entering the war, Rovere and Schlesinger pointed out that "the real case against Mac-Arthur in October and November was not that he provoked Chinese aggression but that he failed to prepare for it." MacArthur had crossed the thirty-eighth parallel with the full blessing of the UN, Truman, the State Department, and the Defense Department. But he erred in ignoring the Chinese build-up for a great November offensive. These authors concluded that "he walked straight into a Communist trap and led American arms to one of the most ignominious defeats in American history."

Truman blamed MacArthur for "the manner in which he tried to excuse his failure." As soon as the November offensive stalled, MacArthur became publicly critical of American policy. He complained about the limited military objectives and insisted that his old directives were no longer applicable. He gave a series of interviews, released press notices, and sent reports to Washington in which he gradually outlined a four-point program for victory: a blockade of China, an air and sea attack on Chinese cities, the use of Nationalist reinforcements in Korea, and the encouragement of Chiang to attack in South China. On December 6, 1950 Truman ordered in a directive that all civilian and military personnel should refrain from foreign policy statements. MacArthur disregarded the orders. Despite his prediction that we would be driven from Korea unless his orders were broadened, MacArthur's army held its own. The Eighth Army survived another heavy Chinese offensive launched December 31; by January, under its new commander, Matthew B. Ridgway, the army began to push the Reds back. Enemy supply lines, already over-extended, began to break down and this spelled disaster for the Communists. By March 1951 the UN forces were on the offensive.

On March 25, 1951 MacArthur struck out on his own again. In a statement from Tokyo, he offered to accept the enemy's surrender in the field and claimed that if surrender were not made at once the Chinese might be subjected to a full UN attack on the homeland. Truman instructed the Joint Chiefs of Staff to order MacArthur to refrain from further statements and to obey the December 6 directive. But MacArthur, on March 20 answered an earlier letter from House minority leader Joseph Martin of Massachusetts. On April 5 Martin rose and read the letter to the House. In part it read:

"It seems strangely difficult for some to realize that here in Asia is where the Communist conspirators have elected to make their play for global conquest, and that we have joined the issue thus raised on the battle-field; that here we fight Europe's war with arms while the diplomats there still fight with words; that if we lose the war to Communism in Asia the fall of Europe is inevitable, win it and Europe most probably would avoid war and yet preserve freedom. As you point out, we must win. There is no substitute for victory."

Truman had had enough. Acheson, Bradley, Marshall, Harriman and the Cabinet were consulted and the feeling was unanimous that MacArthur had to go. The President had already made this decision. General Matthew Ridgway was asked to assume command and MacArthur was notified of his removal by wire.

Five days later MacArthur returned to the United States for the first time in many years. He landed in the midst of what Senator James Duff of Pennsylvania called "a great emotional binge." Millions of people followed the general's progress from San Francisco eastward. They listened to him as he spoke before a joint session of Congress on April 19. They digested many of the 2,045,000 words of testimony given between May 3 and June 25 before joint Senate committees called to investigate MacArthur's dismissal. Although MacArthur insisted that he intended to "fade away" like all old soldiers, he remained conspicuous for many months. He toured the country delivering successive blasts against the administration.

In his memoirs Truman said he had not been disturbed about the acclaim given to MacArthur but that he was annoyed at the investigation because the secret military information thus revealed was a windfall for the Communists. He commented, "While some of the senators were busy trying to prove that I had kept General MacArthur from scoring major successes on the battlefield, his successor in Korea was doing a fine job of carrying out the administration's policy." Those who condemned Truman for firing MacArthur were amazed to discover that the Joint Chiefs of Staff sided with the President. They rejected the total warfare policy of their fellow West Point alumnus and sided with the Missouri volunteer captain of artillery. Their point was that MacArthur's policies would mean a major war for which we were not prepared. The whole issue was summarized succinctly by General Omar Bradley who, during the investigation, said that MacArthur would "involve us in the wrong war, at the wrong place, at the wrong time, and with the wrong enemy."

. . . conditions finally seemed ripe for negotiation.

After removing MacArthur Truman went on the air to report to the country. "In the simplest terms what we are doing in Korea is this: We are trying to prevent a third world war," he said. "So far, by fighting a limited war in Korea we have prevented aggression from succeeding, and bringing on a general war." He continued later, "If the Communist authorities realize they cannot defeat us in Korea, if they realize it would be foolhardy to widen the hostilities beyond Korea, then they may recognize the folly of continuing their aggression. A peaceful settlement may then be possible."

It did not look as if this peaceful settlement would ever come. As the war lengthened into months and the months into years, popular criticism increased. Many became convinced of the MacArthur theory that the Communists would negotiate only if their power were broken by all-out war. The Communists launched major offensives in April and May 1951 only to be thrown back with frightful losses. Now, with the Communists exhausted and the UN forces near the thirty-eighth parallel again, conditions finally seemed ripe for negotiation.

With the changed military situation thirteen nations in the UN proposed a resolution, adopted December 14, 1950, which led to the formation of a committee to discuss a cease-fire. China refused unless the cease-fire negotiations included other Asian problems. She asked for the withdrawal of all foreign troops from Korea, the withdrawal of American aid to Chiang, a seat in the UN and a Chinese-approved treaty with Japan. These terms were unacceptable and on February 1, 1951 Secretary Acheson succeeded in getting the UN to brand Red China as an aggressor. This action was based on a suggestion made by the United States in September 1950. When the veto problem arose again with the return of Russia to the Security Council, America had to resort to the General Assembly for support. A "Uniting for Peace" resolution was adopted on November 3 permitting the General Assembly to take steps to insure peace when and if the Security Council could not act. It was under the terms of this resolution that the General Assembly branded China an aggressor and began to take action to restore peace.

In May Secretary Acheson induced the UN to place an embargo on shipments of vital war goods to the Chinese. He also re-asserted America's opposition to China's admission to the UN and to Communist attempt to take Formosa. Since the Red Chinese were not represented in the UN, it was necessary for Russian delegate Jacob Malik to convey their willingness to negotiate to the Security Council on June 23, 1951. On July 10 negotiations began between General Ridgway and the Communist commanders at Kaesong; later resumed at Panmunjon. They were torturous and continued for many months during which the UN forces fought a holding action along the thirty-eighth parallel. It was possible to drive northward to the Yalu because the Communists had suffered more than a million casualties, but it was decided merely to concentrate on holding the line at approximately the old border. In many places UN forces were slightly north of the line, but the fact that Panmunjon was actually south of the parallel gave the Chinese a small propaganda advantage for they could claim that they were negotiating in South Korean territory. Many issues stood between the two negotiators. The first was the boundary. The Communists demanded the restoration of the thirty-eighth parallel but the Americans insisted on the present battle line. Next, and most important, was the question of prisoners. The UN forces held 132,000 Communists, many of whom had surrendered on promise of safety and fair treatment. It would have been a breach of faith to repatriate them forcibly as the Reds requested. On December 18, 1951, the Communists presented Ridgway with a list of 11,559 UN prisoners of whom only 3,198 were Americans. Since our official records showed 11,224 Americans missing in action the Communists apparently could not or would not account for nine thousand of our men, thus complicating the negotiations even more.

Negotiations were broken off in 1952 and resumed in April 1953 after Eisenhower was inaugurated. In the armistice signed on July 27, 1953 the Americans had won most of their demands. The military line became the boundary between North and South Korea and commissions were established to enforce the cease-fire regulations. A Neutral Nations Repatriation Commission was entrusted with the repatriation of prisoners, each of whom could freely determine whether he wished to be sent home or not. Several thousand Communist prisoners chose to remain in South Korea but a handful of American youths preferred to stay with their captors. Those few were of inestimable propaganda value to the Communists. When the armistice was signed, 25,604 Americans had been buried in a rough terrain few of them could have located on the map before June 1950. Ten thousand more were missing. More than a hundred thousand had been wounded. Why? Truman said the future judgment of history would vindicate his actions in entering the war and in refraining from expanding it; that the greatest accomplishment of his administration was the avoidance of a third world war. He contended that the timely intervention in Korea restrained the Communists from further aggression and violence.

There is no quarrel with Truman's claim that a third world war had been avoided, although it does not necessarily follow that intervention in Korea prevented it. Nevertheless, the Korean War did serve notice on the Communists that the day of easy pickings was over and, after 1950, the Communists were infinitely more circumspect in their dealings with the United States. The war was a long one and peace negotiations consumed many months of stalemate and indecision. However, it is impossible to prove that we would have gained a quicker settlement by the all-out attack on China that MacArthur suggested; he might have involved his country in an even larger and longer war. One regrettable aspect of the whole affair was that the McCarthyites were able to identify the administration in the public mind with treason and appeasement. It was therefore impossible for Truman's administration to conclude a peace in Korea on the basis of any compromise settlement. When Eisenhower became President he concluded a peace on exactly the same terms Truman had been willing to accept. Eisenhower was hailed as a statesman; Truman, settling on the same terms, would have been called an appeaser. Such are the vagaries of history.

The Korean War ... marked the beginning of solidification.

Even before John Foster Dulles spoke of the need for an "agonizing reappraisal" of American foreign policy, changes were underway as a result of the Korean War. Government policies are always subjected to revision in the light of new conditions and, in a democratic society, such revisions are invariably accompanied by open discussion. In their book, *United States Foreign Policy, 1945-1955*, on foreign policy, Reitzel, Kaplan, and Coblenz point out that, under containment, American long-term objectives were subordinated to short-term considerations generated by the Korean War. These caused the military aspects to be stressed at the expense of the economic and political. Before the Korean War America had moved slowly toward rearmament because, at that time, we were convinced that the Soviet was not a military menace. After 1950 the danger increased; America began to rearm both here and abroad. Had the Russians wished to attack the United States they missed an excellent chance in 1950-51 when we were involved in Korea. It can be argued that their decision not to do so (assuming that they really wanted to attack then) was deferred because of America's temporary advantage in stockpiling atomic bombs.

Our decision to speed up European rearmament brought us face to face with the problem of Germany. France still opposed German rearmament and the diplomats wrestled with the difficult questions of how to fit Germany into NATO, the degree of sovereignty to which she was entitled, her place in the European political structure, and the degree to which America could gauarantee Europe against a resurgent Germany. There was also the difficult question of how German troops were to be incorporated into the NATO armed forces. These questions came before the North Atlantic Council at Lisbon in February 1952, where it was decided that Germany would be brought into the European Defense Community (EDC) which, in turn, would be brought within NATO.

Nevertheless, a compromise had to be arranged to satisfy both French and German reservations. In the first place the EDC treaty had to be ratified, its precise relations with NATO had to be defined, and the exact terms of the Franco-German compromise had to be decided. The ratification of the EDC treaty bogged down hopelessly in Germany and in France; and Russia tried to hamper developments by pressuring the West for a conference to consider Germany unification. Furthermore, the two sides could not agree upon conditions for calling the conference. America dared not reject the Soviet offer entirely for fear of enraging the Germans, but at the same time, there was some allied opposition to a conference of any kind. The American position was that there could be no talk with the Russians until Germany had been successfully integrated into the western alliance, consequently the matter drifted until after the November elections.

As the United States moved to solidify the Western bloc after 1950, Russia was also tightening her hold over her satellites. Although theoretically the satellites were sovereign states they were actually directed from Moscow through the international Communist parties and by various economic and military pressures. If the United States sought to build up

Germany to counter Russia in Europe, the Russians replied by strengthening China in Asia. For a time it looked as if China might go its own Communist way; as though there were some hope for Chinese "Titoism" under Mao, but those who hoped forgot that China already had had a Tito in the person of Chiang who had broken with the Reds in the 1920's. There was little chance of another. The Korean war, America's inflexible attitude against recognizing the Chinese Reds, and our unwillingness to admit China to the UN drove her into closer cooperation with Russia.

NATO did not seem to be as secure as the Communist bloc, since its flanks were exposed to the enemy. America succeeded in bringing Greece and Turkey into NATO in March 1952 and the next year the Yugoslavs, under Tito, the Greeks, and the Turks were induced to sign a treaty of friendship. Yugoslavia was offered military assistance. This was part of the American policy of extending our alliance system into the Middle East. In October 1951 the Americans, British, French, and Turks proposed the creation of a Middle East command which would include Egypt as a full partner. Egypt rejected these proposals and joined with other Arab states in expressing their satisfaction with the Arab League. In July 1952 a coup ousted King Farouk of Egypt and power passed to a military junta. This group activated the Arab League to fight against colonialism and the new state of Israel. Egyptian aid was extended to anti-French rebels in Tunisia and Morocco, where the French were having a difficult time. In April 1951 Mohammed Mossadegh, prime minister of Iran, embarrassed the West by nationalizing British oil interests. This crisis dragged on into 1952 without settlement and by October the two states had severed diplomatic relations.

The United States also attempted to strengthen its alliance system in the Pacific. On August 8, 1951, forty-nine countries signed a Japanese peace treaty at San Francisco and, on the same day, the United States and Japan concluded a bilateral security pact. On August 31 we signed a mutual defense pact with the Philippines and, on September 1, concluded a similar pact with Australia and New Zealand (ANZUS). These alliances plus NATO and OAS (Organization of American States) were not related except that the United States was a party to each and supplied most of the money for their continuation.

In other Far East areas our efforts were not as successful. Nevertheless, in spite of our assistance to Formosa, to France and to Indochina, there were, by 1952, substantial increases in Communist strength in Indochina, Malaya, Thailand, and Tibet. Although American spokesmen continued to discuss a bipolar world, there were countries which did not fit into either camp. India was the most important uncommitted state and drew much support from Burma, Ceylon and Indonesia. There were more such states by 1952 but their lack of organization limited their influence. Although the uncommitted states had little power, they still had to be considered. In the event the United States and Russia were to reach an even atomic balance, it was entirely possible that a weaker third party might play a decisive role in world affairs. Since American diplomats had de-emphasized the economic and political in our alliance system, it was inevitable that they should conclude agreements involving right to military bases. Examples were bases in Iceland, Greenland, Saudi Arabia, Morocco and the Azores.

The Korean War not only forced America to reconsider its foreign policy, but it also marked the beginning of solidification. The Russians learned that, if provoked, America would fight and we learned that the Communist bloc could not be cracked by anything less than a major war. Since the United States and Russia were unprepared to fight each other, both concentrated on strengthening their blocs and augmenting their internal strength. This explains the feverish diplomatic activity to strengthen the alliance system in 1951-52 and later under Eisenhower.

The new look in American foreign policy merited careful scrutiny. From 1945 to 1950 America labored to create a situation in which several states of near equal power might counterbalance each other at the top of the greased pole of world dominance. By 1950 it was evident that we were leaning on broken reeds. France and China had fallen out of the race and the British Commonwealth had slipped several notches. So the United States found itself alone sharing the top of the pole with the Soviet Union. Five years' work to rebuild American friendships had produced little in tangible results. We were then forced to redouble our efforts to build up the military strength of our allies as well as ourselves. Consequently, after 1950, we embarked on a rearmament program with a vengeance. Under the containment policy we held to the theory that if the West built up to a certain point of strength, the Soviet bloc would be properly impressed and negotiate. In other words, strength had not been sought simply because it was desirable *per se,* but because it would lead to an American-Soviet accommodation. Under the new system negotiation was reduced in importance and, in time, became virtually impossible. After 1950 strength was sought to insure security. There no longer seemed to be an end in sight; the armament escalator presumably not only went to the top floor but also kept on going. Since this new dispensation ruled out negotiation it was evident that an unbridled arms race would eventually mean atomic stalemate, the reduction of both sides to little more than armed camps, and/or a war of unprecedented destructiveness.

The decision to concentrate on rearmament set off a chain reaction of secondary considerations, many of which ultimately became major problems themselves. There were three choices for American military planning after 1950: concentrate on building up American power, rearm our allies, or do both. The "got-it-alone" approach was apparently unacceptable. Those of the "go-it-alone" school argued that alliances were a handicap. Those who defended an alliance system maintained that we needed not fewer but more alliances—so many that the Soviet would finally be completely girdled by alliances. The result of the multiplicity of agreements concluded after 1950 was the sacrifice of freedom of action in those areas, particularly in Asia, where we had formerly enjoyed much freedom. Since, under alliances, we demanded that our allies support our redefined foreign policy, we precipitated trouble with each one.

On the home front ticklish constitutional questions were raised about the right to send troops abroad and to commit the nation to a quasi-war without congressional approval. The debate also produced serious questions about the type of armament needed. If America were going to "go-it-alone," we needed an army as well as an air force and navy, but if we were going to rely on alliances, we could confine ourselves to an air force and a navy and de-emphasize the army.

Between 1945 and 1950 there was little friction between the United States and her friends. Everyone agreed on matters of reconstruction, rehabilitation, political stability, the restoration of trade, and access to raw materials. When America began to show a concern over security, the differences with our allies became more noticeable. We tried to gain support for our security aspirations but our allies often found these incompatible with their national interests. America sought uniformity in the face of conflicting national interests, and the other states had to decide at what point our policies would not jeopardize their national interest or at what point we would be angered into withdrawing our military and economic assistance.

When the fear of all-out war against China or the fear of Russian intervention began to wane in 1952 predictions were then made that the Soviets would not precipitate a general war. This opened the question of the kind of rearmament needed. Even though a major war with Russia seemed remote by 1952, the possibility could not be disregarded. If a major war was less likely there was still the possibility of smaller wars. Might there not be a series of "Balkan incidents" like those which preceded World War I, or some Hitler-like "Saturday surprises" which preceded World War II? These might mean a series of "police actions," and also revive the possibility of a major war.

Should we prepare for a major war only or extend our armament program to cover everything from an uprising of hillsmen in some half-forgotten colony to an all-out nuclear war with Russia? The question that caused admirals and generals to fight knock-down battles from 1950 to 1952 was deeper than mere inter-service rivalries. These men held the future of the country in their hands and any mistake in judgment would mean disaster. The correctness of their decisions could be determined only by war. The problems covered types of armament, dispersement of manpower, location of future bases, types and amount of research, and allocation of funds and resources. In the race between Russia and the United States the latter had to be assured of access to strategic raw materials and at the same time deny them to the Russians. Since the United States was the center of a tremendous alliance system we could not afford to be knocked out, even momentarily. As long as America was intact Russia would not dare strike other powers for fear of retaliation.

The core of military thinking was the atom bomb. The free nations lived in terror that America might use the bomb and precipitate wholesale Russian retaliation. Their fears were intensified by American insistence that the atom bomb was the trump card, and that since this was all that prevented a Russian attack, we could not permit outside interference in our decision to use it. Even before Secretary Dulles used the term widely, the "instant retaliation" concept was firmly rooted in military thinking. Outnumbered, Americans' only hope for victory rested upon instant availability of atom bombs and a willingness to use them. But now, since the Russians were equally armed with atom bombs, American strategy had to depend upon technological and industrial superiority. With the shift in emphasis after 1953 to nuclear-type weapons the scientific research and development absorbed more and more of our energies, budgets and personnel. At the same time, and for sound strategic reasons, the UN figured prominently in America's new foreign policy. Truman realistically guided his administration's diplomacy through both regional alliances and the UN, relating the former to the latter whenever possible. This was open recognition that collective security under the UN had to

111

be modified, at least temporarily, in favor of more immediate problems. If we neglected the immediate problems to pursue the illusion that the UN could be made to work at once, we ran the risk that ultimately the UN might become an agency of the Communists.

The Fair Deal Years

. . . successful with so much of his Fair Deal.

Although Truman had thrown down the gauntlet to the conservatives in 1945, there were no assurances that he actually spoke for the people until he was elected in his own right in November 1948. Truman interpreted the election as a mandate to pursue relentlessly the twenty-one point domestic program that he had outlined in 1945. The program came to be known as the "Fair Deal." This term, which gained currency after the State of the Union message of January 5, 1949, was publicized by the press and applied to the President's program. Truman had told both houses on that day that "every segment of our population and every individual has a right to expect from his government a fair deal." Actually he added little in 1949 to what he said in 1945. In the final analysis he advocated little that had not been advocated previously by the New Dealers. During his first term only a fraction of the program had been written into the statute books. The big question was whether he would be more successful in 1949.

Truman's Cabinet by this time consisted of: Dean Acheson, Secretary of State; John W. Snyder, Secretary of the Treasury; James Forrestal, Secretary of Defense; Thomas Clark (destined soon for the Supreme Court), Attorney General; Jesse Donaldson (who had succeeded Hannegan in 1947), Postmaster General. Charles Brannan continued in the agriculture post to which he had been appointed in 1948. Julius Krug was Secretary of the Interior but was replaced by Oscar L. Chapman later in 1949. Charles Sawyer and Maurice Tobin, who had replaced Harriman and Schwellenbach in 1948, continued in the Commerce and Labor posts.

Truman was only slightly more successful in dealing with the Democratic Eighty-first and Eighty-second Congresses than he had been with the discredited Republican Eightieth. The reason was the same. Although bipartisanship was a common term it was not applicable to domestic affairs. Truman could count on little Republican support and the loss of much Democratic support. Seldom did the Democrats vote solidly as a party except on routine partisan matters such as electing Sam Rayburn to the speakership. The southern Democrats controlled approximately one hundred seats in the House and twenty in the Senate. They usually voted with the conservative Republicans against Truman's program. With the Democrats in control southern strength was even increased since many southern congressmen held key committee chairmanships and could therefore block any Truman proposal they did not like. In 1949 Senator John Bricker of Ohio even proposed a formal coalition of southern Democrats and Republican conservatives, particularly since the rift in the Democratic party caused by the "Dixiecrat" rebellion continued after the election.

The four years (1948-52) that Truman was an elected President were two years of some small success with his Fair Deal program, and two years of the Korean War. Although Truman regularly presented his Fair Deal requests during the war years, he saw them knocked down just as regularly while Congress concentrated on war problems and investigations. In his inaugural message on January 20, 1949, Truman called for the immediate enactment of his Fair Deal program. He worked with Democratic leaders in an effort to guide his program through Congress. The results were often disappointing. However, Truman did much to exert an indirect influence on public opinion and events. By constant insistence upon progressivism he kept the fight alive in an effort to wear down the conservatives' resistance. Much that was done on the state level was undoubtedly influenced by Truman's example, and some of the accomplishments of the early days of the Eisenhower administration are traceable to seeds sown by Truman.

Of all the issues none was hotter than that of civil rights. Truman continued to press for adequate legislation. He asked for laws to prohibit the poll tax, lynching, and discrimination in interstate transportation. He asked that all federal funds for housing and education be withheld unless the recipients permitted equal treatment for all. He also asked for a permanent Federal Employment Practices Commission. Truman was well aware that one of the serious barriers to civil rights legislation was the Senate's cloture rules that permitted a filibuster. At his instigation several Democratic leaders amended the rules but the end result was a strengthened cloture rule rather than one that relaxed the hold of the southerners over civil rights debate. Although a civil rights measure would often pass in the House it would expire ingloriously, smothered by a Senate "talk-athon."

Since the President was unable to influence favorable action in Congress, he resorted to executive action. By executive order the Federal Housing Authority refused to finance new housing and apartment projects where racial or religious discrimination was permitted. In December 1951 Truman created a watchdog committee to make certain that no government defense contracts were awarded to firms which permitted discrimination. Since war orders were such an important part of the economy at the time, so Truman's action, in effect, created an FEPC for industry. Government attorneys and attorneys for the National Association for the Advancement of Colored People took their cases to the courts and won many important decisions on civil rights. Efforts were made to invoke the Fourteenth Amendment to end various forms of segregation and discrimination. On the state level many leaders followed Truman's example in the fight for civil rights. Several states, by 1952, had legislated against poll taxes, lynching, and the wearing of masks.

Although unsuccessful in amending the Social Security Act before 1948, Truman renewed his efforts in 1949 and 1950. In the latter year Congress finally acted and added another ten million persons to the thirty-five million already covered by the program. Those added included self-employed businessmen, state and municipal employees, domestic help, employees of non-profit organizations, and certain types of agricultural workers.

Truman was justly dissatisfied with the housing legislation adopted during his first term and he renewed his fight against what he called the "Real Estate Lobby" in a lengthy letter to Speaker Rayburn. The struggle in Congress was particularly severe but Senator Taft, always friendly toward housing legislation, was one of the President's ablest aides. Housing legislation proved to be one of the most important Fair Deal triumphs. Although Truman blamed the Republicans for opposing housing legislation, the liberal Republican support of his 1949 measure was responsible for its adoption. Under this act the federal government was to embark upon a five-year urban slum clearance program and a four-year rural housing program. The act also provided a six-year program of federal aid for the construction of 810,000 single housing units. Under the new housing acts the Housing Expediter was given more power to enforce rules. Rent control was extended until June 30, 1950 without the 1947 provision that a voluntary fifteen per cent increase in rents was permissible upon agreement between landlord and renter. However, Truman's recommended financial assistance for housing cooperatives was ignored by the Eighty-first Congress.

Truman continued to campaign for a liberalized Displaced Persons Act. In 1949 a bill passed the House abolishing the anti-Jewish and anti-Catholic features of the earlier measure and raised the quota from 205,000 immigrants in two years to 339,000 in three years, but Senator Pat McCarran of Nevada still blocked the bill in the Senate. However, during 1950 the administration was more successful and in June Congress approved an act to admit 415,744 persons in three years and the objectionable features of the earlier measure were eliminated.

The farmer population had contributed heavily to Truman's election victory, and something had to be done to strengthen their position in the economy. The new Secretary of Agriculture, Charles Brannan, devised a plan to bolster farm prices and also relieve harrassed consumers. Basically the Brannan Plan was a return to supply and demand whereby nonperishable produce would continue under the established system of supports, crop loans, and government storage, but perishable items would sell at an open market price. The consumer would thus buy meats, eggs, and dairy products at non-support prices. Meanwhile, the government reimbursed the farmer for the difference between market and support prices. Many farm organizations which drew their support from large-scale operators disapproved of this measure which presumably was designed to aid the small farmer. Raising the old bogies of socialism and regimentation, the farm organizations induced Congress to reject the plan. Although the Brannan plan was not adopted, the Agricultural Act of 1949 provided that ninety per cent of parity prices were to prevail until 1950. In 1951 these would be replaced by a flexible system ranging from seventy-five to ninety per cent of parity.

In 1949 Herbert Hoover's Commission on Organization of the Executive Branch of the Government presented a series of reports embodying 277 recommendations. The Hoover proposals and suggestions were hailed as an achievement of major importance and in June Congress empowered the President to translate them into action. Truman began at once to reorganize the executive department. Although most of his recommendations were instantly endorsed by Congress, there was stout and successful opposition to Truman's plan for a new federal Department of Welfare. It was opposed for fear Truman would use it to carry on an extensive propaganda campaign for his national health insurance plan. On this point Truman had not accepted the Eightieth Congress' verdict but, in 1949, renewed the fight for a 1½ per cent payroll tax to provide health insurance coverage for an estimated 85,000,000 persons. The basic details of his 1949 proposals were the same as his earlier ones. The American Medical Association brought out its heaviest artillery and the measure was demolished in Congress on the charge of socialized medicine.

The same fate befell Truman's plan to provide federal assistance to education. In May 1949 a Senate-approved bill to appropriate three hundred million dollars, to be spent on education at the discretion of the states, ran into trouble in the House when efforts were made to limit its use to public schools. Not only was the cry of socialism raised against the measure, but it also ran afoul of the civil rights and church *vs.* state issues. Cardinal Spellman and Mrs. Eleanor Roosevelt engaged in a vigorous exchange of opinion on this question, a dispute which accomplished little more than a further beclouding of the issue.

In 1948 Truman had promised labor he would try to restore the Wagner Labor Act and repeal the Taft-Hartley Act. The chances seemed good since there was much criticism of the new law and even Senator Taft was not entirely satisfied with the act. He had indicated his willingness to compromise by incorporating several pro-labor provisions. However, Truman and his labor advisers demanded all or nothing; they were satisfied only with repeal and in the end they had to accept nothing. The Eighty-first Congress made no serious effort to repeal the act although, under Taft's direction, the Senate moved toward amending it. However, Truman redeemed himself with labor by securing an amendment to the Fair Labor Standards Act which raised the minimum wage from forty to seventy-five cents. An additional five million workers were included under this new act.

An expansion of public power facilities and the conservation of natural resources were basic planks in Truman's Fair Deal. He continued to urge broader federal participation in the construction of a St. Lawrence Seaway as well as new projects in the Columbia and Missouri river valleys. These proposals were rejected although Congress was willing to increase appropriations for the Tennessee Valley Authority (TVA) and the Rural Electrification Administration (REA).

It is amazing that Truman was successful with so much of his Fair Deal program in a Congress which, although it represented his own party, was essentially hostile. Truman was pleased with the results achieved by the Eighty-first Congress and at the end of its first session he praised its accomplishments. On the other hand, Guy Gabrielson, Republican National Chairman, had a different impression. To him Congress had a "far less impressive record than that established by the Brooklyn Dodgers in the recent World Series." Like its immediate predecessor, the Eighty-first Congress scored its most notable achievements in foreign affairs. The vote had been bi-partisan and included ratification of the NATO agreement, the continuation of the Economic Cooperation Act, the adoption of the Mutual Defense Assistance Act, the Point Four Program, and the extension of the Reciprocal Trade Agreements Act. In this last instance Congress returned to the broad concepts of the late Cordell Hull and allocated to the President the power to negotiate trade agreements on the basis of a fify per cent tariff reduction.

. . . problems of national defense and a brief economic recession.

During the first eighteen months of his new term Truman had to face difficult problems of national defense and a brief economic recession. The National Military Establishment, created by the 1947 act, proved unworkable. Secretary of Defense Forrestal found his position an impossible one. The three service secretaries, by virtue of their power and membership on the National Security Council, were difficult to handle; each sought the lion's share of military appropriations for his own service. The Joint Chiefs of Staff did the same thing and, in the absence of a presiding officer, any agreement among them was out of the question. The confusion was dramatically accentuated when Forrestal, broken in body and spirit by the unequal fight, resigned and soon after leaped to his death from a hospital window.

With the evidence before it, the administration moved to eliminate the weakness of the 1947 act by substituting a new one which passed August 2, 1949. The National Military Establishment was changed to the Department of Defense; the service secretaries were subordinated to the Secretary of Defense and removed from membership on the NSC. The Secretary of Defense was further strengthened by the appointment of a Deputy Secretary with more power than the now displaced undersecretary. Three new assistant secretaries were made responsible to the Secretary of Defense. The new act also provided for a non-voting chairman for the Joint Chiefs of Staff. Truman's first appointment to this position was General Omar N. Bradley.

As Forrestal's successor Truman appointed Louis Johnson. He soon found that the new organizational set-up did not solve all problems. A continuing and basic cause of friction was the question of strategy. Johnson launched a drive for economy in the armed services. Drastic and, as was later demonstrated, foolish personnel cuts followed. The main defense argument arose between the Navy and the Air Force. The battleship admirals of the 1930's had given way to the carrier admirals of the 1940's, who argued that it was wrong to give strategic bombing operations to the land-based planes of the Air Force. A much more effective attack could be launched, they maintained, from the "floating islands" of the fleet. To further this purpose the Navy began construction of a huge super-carrier, the *USS United States*, to accommodate the larger and speedier jet planes. When Johnson stopped construction on this ship he served notice that he was siding with the Air Force. Funds were diverted from the other services to build up the Air Force's fleet of B-36 bombers. The "Fancy Dan" admirals, as Bradley called them, revolted and dramatically broke the long-smoldering inter-service feud into the open. The ensuing "Battle of the Pentagon" was embarrassing to all concerned, and finally in 1950 Truman dismissed the recalcitrant Chief of Naval Operations, Louis E. Denfield, and the Secretary of the Navy, John Sullivan, resigned.

Secretary of Defense Johnson also became involved in a public debate with Acheson over the question of aiding Nationalist China, but it was the Korean War which wrote finis to Johnson's stormy career. He had publicly boasted that if the Russians created any trouble, the United States Air Force would blast them into submission within an hour. This statement looked foolish indeed when his country became involved in a war in which the atomic bomb and strategic air bombardment force were worthless. His drastic cuts in personnel left the country pitifully unprepared to fight even a tenth-rate power. On September 1, 1950 Johnson resigned and, to restore confidence in the Department, Truman prevailed upon Marshall to come out of retirement to serve as Secretary of Defense.

The boom, which had been gaining momentum since 1945, showed definite signs of slackening off early in 1949. Unemployment rose to approximately four million early in the year and there was a corresponding decrease of about two per cent in gross national production during the first half-year. However, despite some soft spots in the economy, the basic construction, automotive, and steel industries remained prosperous, and before the end of the year there were encouraging signs of recovery. There is little doubt that the recession reduced congressional support for

119

the Fair Deal and that Congress refused Truman's request for increased taxes to balance the budget for the same reason.

The recession did not discourage labor from launching a drive for a fourth-round increase in wages. During 1949 labor strife centered on the steel and coal industries. The steel workers not only demanded substantial wage increases but also pension, health, and insurance plans as well. When agreement became impossible, a federal fact-finding board proposed that wage increases be withheld but sanctioned the other demands. This compromise was acceptable to the unions but it was flatly rejected by the operators. A month-long strike followed in October resulting in substantial gains for the workers. Throughout 1949 John L. Lewis continued his obstructionist tactics. There were no strikes, but during most of the year he held his miners to a three-day week by means of forced holidays. The net result was that Lewis lost stature in the labor movement by failing to secure many benefits for his union. In contrast, both Murray and Reuther secured substantial gains for their unions during the same year.

By 1950 the economy was fully recovered. Unemployment dropped to about 3,500,000, which was considered an almost irreducible minimum. The 150,697,361 Americans—the population shown by the 1950 census— enjoyed a prosperous year marred only by a few disturbances in the coal, automotive, and railroad industries. The country was on its way out of the recession when the Korean War began in June.

The very prosperity of the times hampered the war effort. With barely three million unemployed workers to draw upon, industry was hard pressed to find sufficient labor to produce the needed war goods. Shortages developed quickly and inflation followed in their wake. In July Truman asked Congress to provide new controls on the civilian economy and two months later the Defense Production Act was passed. This act gave Truman power to impose wage, price, and ration controls, as well as establish allocation and priority systems and impose credit limitations. At first Truman was content to try a system of voluntary controls rather than invoking the powers granted by the act, but he soon found the voluntary system unworkable. The Federal Reserve Board increased both the downpayment for automobile purchase and the bank rediscount rate. It likewise limited the maturity dates of mortgages. But such restrictions were unavailing.

When Truman proposed his budget for the year July 1, 1950 to June 30, 1951, he estimated expenditures at about forty-two billion. He asked for additional taxes in order to balance the budget and hold the national debt at its June 30, 1950 figure—$257,376,855,385. The Korean War increased expenditures rapidly and by the time Congress adjourned the fifty-billion mark had been passed. The war alone added another seventeen billion to the budget during 1950. A staggering deficiency loomed but income and corporate levies were increased on October 1 in hopes of raising another five billion.

The war caught Congress with its political fences down. Unfortunately it was unable to adjourn until September 23. Meanwhile, Truman began another series of "whistle stop" speaking tours early in May. Following the elections Congress reassembled on November 27. Lame-duck legislators eased into the final months of their terms. There was no expectation that Congress would be called upon to consider any new crisis, when suddenly the Chinese Communists came into the Korean War "with both feet." Congress was forced into action immediately. Rent controls, due to expire at the end of the year, were continued until March 31, 1951 and new tax levies were provided to bring in an estimated four billion. On December 16, 1950 Truman proclaimed a state of national emergency, asked for an increase in the armed forces to 3,500,000 men and appointed Charles E. Wilson of the General Electric Company to head the Office of Defense Mobilization. Voluntary controls to aid the war effort had proved unworkable, but it was difficult to find any group willing to support the rigid controls that were needed.

The Korean War caused scarcely a ripple ....

The Eighty-second Congress, which assembled in January 1951, concerned itself almost exclusively with the Korean War. It paid little attention to President Truman or his Fair Deal program. Before the year 1951 was over, Truman was denounced vehemently. There was even talk of impeachment. Nevertheless, he continued to press for his Fair Deal. Even so, his main concern—like Congress'— was to build up the country's armed strength.

During the year a slight modification was made in the Taft-Hartley Act to legalize union-shop agreements without elections among employees approving union shops. This step was made necessary by the Supreme Court's decision in *NLRB v. Highland Park Manufacturing Company*. Even though a gain from labor's point of view, this was still not the type of amendment labor demanded.

The new Congress, unlike its immediate predecessors, was not called upon to endorse any bold new programs on foreign policy. The "Great Debate" ended in a partial victory for the President; he was granted authority to send troops to Europe, but it was understood that congressional approval would be needed if more were to be sent later. Congress also created the Mutual Security Agency to coordinate the various foreign-aid programs under one head. ECA was to expire on December 31. The Reciprocal Trade Agreements Act was continued although Congress denied tariff reductions to Communist states. The Displaced Persons Act was extended slightly for several thousand immigrants who had missed the deadline specified in the original act.

In 1952 Congress passed, over Truman's veto, the McCarran-Walter Immigration and Nationality Act, which set, as a quota for each country, one-sixth of one per cent of the number of such nationals residing here in 1920. No fewer than one hundred persons from each country were to be admitted. Under this system priority was given to those persons of northern European extraction. Although Asiatics were now permitted to enter in small numbers, the act generally discriminated against those groups which were at one time called "unassimilatable." The Attorney General was also given power to deport undesirables and the naturalization laws were tightened to control alleged undesirables or subversives.

The Korean War not only continued inflation but intensified it. An Economic Stabilization Agency had been created to hold price-wage lines, but in January 1951, its director, Alan Valentine, resigned because the voluntary control program had been a dismal failure. He was replaced by Eric Johnston, who with Director of Price Stabilization Michael V. DiSalle and Chairman Cyrus S. Ching of the Wage Stabilization Board, sought to devise a new system. On January 26, 1951 Ching abandoned the voluntary program and announced that no further wage increases were to be permitted without the board's permission. Price ceilings were also set to hold the line at the highest level between December 10, 1950 and January 25, 1951. The reaction was immediate. In February despite appeals from Director Wilson of the Office of Defense Mobilization, there was a strike involving several railroad brotherhoods. Truman promptly ordered the Army to operate the rail lines but the soldiers were hampered by a strange malady which seemed to afflict railway switchmen and no one else. Finally, as the number of switchmen on "sick leave" increased, the Army issued a "work-or-else" order. Although the brotherhoods returned to work this did not bring peace on the labor front. The labor representatives on the Wage Stabilization Board boycotted the meetings and ultimately

Truman was forced to adopt an escalator arrangement which thawed the wage freeze. The boycott ended in April when Truman reorganized the Wage Stabilization Board with power not only over wage controls but also over disputes involving collective bargaining. The old board had held rigidly to ten-per-cent-raise ceilings over January 1951 levels but the new board was more flexible.

Price controls, permitted under the Defense Production Act, were scheduled to end in June. Truman requested well ahead of time that they be renewed and that additional authority be granted to control installment credit, rents, and food prices. In March 1951 the administration announced a twenty per cent reduction in steel allocations for the production of autos, appliances, and other civilian goods. Prices shot up at once, but by June there was a tendency for them to level slightly. There was a battle in Congress because the consensus of opinion was that Truman should be granted less rather than more power over price controls. DiSalle was denounced because, during the spring, he rolled back beef prices. When price controls expired on June 30, Congress had not yet acted. A temporary measure continued control until July 31 but in the meantime, Congress passed a permanent measure which Truman finally signed although he pronounced it the worst bill ever presented to him. The Defense Production Act was extended to June 30, 1952. DiSalle's price rollback was sabotaged by congressional action prohibiting rollbacks exceeding ten per cent on farm products. A feature particularly objectionable to Truman was the Capehart Amendment, which permitted rollbacks on manufactured goods but also provided that ceilings could be raised if costs increased. Cattle slaughtering quotas, imposed previously by the administration, were scrapped, and restrictions on installment credit were relaxed. Residential rent controls were imposed but only with the understanding that landlords be permitted to make a twenty per cent increase in some cases. The act had the overall effect of nullifying any program for effective controls.

In a special message to Congress in February 1951 Truman called for tax increases totaling ten billion to be collected through income, corporate, and excise levies. It was not until October that Congress acted but then it halved what the President had requested. At the same time he had asked for increases in the postal rates to cover the usual post office deficit. These were finally voted and became effective on January 1, 1952.

Since the armed forces were being increased to 3,500,000 men, some changes became necessary in the draft legislation. A movement to draft eighteen-year-olds was opposed on the ground that eighteen was too young for the rigors of military life. Eventually, when the Universal Military Training and Service Act was signed on June 19, 1951, a compromise was reached. This extended the draft until June 1, 1955, and provided that men between eighteen-and-a-half and twenty-six were to be called for twenty-four months' service. The older men would be taken first.

All branches of the armed services were expanded rapidly. The Navy was permitted to go ahead with its super-carrier, the *USS Forrestal;* Truman asked for funds to construct the first atomic submarine, and also five billion dollars to support research in developing a new arsenal of "fantastic" weapons.

During 1951 General Marshall again retired from public life and turned over his portfolio of office to Robert A. Lovett who continued as Secretary of Defense for the remainder of Truman's administration. Lovett guided many significant developments in military strategy.

As early as December 31, 1946, the Atomic Energy Commisison had taken over full control of atomic production as well as research and development. There were other agencies with their finger in the atomic pie including the Joint Congressional Committee on Atomic Energy; the Military Liaison Committee, appointed by the President from top-ranking civilian scientific and technical experts to advise the AEC and the Military Liaison Committee. But, it was not until 1949 the Atomic Energy Commission began to function smoothly. Truman then created a committee composed of the Secretaries of State, Defense, and the chairman of the AEC to study special problems in connection with atomic energy. One of the most important was the production of an explosive hydrogen device after it was discovered that Russia had an atomic bomb. The hydrogen bomb was theoretically possible but there were misgivings that it might not work. David Lilienthal, of the AEC, and Senators Brien McMahon and Bourke Hickenlooper of the Joint Congressional Committee on Atomic Energy, recommended that the step should be undertaken even though success was uncertain. The President approved the project in January 1950. After tests conducted in the Pacific indicated the feasibility of the bomb in March 1951, research was pushed as rapidly as possible. During the summer of 1952, Gordon Dean, new head of AEC, recommended the establishment of test sites for hydrogen bomb research near Las Vegas, Nevada. Finally, in November 1952, the hydrogen bomb was successfully detonated; once again American military power moved ahead of the Soviets.

While experiments were being conducted to perfect a new and more terrible explosive, work was also being rushed on the *Nautilus,* the first atomic-powered submarine. It was expected that this vessel would prove the practicability of the new power for a whole fleet as well as point the way to peaceful uses for atomic energy.

The year 1952 was again a year of labor strife in spite of the war. The Department of Labor reported more work stoppages than in any year since the high point of 1946. The major disturbances occurred in the coal, oil, telephone, and steel industries. As a result of the steel strike, Congress reorganized the Wage Stabilization Board but denied it further authority to interfere in wage disputes. When union demands for wage increases were rejected by steel management, the union served notice that it would strike when the then current contract was to expire on December 31, 1951. Truman was deeply concerned especially when Secretary Lovett warned that any steel stoppage would weaken the war effort. To avert trouble, Truman referred the question to the Wage Stabilization Board and the union agreed to postpone the strike until the matter could be investigated fully. On March 20 the board recommended increases of eighteen cents without price raises. Truman fully agreed that wage increases could be made even though prices remained the same, but Charles Wilson warned him that the owners would take a dim view of his logic. When Truman stood by his guns, Wilson resigned as Director of Defense Mobilization. John Steelman, who became acting director of ODM, labored with the operators and union leaders until all hope of a settlement faded. At last, on April 7, the union said that a strike had become inevitable.

With the advice and consent of most of his Cabinet, Truman moved on April 8, 1952 to seize the steel mills. Since ninety-two companies and 600,000 workers were involved, the President defended his action as necessary to avoid a stoppage in a vital industry during wartime and based his authority on "inherent" powers. He insisted that no price increases should be permitted. If they were, he said, "you could say goodbye to stabilization. If we knuckled under to the steel industry, the lid would be off. Prices would start jumping up all around us." He recommended that Congress should approve the move at once.

Truman refused to invoke the Taft-Hartley Act. This act, he argued, was designed for peacetime labor disputes and he preferred to use the provisions of the Defense Production Act, which he considered more effectively adapted to meet the wartime situation. The eighty-day waiting period provided in the Taft-Hartley Act did not guarantee that strikes would be prevented and Truman further argued that by postponing its strike since December 31, the union had actually waited ninety-nine days.

In the meantime, Judge David Pine of the U. S. District Court in the District of Columbia had ordered Secretary Sawyer to return the mills to the owners, and on June 2, 1952 this decision was upheld, six to three, by the Supreme Court in the case of *Youngstown Sheet & Tube Co. v. Sawyer*. Truman was deeply chagrined that the court had found his seizure illegal, but he ordered prompt compliance with its directive.

On June 10 Truman asked Congress to pass legislation to deal with the steel strike, but all Congress did was to provide, in the new Defense Production Act, that the provisions of the Taft-Hartley law would apply. The country experienced a fifty-three day steel tie-up before the strike finally ended with sixteen-cent-wage and $5.20-per-ton price increases. There were serious munition shortages at the Korean front as a direct result of the strike.

During the last year of his term Truman continued to press for certain features of the Fair Deal program. On December 29, 1951 he had appointed the President's Commission on the Health Needs of the Nation to study this important question under Paul B. Magnuson, medical director of the Veterans Administration, and on December 18, 1952 the commission submitted a report. It was too late for Truman to revive his national health plan but the committee's report, based on a year of study, suggested a health plan combining some of Truman's earlier proposals and the voluntary insurance systems then in use. The Commission also recommended the creation of a cabinet post for health and security, a special federal health commission, federal assistance to medical schools, and government financial assistance to those who could not afford voluntary health insurance plans.

In 1945, by proclamation and executive order, Truman had asserted the federal government's control over offshore oil reserves, and in 1947 the Supreme Court in the case of *U. S. v. California* had ruled that the federal government had paramount rights in all resources lying between the coast and the three-mile limit. Texas, Louisiana, and California, with extensive offshore oil reserves, had been leasing drilling rights to private operators for years. They used every means to circumvent the Supreme Court's decision until finally, in 1952, Congress passed a bill transferring title to these resources to the states. Such a move "would be robbery in broad daylight," said Truman, as he pounced on the measure at once and vetoed it on May 29.

Truman was ignored, rejected, and forgotten during the closing days of his administration as both sides prepared for the election of 1952. However, he seemed no more forgotten than the "police action" in distant Korea. The Korean War caused scarcely a ripple on the main stream of American life. Most people went along on a business-as-usual basis. Labor leaders continued to wrangle for a few extra pennies, businessmen insisted upon substantial price increases at every turn and consumers apparently assumed a war could be fought with one hand while with the other, cars, appliances, and civilian goods could be produced in an undiminished stream. National production hit $357,000,000,000 and employment stayed steadily above the sixty million mark. All suggestions that inflation should be controlled encountered opposition from every self-interest group.

Index

129

UNITED STATES COLLECTIVE DEFENSE ARRANGEMEN

REPUBLIC OF KOREA TREATY

JAPANESE TREATY

REPUBLIC OF CHINA TREATY

PHILIPPINE TREATY

NORTH PACIFIC OCEAN

SOUTHEAST ASIA TREATY

ANZUS TREATY

INDIAN OCEAN

NORTH ATLANTIC TREATY (15 NATIONS)

A treaty signed April 4, 1949, by which "the parties agree that an armed attack against one or more of them in Europe or North America shall be considered an attack against them all; and . . . each of them . . . will assist the . . . attacked by taking forthwith, individually and in concert with the other Parties, such action as it deems necessary including the use of armed force . . ."

1 UNITED STATES	9 LUXEMBOURG
2 CANADA	10 PORTUGAL
3 ICELAND	11 FRANCE
4 NORWAY	12 ITALY
5 UNITED KINGDOM	13 GREECE
6 NETHERLANDS	14 TURKEY
7 DENMARK	15 FEDERAL REPUBLIC
8 BELGIUM	OF GERMANY

RIO TREATY (21 NATIONS)

A treaty signed September 2, 1947, which provides that an armed attack against any American State "shall be considered as an attack against all the American States and . . . each one . . . undertakes to assist in meeting the attack . . ."

1 UNITED STATES	22 EL SALVADOR	29 PERU
16 MEXICO	23 NICARAGUA	30 BRAZIL
17 CUBA	24 COSTA RICA	31 BOLIVIA
18 HAITI	25 PANAMA	32 PARAGUAY
19 DOMINICAN	26 COLOMBIA	33 CHILE
REPUBLIC	27 VENEZUELA	34 ARGENTINA
20 HONDURAS	28 ECUADOR	35 URUGUAY
21 GUATEMALA		

ANZUS (Australia–New Zealand–United States) TREATY (3 NATIONS)

A treaty signed September 1, 1951, whereby each of the parties "recognizes that an armed attack in the Pacific Area on any of the Parties would be dangerous to its own peace and safety and declares that it would act to meet the common danger in accordance with its constitutional processes."

1 UNITED STATES
36 NEW ZEALAND
37 AUSTRALIA

PHILIPPINE T (BILATERAL)

A treaty sign 30, 1951, by parties recog an armed att Pacific Area o the Parties wo gerous to its and safety" party agrees t act "to meet t dangers in with its cor processes."

1 UNITED S
38 PHILIPPI

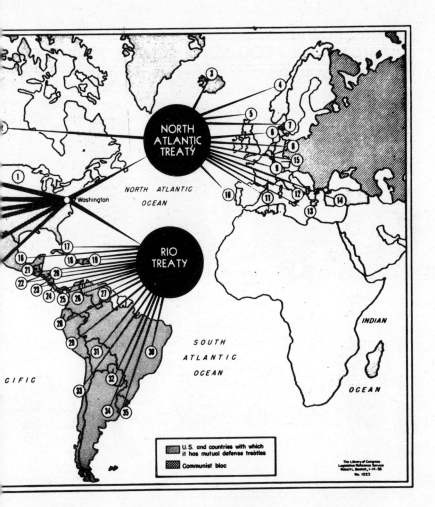

U.S. and countries with which it has mutual defense treaties

Communist bloc

The Library of Congress
Legislative Reference Service
Robert L. Skelton, L.-14-'55
No. 1223

JAPANESE TREATY (BILATERAL)

A treaty signed September 8, 1951, whereby Japan on a provisional basis requests, and the United States agrees, to "maintain certain of its armed forces in and about Japan . . . so as to deter armed attack upon Japan."

1 UNITED STATES
39 JAPAN

REPUBLIC OF KOREA (South Korea) TREATY (BILATERAL)

A treaty signed October 1, 1953, whereby each party "recognizes that an armed attack in the Pacific area on either of the Parties . . . would be dangerous to its own peace and safety" and that each Party "would act to meet the common danger in accordance with its constitutional processes."

1 UNITED STATES
40 REPUBLIC OF KOREA

SOUTHEAST ASIA TREATY (8 NATIONS)

A treaty signed September 8, 1954, whereby each Party "recognizes that aggression by means of armed attack in the treaty area against any of the Parties . . . would endanger its own peace and safety" and each will "in that event act to meet the common danger in accordance with its constitutional processes."

1 UNITED STATES
5 UNITED KINGDOM
11 FRANCE
36 NEW ZEALAND
37 AUSTRALIA
38 PHILIPPINES
41 THAILAND
42 PAKISTAN

REPUBLIC OF CHINA (Formosa) TREATY (BILATERAL)

A treaty signed December 2, 1954, whereby each of the parties "recognizes that an armed attack in the West Pacific Area directed against the territories of either of the Parties would be dangerous to its own peace and safety," and that each "would act to meet the common danger in accordance with its constitutional processes." The territory of the Republic of China is defined as "Taiwan (Formosa) and the Pescadores."

1 UNITED STATES
43 REPUBLIC OF CHINA (FORMOSA)

GPO 9

courtesy of The Library of Congress: Legislative Reference Service.

AMERICA at MID-CENTURY

The Eisenhower Administration

CONTENTS

The Eisenhower Administration

The End of an Era

. . . Taft was certain of victory.

The presidential election of 1952 was one of the most significant in American history. Much was at stake. The new foreign policy, so patiently forged from 1945 to 1952, the economic and social gains since 1933, and many other accomplishments of what Eric Goldman in *The Crucial Decade* had called the "Half Century of Revolution" were on trial. The Republicans had missed the call in 1948 but there could be no mistaking the trend in 1952. It was inconceivable that they could lose if they nominated a reasonably popular candidate. There seemed to be no obstacle in the way of victory; Harry Truman's popularity had never been lower and he was dragging his party down with him.

Robert A. Taft of Ohio was a leading contender for the Republican nomination after his re-election as senator in 1950. The full support of the conservatives and the isolationists rallied behind him. His press backing was significant and many political machines throughout the Middle West and the South were in his corner. The eastern party leaders, who had dominated Republicanism for twelve years, were resolved to defeat Taft and they found ready allies among western Republicans. This was the group that accepted, in principle, the major accomplishments of the New and Fair Deals, as well as most of Truman's foreign policy. They needed a powerful candidate to supplant Taft. Unable to accept either Thomas E. Dewey or Harold E. Stassen, former governor of Minnesota and then president of the University of Pennsylvania, they turned to Dwight David "Ike" Eisenhower, commander of NATO and president of Columbia University.

Eisenhower had been before the public as a possible presidential candidate since 1945 but there was some question about his political affiliations. Both parties claimed him. Presumably, Truman offered to assist him in securing the Democratic nomination in 1948 and in that same year Eisenhower had gracefully declined to permit the Republicans to enter his name in the New Hampshire primaries. He had stated that he was "not available for and could not accept nomination to high political office." It did not end there. In 1950 both Senator Henry Cabot Lodge, Jr., of Massachusetts and Thomas E. Dewey of New York said he was their choice for the Republican nomination, but Eisenhower's departure for Europe in December to command NATO troops jolted their hopes.

While Eisenhower remained noncommittal, Taft announced his candidacy on October 16, 1951, and he was soon joined in the race by Harold Stassen and Governor Earl Warren of California. Lodge headed a group campaigning for Eisenhower but there was still no authorization. Finally, in December 1951, Lodge went to Paris and returned with a declaration on January 6, 1952 that he had obtained permission to enter Ike's name in the New Hampshire primary. Eisenhower had cast his lot with the Republicans but Taft's biographer, William S. White, noted that many conservatives still felt he was more Democrat than Republican. According to Merlo Pusey, Eisenhower's biographer, his decision to identify himself with the Republicans was based on his family's past association with that party, his boyhood Kansas days lived in an environment of Republicanism, and his belief that only a change of parties in Washington could root out the political corruption. Eisenhower did not doubt that Taft could clean house in the capital but he was unwilling to see the Ohioan in the White House because of his views on foreign policy. For these reasons, according to Pusey, Eisenhower decided to be a candidate. During the summer of 1952 Eisenhower told a group of reporters in Denver that his sole reason for accepting the call was to defeat Taft.

Eisenhower's conclusive primary victory in New Hampshire, where he had not campaigned, strengthend his support. An equally impressive write-in campaign in Minnesota, where he had even exceeded former Governor Stassen's total vote, added to his prestige. However, a few votes in the primaries meant nothing; the important thing was delegates pledged to his support at the convention. In this respect Taft was far ahead. On June 1, 1952 Eisenhower was relieved of his duties in Europe and he returned to campaign actively. The jockeying for convention votes continued and when the selection of delegates was completed Taft claimed 588 of the 604 needed for the nomination.

By the time the convention met in Chicago on July 7 Taft was certain of victory. He claimed 607 votes and his men dominated the machinery of the convention. Pro-Taft Senator Bricker of Ohio arose at the convention and offered a resolution to the effect that until a permanent organization was chosen the 1948 rules should be operative. The Eisenhower men then made their move. Governor Arthur B. Langlie of Washington countered Bricker's resolution by proposing that contested delegates from Georgia, Texas, and Louisiana should be denied the right to participate in the convention until their credentials were clarified. Texas was the big issue because it was in this state that the Eisenhower men claimed Taft had "stolen" the delegates. In the ensuing delegate contest Taft was defeated and Eisenhower won the nomination on the first ballot. Taft's friends hoped the party could be reunited by nominating him for Vice President but Eisenhower's backers were unwilling. They wanted a young westerner, and a governors' conference, headed by Herbert Brownell, an attorney from New York, proposed Richard M. Nixon, whom Eisenhower had already endorsed as one of several acceptable candidates.

. . . *Stevenson finally reconsidered.*

Although Truman withheld the announcement that he would not run again until March 30, 1952, there were many claimants for the Democratic nomination before that date. The President felt that Chief Justice Fred Vinson of the Supreme Court would make an admirable candidate but Vinson demurred on the ground that he would not use the Supreme Court as a stepping stone to political position. Senators Richard Russell of Georgia, Robert S. Kerr of Oklahoma, Vice President Alben Barkley, and W. Averell Harriman of New York were self-admitted candidates. Among the most powerful contenders was Senator Kefauver of Tennessee who had won a national reputation through his conduct of his crime investigation committee. He turned against the Truman administration and in a whirlwind, highly personal campaign, toured the country seeking support.

It was generally understood that Barkley would be supported at the convention but at a meeting on July 21 he was told candidly that in view of his advanced age it would be wiser for him to withdraw. Moreover, there was much opposition to his candidacy among labor leaders. Kefauver was the leading contender as the convention opened. However, the real choice of the northern and mid-western party leaders and of Truman, was Governor Adlai E. Stevenson of Illinois. Although he had declined

3

to consider himself a serious candidate, Stevenson finally reconsidered. He was nominated on the third ballot and Senator John J. Sparkman of Alabama was chosen as his running-mate.

> *. . . creeping socialization and the five per centers.*

For the first few weeks Eisenhower tried to conduct a campaign above partisan politics. Stevenson took advantage of Eisenhower's aloofness and dazzled the public with a series of brilliant speeches in which his wit, piercing satire, and masterful prose enlivened an otherwise dull campaign. Eisenhower had had little opportunity to address the general public during his career, although he was known to be unusually persuasive in intimate gatherings. Through inexperience Eisenhower made a poor showing on the platform and before the TV cameras and as a result his sincerity and warm personality were often not communicated to his listeners. After allowing his opponent an initial advantage, Eisenhower changed his tactics suddenly, stepped up his campaign, and sought to heal the party breach by winning Taft's support. The Senator was rusticating in Canada, aloof from the campaign, when he was invited to Columbia University for a conference. Taft brought a document with him and he and Eisenhower went over it carefully. They announced that they were in substantial agreement on domestic policies; there was some difference over foreign policies, but as Taft said, it was a "difference of degree." The real issue was, in the opinion of both men, "liberty against creeping socialization." The Democrats sought to create the impression that Eisenhower had consummated a secret deal and they referred to the meeting as the "Surrender at Morningside Heights"—the location of Columbia University—but the truth of the matter was simply that at the meeting Taft, who had long considered Eisenhower a "me too" Republican in the Dewey mold, was reassured that the General was in sympathy with much of the conservatives' credo.

One of the major issues of the campaign was corruption in Washington. Ike had promised to sweep the five per centers and grafters out of the capital. In 1949 it was revealed that for a fee of five per cent certain opportunists in Washington guaranteed to obtain contracts and other favors from the federal government. Truman's friend and military aide, Major General Harry H. Vaughan, was directly implicated. He was alleged to have interceded to secure lumber for a race track at a time when lumber was in short supply. This was only one of various charges against him. In fact, he was linked with so many other improprieties that when anything questionable occurred it would bring forth a Washington pun, "cherchez la Vaughan." In 1952 irregularities were revealed in the Reconstruction Finance Corporation. Senator J. William Fulbright's sub-committee of the Senate Banking and Currency Committee discovered that a company which had been denied a loan on three occasions was suddenly found worthy of one after Democratic National Chairman William Boyle became one of its attorneys. The Republican Chairman, Guy Gabrielson, had also sought advantages for a company in which he was interested. On Fulbright's recommendation, Truman undertook to reorganize the RFC.

Senator Estes Kefauver's Special Committee to Investigate Organized Crime in Interstate Commerce also turned up an alarming degree of liaison between big city politicians and crooks. Then came a series of revelations. Even the Bureau of Internal Revenue had fixed tax evasion cases in return for mink coats, appliances and other gifts. In February 1952, after Assistant Attorney General T. Lamar Caudle had been removed for mishandling tax cases, Truman appointed a Republican, Newbold Morris of New York. Morris resigned when Attorney General J. Howard McGrath refused to cooperate. Truman then dismissed the Attorney General and replaced him with James P. McGranery who permitted the investigation to lapse. As Eisenhower was promising "to throw the rascals out," a report was circulated that vice presidential candidate Nixon had an expense fund of more than $18,000 contributed by California businessmen. Although Nixon insisted the fund was used to fight Communism and was not for personal emolument, his actions were criticized and there was talk of dropping him from the ballot. Governor Sherman Adams of New Hampshire made the point publicly that it was necessary for the Republicans to be as "clean as a hound's tooth." It was decided to put Nixon on the air September 23 and on that day he told a national TV audience about his boyhood, his school days, his courtship, his marriage, his war experience—in fact almost every aspect of his private life—even about the family dog.

Those who regarded this as a maudlin display of sentimentality, contrived to arouse traditional sympathy for the underdog, were outnumbered by those who were willing to overlook the existence of a private fund because it had been used in a good fight against subversive influences. Thousands of telegrams favoring the retention of Nixon on the ticket poured into Republican headquarters. While Nixon was explaining himself

5

to the public, Eisenhower was speaking in Cleveland. Casting aside his prepared speech, the General praised his young associate and invited him to a conference in Wheeling. Nixon "came to Canossa," where he found Eisenhower enthusiastic in his desire to continue their partnership. In the meantime the Republicans made capital of a discovery that Stevenson also had a secret fund which he said had been employed to supplement the salaries of state employees assisting in the campaign. The whole controversy ended on a humorous note with every candidate hastening to reveal income-tax returns.

. . . the biggest [foreign policy] issue . . . the Korean War.

No issue was more significant than foreign policy in 1952. Although both parties were in substantial agreement on general outlines, there were many points on which they differed. Although isolationism was always in the background, the biggest issue was the Korean War. Eisenhower said that Truman had acted wisely in aiding South Korea, but he blamed the President for creating a situation in which the Communists were induced to attack. He also blamed him for failing to conclude an honorable peace. On October 25, at Detroit, Eisenhower hurled a bomb-shell. Presumably acting on a suggestion of Harry Kern of *Newsweek,* he promised, if elected, to go to Korea and expedite the conclusion of peace. As it turned out, the eventual visit was destined to accomplish nothing, but as a political device it was unbeatable. It was a masterstroke comparable to Truman's when he called the Eightieth Congress into special session in the summer of 1948. Truman countered Eisenhower's promise to go to Korea by releasing a top-secret document written on September 26, 1947 in which Eisenhower, as Army Chief of Staff, had concurred in the judgment current at that time that Korea was of no strategic value to America. But even this could not offset Eisenhower's dramatic announcement.

John Foster Dulles had induced the Republicans to include a plank in their platform calling for the liberation of all former sovereign countries now under Soviet domination. The Republicans thus served notice that they no longer considered containment as an acceptable policy but, if elected, they intended to substitute a policy aimed not only at holding the line against further Communist expansion but also at rolling it back.

Internal security and civil liberties . . . .

Internal security and civil liberties continued as major issues in the 1952 campaign. Both parties took a stand on the recently enacted McCarren Act, but as an issue this was overshadowed by the intense debate over Senator McCarthy of Wisconsin. On June 14, 1951 he had risen in the Senate to attack General George C. Marshall, former Secretary of State under Truman. Marshall, he said, was connected "with a conspiracy so immense, an infamy so black, as to dwarf any in the history of man." Then, in 1952, Eisenhower was asked to support McCathy, a man who had all but used the term "traitor" in describing his friend and the one superior officer directly responsible for his promotion to the top of his army career. Eisenhower did not agree with the McCarthy faction. He defended our Korean intervention and he condemned the attack on his former mentor, Marshall. He favored removing subversives and security risks from office, but he insisted that it had to be done in a just, fair, and completely legal manner. But probably through Taft's persuasion, Eisenhower was made to see that it would be impossible for him to oppose a Republican candidate, even though he found that man personally distasteful. Party solidarity was essential and the magic of the Eisenhower name was desperately needed by other Republicans seeking gubernatorial or congressional posts. Ike campaigned in Indiana where William Jenner, one of the staunchest McCarthyites, was standing for re-election, but he gave Jenner only nominal support. When he appeared in Wisconsin many advised him to renounce McCarthy, but Eisenhower yielded to Governor Walter J. Kohler's suggestion and deleted some references to Marshall from his Milwaukee speech which could have been considered critical of McCarthy. Throughout the campaign Eisenhower followed a middle course on all matters and refused to criticize his fellow Republican candidates even though he objected to some of their policies.

There were many other issues in the campaign; government finance and fiscal policy, the Taft-Hartley Act, farm policy and parity prices, conservation of natural resources, public power development, the ownership of tideland oil, and civil rights. These, however, were overshadowed by the important questions of foreign policy, corruption, and internal security. It was these latter issues that proved to be the decisive ones. Both parties participated in mudslinging. The Republican press blamed Truman because he had tried the "give 'em hell" approach which had worked so successfully in 1948. Stevenson was loath to accept Truman's assistance and established his campaign headquarters in Springfield, Illinois, partly to disassociate himself from the administration in Washington.

As election day approached Stevenson seemed to be gaining against odds in popularity and prestige, but the extent of the swing was difficult to guage and it came too late to effect the final result. The Republicans were not to be denied in 1952. The team of Eisenhower and Nixon was a combination the people wanted; it symbolized America in that year. Stevenson's brilliant intellectualism aroused the fervid applause of those who were to become known as eggheads, but Eisenhower's emotional appeal was much more persuasive. He was the military hero of World War II returning home to set everything right. He was above partisanship; he was reticent (therefore wise) and humble (therefore strong) with an infectious grin which denoted understanding and an essential quality of humanity. He was a man of the people as opposed to a man of the discredited intellectuals. Stevenson smacked too much of the same smart aleck intellectualism the public found distasteful in Dean Acheson.

Nixon was the embodiment of the typical young man of the 1950's. Jaunty, clean, well-fed, and confident, he epitomized the era of men who had a secure job, a mortgage, a good credit rating, and an unlimited horizon of opportunity—a young man who would go as far as ambition and ability dictated. While the Democrats bore down on the follies of Herbert Hoover's administration and warned the voters that a vote for Republicanism meant a vote for depression and a swing to the right, they were speaking a language as unintelligible as ancient Hittite. A younger generation did not remember a time of bread lines, apple sellers, and men leaning on shovels; the word depression did not exist in their vocabulary. Such things had no place in the chrome-plated, lanolin-smooth world of 1952. The Great Depression of the early thirties was as remote in thought and time as the Great Blizzard of '88.

On election day Eisenhower polled 33,936,252 votes to Stevenson's 27,314,992. The electoral college vote was 442 to eighty-nine. The Republicans won control of the Senate with forty-eight seats to the Democrats' forty-seven and the House 221 to 212. Eisenhower won on a combination of personal and historical circumstances. It was a personal victory for a man who embodied all the virtues which Americans admired, but the victory was partly a result of disunity within the Democratic party. The Korean War, the civil rights issue, corruption in Washington, the treason and subversion issues, inflation, and fear of new taxation were all forces which compelled many people who had formely voted Democratic to cross party lines and endorse Eisenhower. The South, although traditionally Democratic, disliked the civil rights and tideland oil stands of the administration and so, for the first time since 1928, a Republican captured electoral votes in this area. Organized labor, farmers, Catholics, and immigrant groups, all of whom had formerly tended to support the Democrats, also crossed party lines.

But the Democratic party was not seriously weakened by the outcome of the election. The Republicans had run the most prominent man in the United States in 1952, but his victory was no landslide. They had expected to win complete control of Congress, but when it was all over they barely managed to control the House; and when Republican Senator Wayne Morse voted with the Democrats, they had to be satisfied with a tie in the Senate. The isolationists, who had hoped to undo the foreign policy inaugurated in 1947, and the conservatives, who wanted to turn the economic clock back to 1929, could take little comfort in the outcome of the election.

Between November, 1952 and January 1953, Truman had prepared for an orderly transfer of authority to his successor. During the campaign Truman had invited Eisenhower to the White House to participate in a Central Intelligence Agency briefing on foreign affairs, but the General had declined, explaining that he did not wish to appear as if he intended merely to continue the policies of his predecessor if he became president. "I'm extremely sorry that you have allowed a bunch of screwballs to come between us," wrote the President in expressing his chagrin over Eisenhower's refusal. But, when the election was over it was a different story. This time Eisenhower chose Senator Lodge and Joseph M. Dodge, who was to be his Director of the Budget, to represent him in Washington and cooperate with the outgoing administration in order to bring about the change in an orderly manner. On December 2, 1952 Eisenhower flew to Korea. He returned to announce that he had no quick solution for the peace negotiations.

On January 20, 1953 the first Republican President took office since Herbert Hoover was inaugurated on March 4, 1929.

. . . a worthy successor of the two Roosevelts and Wilson.

If Truman seemed too small for Roosevelt's chair in 1945, his stature had diminished even more by 1952. It is probably true that future Americans will judge Harry S. Truman more favorably than many of his contemporaries. During the critical years, from 1945 to 1952, his administration initiated and implemented many important policies. It is unfortunate that Truman could not sell himself to his own generation. He had only himself to blame for some of the adverse opinion, but much was also due to historical circumstances. He was unfortunate in having to succeed one of the most impressive, devastating, irrestistible, and arresting personalities ever to occupy the White House. By comparison, anyone would have appeared smaller. Without the commanding presence and aristocratic air of Roosevelt, Truman could neither inspire the confidence nor engender the devotion accorded his predecessor, although, like him, he could be the center of controversy. Physically small, myopic, self-effacing, humble, and without an impressive speaking voice, he seemed completely insignificant. In addition, his personal shortcomings contributed to the adverse appraisal. Although personally above reproach, he often surrounded himself, like Grant, with men whose principles were open to question. His insistence upon retaining the company and defending the actions of unworthy associates was commendable as personal loyalty, but it was suicide politically. His willingness to stand by his old friend General Vaughan is a case in point. His intense political partisanship and his reluctance to recognize the extent of subversion and corruption cost him many friends and many votes. His parental fury at music critics, who were something less than enthusiastic about his daughter Margaret's voice, seemed petty and unworthy of a chief executive. His robust speech, his occasional lapses into scurrility, and his predilection for the rough and tumble invective of a bygone era reduced him in public esteem. His use of the abbreviation S.O.B. in speaking of his critics did not comport with the high requirement of his position.

There were assets to counterbalance the shortcomings. Truman was a man of integrity and honesty. Tutored politically under the Pendergast machine, and Senator and President during a period of unprecedented laxity, Truman was never guilty of any personal impropriety. He hated pretense, intolerance and bigotry. Throughout his career he was the champion of religious and racial minorities. Although he sometimes appeared hesitant and confused, Truman amply demonstrated the capacity and courage for making momentous decisions; to use the atomic bomb, to chart an unprecedented course in foreign policy, to go to the aid of South Korea, to discharge one of the most popular generals in American history, and to pursue a progressive domestic policy in the face of congressional opposition. These decisions—a single one of which could easily have broken a lesser man—were made without equivocation or misgiving.

In foreign affairs Truman demonstrated that he was of sufficient size to fill Roosevelt's chair. Our policies of military and economic assistance to those countries resisting Communism and our willingness to join the United Nations and regional alliances were all major departures from the American tradition. In the dark days from 1945 to 1952 it was America's atomic strength, wealth, political stability, democratic faith, technological, industrial, and scientific preeminence that made it the bulwark of the free world. Yet these moral and physical resources were nothing in themselves—they had to be mobilized and given direction. Truman and his top advisors had the ability to make decisions in the defense of freedom.

Truman presented the kind of imaginative, bold program necessary to rally a democracy. Although personally unpopular throughout most of his administration and opposed by most of the press, Truman was able to carry his policies to fruition. It is relatively easy for a popular president to get what he wants, but when an unpopular executive achieves his goals, it must be by the most inspired and subtle kind of leadership.

On the domestic front Truman was a worthy successor of the two Roosevelts and Wilson. All of them carried forward the banner of liberalism during the "Half Century of Revolution." Truman was vigilant against the conservative reaction that follows wars and, thanks to his efforts, the achievements of the New Deal were secured by the policies of the Fair Deal against the rightwingers of both parties. He kept the presidency strong by insisting that only the chief executive spoke for all the people, and Truman was never reticent in voicing what he felt their interests and rights to be. At a time when the liberal cause seemed to be losing ground, Truman appeared its spokesman. In the end, however, the people refused to accept him as their advocate.

When he reported to the Congress on January 15, 1953 under the requirements of the Employment Act of 1946, Truman summarized the achievements of the New and Fair Deals as well as his philosophy of the role of government in business. Truman looked into the Republican future and predicted that we would have an unprecedented growth in ten years. A labor force of eighty million with an annual production of $500,000,-000,000 might be possible, he insisted. This would mean an increase in per capita income of forty per cent.

The America Truman bequeathed to Eisenhower was rich and productive, but it was also conservative. Communist predictions that capitalism would collapse had been made and revoked regularly since 1945 as the American economy continued to show its old creativeness and resilience. The organism continued to grow, but it was growing in a decidedly conservative direction.

January 20, 1953 brought to a close an exciting era in American history, when lean young men dreamed big dreams of social betterment and progress. An era of improvisation, exciting social experimentation, and rapid progress was giving way to one of consolidation and domestic contentment. The new age was content to build upon the foundation of the old without departing on any new experiments.

In 1952 both parties were at the crossroads; the choice before them was greater reform or consolidation of gains already made with occasional additions. The latter alternative was accepted by both parties. The Republicans' decision to follow Eisenhower's "middle road" was understandable since their job was to get into office, and this could be assured only by satisfying as many groups as possible. The Democrats had an opportunity to develop a reform program within their own great tradition as the party of progress, but no candidate wished to lead them down that path. As a result, the party which for twenty years had sponsored the cause of reform had now become conservative.

The General and His High Command

"... eight millionaires and a plumber."

WHEN THE NEW ADMINISTRATION had been established in Washington, the President turned for assistance to those men whose support had been most valuable during the campaign. Thomas Dewey's counsel carried much weight and, until his death in July, 1953, Taft's counsel was also highly respected. Although Taft looked upon Dewey as a "metoo" Republican, the New Yorker was typical of those who had, by a process of liberalization, made it possible for the party to survive and return to power. Eisenhower's gratitude was reflected in the appointment of many of Dewey's friends to prominent positions. James C. Hagerty became press secretary and Thomas E. Stephens took over as White House special counsel and acting appointment secretary. With these two powerful Deweyites handling Eisenhower's press relations and appointment book, and with Dr. Gabriel Hauge advising him on fiscal matters, there was no doubt that the New York influence was strong. The position of assistant to the president, with its diverse responsibilities and great power, went to Sherman Adams, the former governor of New Hampshire and one of Eisenhower's earliest and staunchest supporters.

For his Secretary of State, Eisenhower turned to John Foster Dulles, a prominent New York attorney, sometime senator, and since the days of Cordell Hull, a kind of spokesman and liaison man for the Republican foreign policy strategists. His greatest achievement had been the negotiation of the Japanese Peace Treaty.

Republicans contended that both Truman and Roosevelt had been hostile to American business. The new President Eisenhower announced that one of his first objectives would be the restoration of a climate in Washington in which business would receive a full and fair hearing. This sentiment was apparent in Eisenhower's appointment of several business leaders to his cabinet. The Democrats promptly dubbed it a cabinet of "eight millionaires and a plumber." Actually, there were only four who might have been classified as millionaires. George Humphrey, president of the M. A. Hanna Company of Cleveland became Secretary of the Treasury. Arthur Summerfield, chairman of the Republican National Committee in 1952, became Postmaster General, and Sinclair Weeks, who held directorships in several major companies, became Secretary of Commerce. Charles Erwin "Engine Charlie" Wilson, president of General Motors, became Secretary of Defense. (At first there was some confusion because Charles Edward "Electric Charlie" Wilson of General Electric had previously directed the Office of Defense Mobilization during the Korean War.) The confirmation of Wilson's appointment was delayed because of his considerable stock holdings in General Motors. The Senate insisted that unless he disposed of his holdings a conflict of interest might be created and therefore make his confirmation impossible. Wilson regarded this as a reflection on his integrity and, for a time, defied the Senate. Eventually he disposed of his holdings and his appointment was confirmed. Herbert Brownell, a New York lawyer and an Eisenhower pre-convention aide, was appointed Attorney General. Eisenhower had been advised to choose his Secretary of the Interior from the Northwest since waterway and power policies promised to be important issues. He selected Oregon's governor, Douglas McKay. Ezra Taft Benson, long associated with various farm organizations and a distant cousin of Senator Taft, was appointed Secretary of Agriculture.

Many of these men had publicly expressed their conviction that their departments were influenced too much by Democratic socialists and enemies of business. They made no secret of their intention to purge these left-wingers from the government. Secretary Wilson was the most outspoken in his enthusiasm for cooperation between government and business. At one point the news reporters quoted him as having said "What's good for General Motors is good for the country." Although, in actual context, the statement was not as bald as the opposition press tried to make it appear, nevertheless, the implication was evident. Wilson's Republican defenders saw nothing wrong with the attitude, but they took a different view of Secretary Martin P. Durkin's sympathy for labor. Durkin was Eisenhower's plumber: He was president of the United Association of Journeymen and Apprentices of the Plumbing and Pipefitting Industry. His appointment blew up a storm of criticism in conservative

Republican circles since he was not only a labor leader but also a Stevenson Democrat. Senator Taft looked upon the appointment as most objectionable. Durkin made no disguise of his intention to work for the interests of labor. Eisenhower had appointed him in an effort to win permanent labor support and pave the way toward a solution of the Taft-Hartley dilemma. Durkin resigned during the summer of 1953 when he failed to secure amendments to the law. He was replaced by James P. Mitchell.

The cabinet was completed by the later appointment of Mrs. Oveta Culp Hobby to the newly created post (April, 1953) of Secretary of the Department of Health, Education and Welfare. She had had a long and successful career in journalism and radio and had been director of the Women's Army Corps (WAC) during World War II. In 1955 her department became involved in a controversy over the distribution of some contaminated Salk polio vaccine, some of which caused the death of several children. Although she was not personally responsible for the error, Mrs. Hobby was criticized. The incident, together with the illness of her husband, led to her resignation in July, 1955. She was succeeded by Marion Bayard Folsom.

Military Leader—Man of Peace

The President was born in Denison, Texas, on October 14, 1890. His parents had lived in Kansas briefly before his birth and the family returned to Abilene Kansas, where he grew up and attended the local schools. The young Eisenhower wrote to Kansas Senator Joseph Bristow for an appointment to West Point or Annapolis. After qualifying, Eisenhower entered the U. S. Military Academy and graduated with the class of 1915. During World War I he was an instructor and a tank officer. In 1935 he was in the Philippines with Douglas MacArthur, but it was not until 1941, as Chief of Staff of the Third Army, that he attracted the attention of his superiors. He continued his brilliant record in Washington and in Europe and when it came time to choose a commander for all the allied forces in the European theatre, Eisenhower, with the backing of General George C. Marshall, was chosen. He directed the invasion of Europe and accepted the German surrender in May, 1945. After the war he served as Army Chief of Staff, temporary chairman of the Joint Chiefs of Staff, president of Columbia University, and commander of the North Atlantic Treaty Organization (NATO). From the time he entered West Point in 1911 he had never held a non-military position, except for his presidency of Columbia University. Even then he retained his five stars.

For years the prophets of gloom have warned against the military mind in high political positions. They deplored the possible rise of a "man on horseback" who, because of his military indoctrination, might favor a preventive war against the Soviets. Forty-one years of active military life would seem to have prepared Eisenhower for just such a role, but as Eisenhower's character and personality were later revealed, it became evident that these predictions could never come true. He was far from being the embodiment of the potential military dictator.

It would be untrue to suggest that Eisenhower's military experience did not shape his concept of the presidency. As "Mr." Eisenhower he was forced to study the conduct, actions, and duties of a civilian leader. Just as Truman had been forced to master his position when Roosevelt died, so Eisenhower had to master an entirely new way of life. His concept of the presidency and its functions was not what one might expect of a military man. He did not believe that the President should dominate the government; he insisted on an equal partnership for the three branches, recognizing that each branch had a specific function and that overlapping and infringement should be minimized.

According to Merriman Smith in *Meet Mr. Eisenhower,* the President's concept of his job involved four functions. He maintained that the president was chief of state *and* head of the government. In the former capacity it was the president's responsibility to plan the country's foreign policy. The decisions proved to be Eisenhower's but the actual implementation was entrusted to the Secretary of State. In his other capacity, as head of the government, the president was responsible for preparing, approving, and securing the enactment of a suitable domestic policy. Eisenhower regarded these as the two most important functions of the four. The lesser functions were those of acting as ceremonial leader of the country and as titular head of a political party. Eisenhower often complained about the former obligation because too much valuable time was consumed in greeting and entertaining visiting dignitaries and conversing through interpreters.

The goal of Eisenhower's foreign policy was the maintenance of world peace and he soon convinced even the most cynical observers that he was sincere. The conduct of the President was so openly that of a man of good will that his complete sincerity was soon recognized as his outstanding personal attribute. This was his most powerful weapon in the struggle for peace, impressing even a case-hardened opportunist like Nikolai Bulganin when the two men came face to face. It was because of his military experiences that Eisenhower understood the waste, inconclusiveness, and tragedy of war; battle had made him a passionate advocate of peace. Although he was not overly optimistic about achieving a genuine world peace at mid-century, he did strive to prevent a major war. The peace of Eisenhower's day was to be a tenuous one, but that condition made it no less desirable. He wished to reach a *modus vivendi* with the Communists until such time as the diplomats could lay a better foundation for mutual trust. During his administration we passed from a Cold War to a Cold Peace. There were several essential differences.

... that moderation should prevail.

Eisenhower tried consistently to resist the demands of extremists on either side and in both parties on matters of foreign policy. He was anxious to be a healer of wounds, a bridger of gulfs, and a leader who sought the middle way in all things. His striving for the middle road was also evident in his domestic policies. Since he believed that America's strength was the free world's best defense against Communism, Eisenhower set out to encourage industry and business. Those who criticized him for relying too much on the advice of leaders from the business and industrial fraternity failed to see that there was a firm connection in Eisenhower's mind between a strong and successful economy and a strong and successful foreign policy.

Influenced by his conviction that moderation should prevail in all things and perhaps influenced by his youthful Kansas Republican background, Eisenhower also believed that government existed to insure fair play in the economy rather than to direct the economic life of the country. Government should be helpful, if necessary, but it should never take the initiative nor intrude in those areas where private industry or enterprise could go it alone. This theory of government-business relationships is sound and few will quarrel with the doctrine of moderation. But, in actual operation, it has been difficult to draw a line between the areas in which private initiative may function best alone or in company with government.

Actually, Eisenhower's ideas did not seem to be much different from those advocated by Truman in his "Declaration of Independence" of

September 6, 1945, in which he, too, stated the general theory that the government should move only into those areas where it was obvious that private means could not get the job done. In *Affairs of State*, Richard Rovere developed the thesis that Truman and Eisenhower were actually much alike. They had grown up within almost a hundred miles of each other in poor, middle-class, semi-fundamentalist homes, and they had matured into men of courage, integrity, honesty, and honor. Both were undramatic, moderate leaders "essentially unideological, unintellectual, intuitive pragmatists, and feeble verbalizers." However, there was an essential difference between Truman's and Eisenhower's concept of the relationship between government and business. Truman believed that government could move with impunity into any area in which private means had either been unsuccessful or had failed to take the initiative. Eisenhower insisted upon a second qualification, apparent in his remark that, "When it comes to dealing with the relationships between the human in this country and his government, the people of this administration believe in being what I think we would normally call liberal, and when we deal with the economic affairs of this country, we believe in being conservative." Many have tended to overlook this distinction. It meant that sometimes when the government might have acted because of the inadequacy of private means, Eisenhower had remained aloof because he considered these were matters that were largely economic. This might explain his conservative approach to public power policy which he has apparently regarded as essentially economic. On the other hand he has supported public housing and highway programs—obviously economic functions—and despite their economic aspects, although more intimately connected with human relationships, he has been a strong advocate of civil rights, social security, unemployment compensation, minimum wage laws, and federal aid to education.

The general who had unhesitatingly ordered millions of men to assault the beaches of Normandy was expected to show the same firmness and decisiveness as President of the United States, but those who expected these qualities to be hallmarks of the administration were often disappointed. In foreign policy Eisenhower frequently acted with decision, but on domestic policy he often seemed to equivocate. His devotion to what he called "dynamic conservatism"—by which he tried to draw a line between liberalism and conservatism—and his political philosophy—based on the notion that the three branches of government were equal and endowed with specific constitutional powers and rights—were not conducive to forceful leadership or clear-cut policy. Those who had expected Eisenhower to be a forceful president because of his military background were as mistaken as those who had appraised him as a "man on horseback" or an advocate of preventive war. Eisenhower had not always been a general. He had progressed slowly upward through a hierarchy of command. During most of that time he had taken as well as given orders, he had followed channels, and he had recognized a clear division of authority and responsibility throughout the ranks. Forty-one years of such experience does not necessarily equip a man to make swift, firm, and sweeping decisions.

Unlike Truman and Roosevelt, Eisenhower never regarded himself as a politician. There were occasions, he said, when he felt that his non-political background gave him more objectivity in dealing with political questions. He hoped to restore the Republican party to its position of political prestige before 1932, but he soon realized he would have to become interested in political problems if this goal was to be achieved. He found it expedient to accomodate his policies to political considerations. Like all leaders in a democracy, Eisenhower realized that his partisans could be kept in power only through political means.

Those who have written about Eisenhower have spoken of him as methodical and efficient—qualities which were probably outgrowths of his military experiences. Eisenhower stressed the importance of teamwork and of an efficient staff of assistants. He felt consistently that he had surrounded himself with the most capable men of the country and that none of them could be excelled. He also believed that the president should be freed of petty annoyances and minor responsibilities in order to devote more time to the more serious problems. In this he was aided by his assistant, Sherman Adams, who believed that by surrounding the President with aides who could transact most of the business of government it would be possible to leave to the chief executive not more than six or seven major decisions a year. Under the Adams system the President would become, at best, a kind of Byzantine emperor, sheltered from the cares of office by dutiful assistants, or, at worst, a kind of Merovingian do-nothing king. Fortunately the formula proved unworkable, although Adams did, before his resignation in 1958, remove many of the burdensome details and decisions of office from the President's shoulders.

During his Army days Eisenhower was reputed to have had a violent temper but, as President, he quickly taught himself the value of self-control and restraint. His boredom, indifference, anger, and disdain were so well concealed that he appeared to be something of a stoic. In public he was able to display the celebrated grin which aroused in the American people deep bonds of kinship and understanding. In small groups he used his charm and personality to good advantage in carrying his arguments.

To most Americans the President appeared as a great humanitarian, an opposer of foreign and domestic oppression, a compromiser and pacifier, a Christian in the best sense of that elusive term, an idealist who leavened his idealism with good sense, an ever-vigilant protector of "the American Way," a relentless foe of Communism, and one whose sincerity, integrity, and honesty were as abiding as the prairies which had nurtured him. In 1956 the American public gave him the largest number of popular votes ever given to a presidential candidate. Yet, when he spoke, his words were not the clear, ringing call to battle that, coming from Roosevelt, had so lightened the peoples' hearts in the dark thirties; and when he wrote, his words lacked the inspiration, literacy, and logic of Wilson, Jefferson, and Lincoln. He had not, like these heroes and Teddy Roosevelt, advocated sweeping political, social, and economic reforms nor did he perform dramatic and valiant deeds. It is possible that his public appeal was somewhat comparable to Washington's. He was a military leader who was also a man of peace. He was a man of aristocratic tendencies but nevertheless a respecter of democracy. But most important of all, he was a leader in whom the people could repose their full confidence at a time when their previous leaders seem to have led them into a blind alley. Eisenhower restored their confidence and led them back to sanity.

Although he did not add any new domestic policies and made only a few minor modifications in existing foreign policies, there has been a tendency to rank Eisenhower among the greats. War or a major depression could still diminish his prestige before he leaves the historical stage but, as he approaches the final year of his second administration, it remains strong. With a friendly wave and a boyish grin he can restore confidence and reduce tension. He has been able to avoid war with Russia or one of her allies, and the rich harvest of progressivism inherited from his predecessors has been preserved. Whatever mistakes the administration has made have been overlooked by the electorate.

III THE EISENHOWER ADMINISTRATION

A Dynamic Foreign Policy

. . . a new "dynamic approach" to foreign policy.

Although the Republicans controlled Congress in 1953, Eisenhower faced an unusual dilemma. He depended upon Liberal Republicans and Democratic support for the sustained success of his foreign policy. But, if he worked too closely with these groups, he ran the risk of alienating certain powerful Republicans whom Norman Graebner in *The New Isolationism* called the "Neo-isolationists." Senators Taft, Knowland, McCarthy, and Jenner spoke for this group. The members of this clique did not agree on policies among themselves but a composite platform included these planks: increased resistance to Russia, rejection of the UN and NATO in favor of a go-it-alone approach, reliance on atomic bombs and strategic air power to deter aggression, liberation of the satellites, more emphasis on the Orient, and disengagement from military and economic aid programs. Many of these policies were contradictory and self-defeating.

The Republican party insisted that it had discovered a new "dynamic approach" to foreign policy which would bring about security and at the same time save money. They had promised to replace containment with an aggressive foreign policy which would wrest the initiative from the Communists. On February 2, 1953, Eisenhower, in a State of the Union message, promised to devote more attention to Asian affairs, to work with European leaders to insure western unity, to encourage profitable world trade, and to reorganize our defenses to provide adequate protection without straining the economy. In a dramatic gesture, aimed at pacifying the China wing of the party, the President removed the restrictions on Chiang Kai-shek's army so that it could attack southern China. Eisenhower's directive was "unleashing" a chihauhau rather than a mastiff,

21

and any successful Nationalist invasion was years in the future, if then.

The morale of the State Department was at a low ebb in January 1953 because of disloyalty charges. Dulles and the President were faced with the task of restoring an esprit de corps and reorganizing the department. Executive Order 10450 of April 27, 1953 barred persons from employment if they were security risks. It applied to all departments and covered not only disloyalty but also other undesirable characteristics such as drunkenness, drug addiction, sexual perversion, and mental illness. Each department head had the power to determine which persons qualified under these regulations. The demoralization of the State Department gradually abated, but many qualified men left before the situation was rectified.

During the first months of the new term the President and Congress clashed several times over foreign affairs. There was violent opposition to the appointment, later confirmed, of Charles Bohlen as ambassador to Russia. McCarthy launched an attack on the State Department's International Information Administration and the Voice of America. He called for a purge of overseas libraries which he said were stocked with Communist books. The IIA was ultimately replaced by the United States Information Agency which was divorced from the State Department. McCarthy simultaneously attacked our allies for trading with Communist China. On his own initiative he bypassed the State Department and the Mutual Security Agency by negotiating agreements with foreign shippers against handling such goods. Shortly before his death, Taft, in his last major address, belabored the UN and our alliance system. The President replied to him on May 28 and reassured the world that we would not go it alone. In an address at Dartmouth College in June, 1953 he replied to McCarthy by interpolating an admonition to the public not to join the book burners.

On January 7, 1953, Senator John Bricker of Ohio introduced a constitutional amendment which produced one of the more vehement quarrels over foreign affairs in the nation's history. The amendment purported to protect the Constitution from being superseded by treaties or executive agreements. Under the amended Bricker proposals, treaties could not become effective until Congress passed legislation "which would be valid in the absence of treaty." This famous "which clause" produced the controversy, since it was alleged that no treaty could take effect until it conformed to state laws or until each state enacted suitable legislation. The President would not compromise on this proposal, which he said would put the country back to the days of the Articles of Confederation. The amendment was shelved in 1953 but reappeared in 1954 and then failed by one vote only.

While Dulles and Eisenhower proposed a dynamic new foreign policy, one of the assurances to the public was that it could be put into effect with greater economy than previous foreign policies. The Korean War and the menace of a global conflict had influenced our defense concepts in 1952. The nation's defenses were being built rapidly to meet a theoretical danger-date when Soviet threats would be strongest. The President rejected this concept. He preferred a gradual build-up for the long haul. "A very real danger not only exists this year," he told the public, "but may continue to exist for years to come. . . . Defense is not a matter of maximum strength for a single date. It is a matter of adequate protection to be projected as far into the future as the actions and apparent purposes of others may compel us." In line with this policy the administration moved to reduce Defense Department expenditures, but it was severely criticized for deciding to reduce the projected 143-wing Air Force to 120 wings. Secretary Wilson insisted that more defense could be provided with a smaller force through better utilization of personnel and equipment. The nation was being offered "more bangs for a buck" under the new plan.

Realizing that the allies could not assume a greater defense burden unless their economies were strengthened, Eisenhower gave considerable attention to the problem of foreign aid. European countries had made remarkable recoveries since 1945, but many still suffered from chronic dollar-shortages. Congress passed a Customs Simplification Act and renewed the Reciprocal Trade Agreements Act. A provision in the latter act created a Commission on Foreign Economic Policy headed by Clarence B. Randall of the Inland Steel Corporation, which was to make a thorough study of the foreign aid situation. On May 5 Eisenhower asked for a continuation of foreign aid which if "judiciously spent" would be more valuable than "an even greater amount spent merely to increase the size of our own military forces in being." He asked for nearly two billion dollars less than Truman had recommended for fiscal 1954. Not only did the administration reduce the total funds available for foreign aid, but more money was diverted for military assistance and to the Orient. The administration also created in 1953 the Foreign Operations Administration (FOA) which, under Harold Stassen, assumed the duties of the Mutual Security Agency, the Technical Cooperation Program, and other reconstruction agencies which had formerly been affiliated with the then-suspect State Department.

The Soviet peace play and the hydrogen bomb....

The death of Stalin on March 5, 1953 was not followed by the disruption of the dictatorship as many had predicted. The power passed to a protegé, Georgi M. Malenkov, who shared it with other members of the Council of Ministers and Party Presidium, Lavrenti Beria, Vyacheslav Molotov, Nikolai Bulganin, and Lazar Kaganovich, as well as the then-obscure party secretary Nikita Khrushchev. The one-man dictatorship had been replaced by a committee of despots.

Suddenly, late in March, the Russians soft-pedaled their anti-American campaign and began pressing for a resumption of Korean truce talks, disarmament conferences, and a Big-Four meeting on German and Austrian affairs. On April 16, 1953, Eisenhower announced that he would pursue his current policies but would not turn his back on serious proposals for negotiation. He called upon Malenkov to show some evidence that the Russians really wished a settlement, but except for a few flamboyant gestures of good will they made no major concessions. During the summer of 1953 Malenkov encountered the first tests of survival as rioting broke out in Czechoslovakia and Berlin. Dulles had induced the Republicans to favor a policy of liberation for the Soviet satellites and thereby roll back Soviet power along the front of eastern Europe. The rioting gave him an opportunity to aid the unwilling subjects of Moscow but, except for a few moral exhortations and some food shipments, nothing was done. Dulles made it clear that he was not talking about forcible liberation. Nevertheless, the Communists were forced to make some concessions and to reorganize the collective leadership.

The party, army, and police were the great forces of Soviet government but nevertheless, Beria's secret police were apparently gaining too much power. Suddenly, in July, he was ousted and later executed. Since the army took an active part in these incidents, it was concluded that Soviet military threats would possibly increase as the army grew more important in the government. Malenkov announced a "New Course," aimed at increasing production of consumer goods. This was hailed by some as evidence that Russian threats were being reduced, but there seemed to be no cause for rejoicing. Russia, after the purge, was as impregnable and monolithic as ever. The biggest danger was that Russia's soft approach and the New Course might make the West apathetic toward its own defense.

Churchill entered into the spirit of the Russian peace offensive on May 11, 1953 when he called for a summit conference to ease tensions. Dulles preferred a meeting of foreign ministers only. On August 8 Malenkov replied to Churchill's and Eisenhower's earlier speech of April 16 by stating that he saw no reason why capitalism and Communism could not coexist peacefully since there was no "basis for conflict" between his country and the United States. But he coupled this with several demands which made it evident that although there may have been no basis for conflict, neither was there any basis for negotiation. Each side demanded no less than total surrender on those points over which the other party was not prepared to yield an inch.

The impact of Malenkov's peaceful coexistence speech was blunted, however, when he followed it with a dramatic announcement that the Soviet had successfully tested a hydrogen bomb. There could no longer be any doubt as to the skill of Russian scientists for they obviously used techniques unknown to our own scientists. The day of atomic stalemate was fast approaching. As Gordon Dean of the Atomic Energy Commission warned, "It does us no good to reach the point where we would be able to wipe out an enemy twenty times over if he reaches the point where he can wipe us out just once."

The Soviet peace play and the hydrogen bomb announcement came at a time when Dulles was pushing for the ratification of the European Defense Community (EDC) which had been suggested by French Premier René Pleven in 1950 when Secretary Acheson had first proposed that Germany should be rearmed. Pleven's plan called for an integrated European army, but the Germans were to be denied the right to form a general staff and their contingent was to be placed in a subordinate position exclusively under EDC control. After seventeen months of negotiation this agreement was signed in May, 1952 by France, Italy, the German Federal Republic, and the Benelux states, but it had to be ratified by each national assembly before it became effective. The French soured on EDC when the British refused to join and insisted it would have to be amended. Even Dulles' threat that the United States would withhold its foreign aid failed to budge the French. A government crisis in which Joseph Laniel replaced René Mayer as Premier further delayed the ratification. Konrad Adenauer secured the ratification of EDC in Germany. In Italy opposition to EDC was intense and on June 29 Alcide

25

de Gasperi, who had been our strongest ally in Italy for years, was forced to resign as Prime Minister. Dulles took some comfort in the treaty of friendship and consultation against aggression ratified on May 18 by Yugoslavia, Greece, and Turkey. This treaty helped to solidify the exposed southern flank of NATO. A treaty with Spain on September 26, 1953 gave the United States additional air bases against Russia.

The continued wrangling over EDC, the failure to arrange a four-power conference on German and Austrian affairs, and the bomb announcement clouded the atmosphere when Eisenhower journied to Bermuda to meet Churchill and Laniel for a three-day conference on December 4. There were no startling developments but the meeting did serve to remove some of the tensions which had grown up among the Big Three. Eisenhower and his advisers had been cool toward a proposed Big Four meeting but they agreed to a conference in which Russia would be free to discuss the inclusion of Red China as a fifth member. The Bermuda Declaration, issued by all three statesmen, also repeated the unrealistic rollback theory. The liberation of the eastern satellites was to be accomplished by peaceful means. The President also showed Churchill and Laniel a dramatic announcement on atomic energy he had prepared for presentation at the United Nations.

On December 8 Eisenhower went before the UN with his "Atoms-for-Peace" proposal in which he suggested that the governments involved should turn over to a special UN International Atomic Energy Agency some fissionable material which would be "allocated to serve the peaceful pursuits of mankind . . . rather than the fears of mankind." The Russians' reaction, however, was not wholly encouraging, although they admitted that the plan had some merit.

The good will created by the Bermuda conference and the "Atoms-for-Peace" announcement was blunted by continued wrangling over EDC when the North Atlantic Council of NATO met in Paris on December 14. The allies had indicated at the Lisbon meeting of the council in February 1952 that economic conditions made it impossible for them to meet NATO troops commitments for the year, and early in 1953 they had eagerly supported Eisenhower's "long-haul" policy. Only NATO commander Matthew Ridgway had opposed any slowdown in the rearmament pace. The allies found it difficult to understand why the United States spoke of rearmament slowdown on one hand and kept insisting upon a ratification of EDC on the other. Dulles began to apply the "shock treatment." At Paris he warned, "If, however, the European Defense Community should not become effective; if France and Germany remain apart, so that they would again be potential enemies, then indeed there would be grave doubt whether Continental Europe could be made a place of safety." There were few who would dispute this contention, but the Secretary then introduced an ominous note in his address: "That would compel an agonizing reappraisal of basic United States policy." This incipient threat was aimed at the French, but they were in no mood to be bullied into hasty action.

> *. . . The New Look with . . . atomic power.*

By the end of 1953 the Joint Chiefs of Staff under Admiral Arthur W. Radford had developed a new military strategy in line with the long-haul policy enunciated by the President in April. In a speech before the Council on Foreign Affairs on January 12, 1954, Dulles elaborated on the "New Look" in defense policy. "The way to deter aggression is for the free community to be willing and able to respond vigorously at places and with means of its own choosing," he told his audience. This new policy of "massive retaliation" would give the nation "maximum deterrent at a bearable cost." The present administration, he explained, approved of what Truman had done but sought more economy and efficiency in defense " by placing more reliance on deterrent power and less dependence on local defensive power."

Before the Senate Foreign Relations Committee on March 19, 1954 Dulles continued to expatiate on the New Look. Russia would be "hit with everything we have" if she attacked us or our "vital interests." He stressed the fact that the administration did not intend to turn minor wars into major ones by using atomic weapons indiscriminately, and he urged that the New Look actually gave America greater "selectivity" in using its "special resources" to "maximum possible advantage." The new budget reflected increasing emphasis on air power, atomic fire power, and reduced personnel.

The New Look with its emphasis on atomic power was criticized on both sides of the Atlantic. A report in February 1954 revealed the terrible devastation wrought by our Eniwetok tests in 1952. A mock raid over the United States was supposed to have produced thirteen million hypothetical casualties. Eisenhower sought to reassure a jittery world through a Voice of America broadcast on April 5 and Dulles simultaneously published an article in *Foreign Affairs* insisting that the United States would not use massive retaliation in all cases but base its response on the nature of each threat. The new dynamism promised by the Republicans was disappointing because the administration seemed to offer nothing except a threat of brute force. The policy lacked imagination and the flexibility needed to meet the changing tactics of the Kremlin wizards.

If the administration's defense policies were disappointing so were the foreign aid policies which finally emerged as a result of nearly a year's work by the Randall committee. This report agreed with the prevailing Republican sentiment that grants should be terminated as speedily as possible, but it made some excellent suggestions for the improvement of trade. On March 30, 1954 the President presented a program based on this report which called for more overseas investments, expanded world trade, and the facilitation of currency convertibility. During 1954 little of his program was enacted. In June the administration submitted its mutual security program for 1955 which continued the trends of the previous year's program. "We can foresee that military aid will have to be continued," said Senator Alexander Wiley, chairman of the Senate Foreign Relations Committee, "but it's out the window for economic aid."

While the New Look and the Randall Report represented new lines of American policy Dulles did not neglect his old desire to gain ratification of EDC. From January 25, to February 18, 1954, Dulles, Anthony Eden, Molotov, and Georges Bidault met in Berlin for the first foreign ministers conference since 1949. Rival plans for German unification were put forward by Eden and Molotov. While the former plan aimed at free elections, a peace treaty, and a federal constitution for Germany the Russians proposed only an all-Europe security pact to replace EDC. The United States could participate only as an observer and none of the signatories could belong to another coalition. In short, the Russians were proposing to scrap NATO. Dulles left the conference convinced that agreement on Germany was impossible.

EDC and the Saar.

Despite both American and British assurances that they would maintain forces in Europe, the French still opposed EDC. The national assembly rejected EDC on August 30. The rejection of EDC embarrassed the administration since neither the President nor Dulles had an alternative policy available. Dulles was in Manila at that moment and remained there while Eden tried to salvage something from the rubble of

EDC. On September 11 Eden began to visit European capitals for discussion. It was clear that the economic and political unity envisioned by the EDC agreement could not be achieved in Europe but it was still possible to solve the important military problem of rearming Germany. Eden's recommendation was to expand the Western Union created by the Brussels Treaty of March 1948 to include Germany and Italy. This idea had sufficient merit to warrant further international discussions in London from September 28 to October 3. Until the meeting, Dulles remained in the background. He had wisely concluded that it would be better to give the impression that the European powers should work out their own destiny without American interference. In London both Dulles and Eden agreed that American and British troops would be kept in Europe, which went a long way toward reassuring the new French Premier Pierre Mendès-France.

There was still the problem of the Saar which stood in the way of the final agreement. While the Russians intensified their propaganda campaign to split the West, two separate sets of negotiations were concluded. The first of them dealt with Eden's proposals and the second settled the Saar problem. The three occupying powers agreed to terminate their occupation of Germany as soon as the agreements were ratified. The Western Union powers agreed to admit both Italy and Germany to membership in an enlarged organization to be called Western European Union (WEU), and the latter state was also to be admitted to NATO, although her war-making potential was limited. The WEU lacked some of the cohesiveness attributed to EDC but it had the added advantage of British membership and still imposed a measure of control on German rearmament. This pleased the French.

On October 23, Adenauer and Mendès-France were miraculously able to reach a settlement in Paris on the status of the Saar by which it was given autonomous status within WEU. The Saarlanders were to give their approval of this project in a plebiscite in October 1955. Since they voted to reject the settlement, the Saar was returned to Germany on January 1, 1957 in exchange for certain economic concessions to the French.

On December 24, 1954, in the midst of a violent Russian propaganda barrage, the French National Assembly rejected the Brussels Pact revision 280 to 259. Once again the French had failed to respond favorably, but Mendès-France met the crisis with great dispatch. After a few harried days of consultation, threats, and promises, the assembly reversed itself 287 to 260 on December 30. French approval of WEU was a great victory

for Dulles, but the patient skill of Eden, the bustling confidence and un-
failing energy of Mendès-France, and the statesmanlike qualities of Konrad Adenauer were all responsible for arriving at a suitable compromise
which in some ways was stronger than the original agreement. We had put
all our eggs in one basket but after the catastrophic defeat of EDC we
finished with fresh eggs and a sturdier basket. The agreement also
produced an unexpected bonus inasmuch as it weakened Malenkov's
government. Already a serious rift was developing in the Kremlin between
Malenkov and a new clique headed by Bulganin and Khrushchev. The
failure of Russia to prevent German rearmament was merely one more
strike against the portly premier.

Italian ratification of EDC had been delayed by the Trieste dispute
which was finally settled on October 5, 1954. A minor boundary modification was made in Yugoslavia's favor and part of the territory (Zone B)
was given to her; Italy received the rest (Zone A). But the settlement of
the Trieste question did not remove all points of friction on NATO's
southern flank. Violent nationalist disturbances against British rule on
Cyprus caused not only trouble for England but also strained relations
between Greece and Turkey.

. . . concluding the peace in Korea.

During the first two years of Eisenhower's administration the Republicans did not formulate any clear or new policies on Asia. They were
committed clearly to one policy only; the non-recognition, the eventual
destruction, and the denial of Red China's admission to the UN. Such a
policy was difficult to sell to the Free Asian States and was equally unacceptable to many of our Occidental allies. The latter insisted that Americans failed to understand the Chinese revolution and these same allies
had little faith in Chiang. Senator Knowland, the pro-Chiang spokesman
in Washington, led the fight against Peiping's admission to the UN. "The
day that Communist China goes into the UN, the U.S. goes out," he told
his constituents. Opposition to this ironbound policy stemmed not only
from our allies; it arose in Washington too. Arthur H. Dean, who was
one of the negotiators at the Korean armistice talks, insisted that it would
be to our advantage to recognize the Reds in return for concessions. America's inflexible attitude on Red China persisted. While the United States
continued to deny Peiping's claim for admission to the UN, Russia was
left as the principal spokesman for Communism and Asian nationalism in

that body. The admission of China might have, in time, created a rival for Russian leadership in the UN, but America's attitude spared the Soviet this problem.

The immediate problem confronting Eisenhower in Asia was that of concluding the peace in Korea without making major concessions to the Reds. Returning from his Korean visit (December 2 to 5, 1952) aboard the cruiser *Helena* the President discussed the need for resuming negotiations with his foreign policy advisers. It was resolved that if the negotiations failed the war would be fought to victory regardless of consequences. Dulles told Jawaharlal Nehru that if the Chinese refused to resume negotiations the United States would attack north of the Yalu boundary. As Dulles hoped, this information was relayed to Peiping and may have been instrumental in getting Chou En-lai and Mao Tse-tung to reopen the peace talks. The resumption of negotiations on April 26 was followed by an armistice on July 27, following the longest truce talks in history—two years and seventeen days. Arrangements were made for the transfer of prisoners of war.

President Syngman Rhee in violent protest against the prospect of a continued division of his country tried, on June 18, to upset the delicate prisoner-of-war negotiations by releasing 27,000 of them. When word of what he had done reached Washington, Dulles and Eisenhower held a hurried conference; it was decided that should the Communists use this as a pretext for calling off the negotiations the United States would open full-scale war. Dulles claimed that by taking the United States to the "brink of war" he had forced the enemy to negotiate. The gamble paid off, but it was a calculated risk where failure might have meant incalculable losses.

One provision of the armistice called for a political conference to arrange a permanent Korean settlement and when the UN reconvened on August 17, 1953 this question arose at once. After much argument in the UN concerning the composition of the membership and the agenda, the conference met late in 1953 but soon adjourned with nothing accomplished. In the meantime the United States moved to strengthen its position in the Orient. The sixteen UN belligerents issued a statement on July 27 that future aggression in Korea would make it impossible to "confine hostilities within the frontiers of Korea." Dulles signed an American-Korean Security Treaty with Rhee to add weight to this warning and on September 2 he extended the threat of retaliation against China if she continued her aggression in Indochina. The extension of American commitments in Asia was a move made possible by additional support from the governments of Premier Shigeru Yoshida of Japan and President Ramōn Magsaysay of the Philippines.

Trouble in Southeast Asia.

In Southeast Asia the most serious trouble spot was Indochina. After the Korean armistice was consummated there was considerable fear that the Chinese would next move their armies into Indochina. Laos and Cambodia had been quiet, but in the third Indochinese state, Viet-Nam, a nationalist organization, which called itself Viet-Minh, had opposed the French since 1939. After World War II some concessions were offered to Viet-Minh leader Ho Chi Minh, but he was satisfied with nothing less than independence. War broke out in 1946.

With the Communists in control of China, Communist-oriented Viet-Minh could count on more assistance after 1949 and the resistance to the French increased. Paris was driven to offering more concessions and in 1949 set up Bao Dai as ruler. What had begun as an anti-colonial war had become another phase in the struggle against world Communism. American aid was made available to the French. The Viet-Namese were neither satisfied with the French offers, nor would they approve Bao Dai, whom they regarded as little more than a French tool. The military advantage swayed from one side to the other but the French gradually grew weary of the long jungle war of attrition which seemingly had neither purpose nor end.

There were two possible courses open: either the war had to be intensified or major concessions had to be made to the Communists. The United States urged the French to continue the fight. We offered more aid and encouraged the French to come to terms with the Viet-Namese so that they would also fight Viet-Minh. In May 1953 General Henri-Eugéne Navarre stepped up the training of Viet-Namese troops for a planned defeat of the Communists by 1956 and, at the same time, French officials opened negotiations with the three-states for a political settlement. The Navarre plan failed because the Viet-Minh rebels received aid from Red China, and Paris was unable to reach an accommodation with the natives early in 1954. The foreign ministers conference in Berlin came at a time when Viet-Minh had taken the offensive in Laos, and the western foreign ministers were forced to accept a proposal for a conference in Geneva on April 26, 1954 to discuss both Korea and Indochina. The two Korean states, as well as Red China, were to participate. The inclusion of this third state, as an equal with the European powers, obviously was an important diplomatic and propaganda victory for the Communists.

The Reds hoped to place themselves in a better bargaining position before the Geneva meeting. On March 13 Viet-Minh launched a major offensive against the French bastion at Dienbienphu. With complete disregard of losses, the Reds used "human sea" tactics to smother the defenders. The struggle for Dienbienphu became symbolic for both sides, although actually the position was of relatively minor strategic value. Gradually the defenders were worn down by the overwhelming manpower of Viet-Minh. On March 20, 1954 General Paul Ely of France came to Washington to make an appeal for more aid. He wanted the United States to dispatch planes from the Seventh Fleet carriers against the enemy at Dienbienphu, but the administration refused, feeling that it was beyond the President's constitutional powers and was also militarily valueless. Nevertheless, both Dulles and Eisenhower agreed that Indochina had to be saved. The President had spoken of the "falling domino" theory of Asian defense; if Indochina fell, a chain reaction might follow in which the southeast Asian states would topple to the Communists like a row of dominoes.

In a speech on March 29 Dulles prepared to take the nation to the brink of war again as he characterized the Communists advance in Indochina as "a grave threat to the whole free community" which would have to be "met by united action" which "might involve serious risk." On April 3 Dulles conferred with congressional leaders, and on the next day with the President and Admiral Radford. The prevailing sentiment was that Ely's one-shot air strike would be worthless, but that large-scale intervention might be advisable if we could get the support of Britain, Australia, and New Zealand, and if the French would agree to grant independence to Laos, Cambodia, and Viet-Nam. John Robinson Beal, Dulles' biographer, called it a decision "not to go to war—unless" or "to go to war—provided." On April 16 Vice President Nixon, apparently with the administration's approval, explained that as a last resort American troops might have to be sent to Indochina to prevent its fall.

On the eve of the Geneva conference Dulles learned that the British, because of pressure from India, Indonesia, Burma, and other dominions, would not support intervention. Seldom were the Big Three so badly divided. The French wanted to get out of the war as quickly and as gracefully as possible. The British wanted to negotiate to keep the war from spreading, and America wished to delay concessions as long as possible in order to build a new alliance to save the rest of Southeast Asia. It was under such circumstances that the Geneva conference met on April 26, 1954. The conference first considered the Korean problem. Both Chou En-lai the Chinese leader and Nam Il the North Korean leader were confident of their position when they presented the Chinese and North Korean proposals on April 27 and 28. Since they offered no hope for free elections or adequate safeguards if foreign troops were withdrawn from Korea, the United States rejected their proposals. The conference reached no settlement for ultimate Korean unification.

Nine states participated in the Indochinese phase of the conference: the Big Four, Communist China, Viet-Minh (The Democratic Republic of Viet-Nam), Laos, Cambodia, and Viet-Nam. On May 7 came news that Dienbienphu had fallen. While Dulles spoke of possible intervention, Senator Knowland offered his "fullest support" if the President decided to send troops. On May 11 Dulles seemed to reverse his position when he said that if it was impossible to save all of Southeast Asia the United States would try "to save essential parts of it."

The French and Viet-Minh terms submitted by Georges Bidault and Pham Van Dong were unreconcilable. For several weeks the conference continued in deadlock, when suddenly on June 12 Premier Laniel left office. Three days later the Korean phase of the negotiations ended in stalemate. The entire conference seemed headed for disaster, but over-night the situation changed. Chou En-lai, whose stellar role at the conference dramatized the increasing importance of Red China, announced on June 16 that he would drop his earlier demands that France surrender both Laos and Cambodia. The next day the new French Premier, Mendès-France, promised to conclude an armistice within four weeks. The conferees gradually moved toward a plan to neutralize Laos and Cambodia and to partition Viet-Nam temporarily. The United States viewed the so-called temporary nature of the partition with skepticism in the light of what had taken place in Korea and showed its dissatisfaction with the course of events by asserting that no more high-ranking officials would be sent to Geneva.

In Mid-July Dulles met with Mendès-France and arranged a rather unpalatable compromise. Dulles promised to send Under Secretary of State Walter Bedell Smith to Geneva if Mendès-France would fight for the eighteenth parallel rather than the sixteenth parallel as the point of partition for Viet-Nam. It was further agreed that if the conference failed to reach a settlement the earlier plan of united action would be invoked and that if a settlement was reached at Geneva the United States would accept it without signing. When it became apparent to Chou En-lai that the Americans, British, and French were in agreement on united action, he induced the Viet-Minh representative to accept the seventeenth parallel as a final compromise in the agreement signed July 21, 1954. A cease-fire went into effect by August 11 and the regrouping of troops on either side of the line began. It was hoped that elections could be held throughout Viet-Nam by July 1956.to reunite the country but these failed to materialize.

The Viet-Namese refused to sign the agreement since they felt the French had surrendered too much territory and Smith also declined to sign although he announced unilaterally that the United States would not disturb the *status quo* nor permit a resumption of hostilities. The Washington opinion was that, although the agreement gave both sides time to regroup, it offered no assurances of permanent peace in Asia. On July 21 the President explained that the settlement was not appeasement and that it was the best solution possible under the circumstance.

To forestall further Communist moves, Dulles pressed for the conclusion of an Asian treaty. On July 23, 1954 he called upon the "free peoples of Southeast Asia" to join in a pact, but only Thailand, Pakistan, and the Philippines joined Britain, France, Australia, New Zealand, and the United States at Manila on September 6. Two days later they signed the Southeast Asia Collective Defense Treaty (the Manila Pact) which set up the Southeast Asia Treaty Organization (SEATO). In Article II the signatories promised to work individually and collectively to develop their capacity to resist attack "and to prevent and counter subversive activities directed from without against their territorial and political integrity." In Article IV they agreed that armed attack would endanger their peace and security and that each member would meet such a situation in accordance with its constitutional processes. A separate "understanding of the United States" was added which specified that under Article IV we referred only to Communist aggression. We excluded Chiang Kai-shek and sanctioned his period strikes against the mainland. Other provisions of the treaty established a council to plan military, economic, and counter-subversive activities. By separate protocol the protective features of the pact were extended to Laos, Cambodia, and Viet-Nam. Perhaps of more significance than the treaty itself was the Pacific Charter which was adopted at the recommendation of President Magsaysay of the Philippine Islands. This

THE EISENHOWER ADMINISTRATION

was a brilliantly planned maneuver to counter the intensive Chinese and Russian "anti-imperialist" and "anti-colonial" campaigns throughout the Orient. The Charter declared that the SEATO powers would promote self-government and help to secure independence for all those peoples desiring them.

The new Asian pact was a step toward restoring stability in the East but there were still loose ends to tie down. We extended assistance to Laos and Cambodia as well as our older ally, South Korea. Particular care was taken to checkrein Rhee so that he would not attack North Korea. Dulles also partially "leashed" Chiang again with a Mutual Defense Treaty. As in the SEATO pact, both the United States and the Nationalists agreed that an armed attack against the territory of either would be a threat to their security and would be met in accordance with constitutional processes. The most significant portion of this treaty was the deliberate exclusion from the defense zone of several offshore islands which belonged to Formosa. Just as Acheson was alleged to have invited attack by ruling Korea outside our defense perimeter, so now Dulles was also accused of inviting attack on the offshore islands. Despite our alliances, military assistance, and guarantees in the Orient, it was evident, by the close of 1954, that these were not enough. The Orientals still desperately needed economic and technical assistance in coping with soaring birthrates and lowering living-standards. These people wanted not only independence and freedom from fear of atomic annihilation, they also wanted a better life. They wanted capital to develop their countries and greater markets for their products. In 1954 it may have been a tragic mistake not to have sensed the need for more economic assistance to these people. It was against this failure that the Communists directed their heaviest attacks during the ensuing years.

Assured of Rusisan friendship and aid by such notables as Bulganin, Khrushchev, and A. I. Mikoyan, the Red Chinese grew bolder. They began to bombard the offshore islands held by Chiang and sought to line up all the Asian states under the banner of the "Five Principles of Peaceful coexistence." Their "peace offensive" won the hearty endorsement of India, Burma, and Indonesia. The Chinese denounced the American atomic bomb tests in the Pacific and relations with Japan were unduly strained when twenty-three helpless Japanese fishermen became victims of radioactive fallout. Anti-Americanism soared in Japan and a new political alignment brought the less-friendly Ichiro Hatoyama into the premiership.

Throughout Southeast Asia neutralism gained more adherents. A "third force" was being created. Already evident during Truman's administration, this neutralism had become a powerful force by 1954. In 1950 Premier D. S. Senanayake of Ceylon had invited the Prime ministers of India, Pakistan, Indonesia, and Burma to Colombo. From this visit the Colombo Plan evolved the next year for the economic development of Southeast Asia. It was to be supported by funds contributed by many states, including America. The Colombo states met again on December 28 and 29, 1954 at Bogor, Indonesia, to plan a conference at Bandung in 1955. Invitations were extended to all African and Asian states including Red China.

The Middle East, Africa, Central America and South America.

The Republicans' promise that they would replace Truman's Europe-oriented foreign policy with a global policy brought them face-to-face with a great band of states stretching westward from Southeast Asia through the Middle East, Africa, Central America, and South America. Most of these states were uncommitted in the East-West struggle. None of them were militarily or economically strong but they possessed strategic locations, natural resources, and a large share of the world's people. Having suffered from past Western colonialism and imperialism, these states were often anti-West, a sentiment used advantageously by the Communists. Internal rivalries, religious, and racial animosities as well as the political instability of these states were exploited by the Communists. As an ally of Western Europe the United States found it difficult to win the support of these uncommitted states. An additional American handicap was the Russians' greater skill in capitalizing on the various internal tensions existing among these peoples although America actually possessed a potential advantage in that she could supply the technical and economic assistance these people wanted in order to improve their living standards.

Egypt was something of an enigma to the United States in the Middle East. Egypt continued its quarrel with Britain over the Suez Canal and the Sudan, but the latter argument was settled in February 1953. The canal zone dispute centered around the Anglo-Egyptian treaty of 1936 under which the British had remained in possession of the zone. The questions to settle were the number of British technical experts to be permitted after possible withdrawal, their rights, and the conditions under which the British might re-enter in the event of war. After Colonel Gamal Abdel Nasser ousted Mohammed Naguib from control of the country an agreement was reached with the British in October 1954. The British were given twenty months to evacuate the zone.

The settlement of the Suez dispute enabled Dulles to proceed with his plans for the building of an eastern alliance but Nasser, the key figure, showed little interest. It was difficult to convince him that Communism offered any threat to Egypt; rather, he looked with greater fear and disfavor upon his militant neighbors the Israeli. They were the chief obstacle to friendly relations between the West and the Moslem states. Since June, 1953, Dulles had also been trying to build a strong alliance in the northern tier of Moslem states. This was handicapped by the continuation of the Iranian-British oil dispute but, in August 1953, thanks to American undercover operations, Mohammed Mossadegh was ousted. In 1954 a consortium was established to manage the oil to the satisfaction of all parties and Shah Mohammed Reza Pahlevi's government moved into the western camp. In February, 1954 Premier Mohammed Fadhil al-Jamali of Iraq announced that he would seek military assistance from the West. American policy made some headway in Pakistan where the new Prime Minister Mohammed Ali negotiated with Dulles in 1953 for military aid. Nehru criticized this move because he feared Pakistan would use her aid against India in their quarrel over the control of Kashmir.

Westward from the Middle East loomed the great African continent bursting with new energy, nationalism, and hatred of colonialism. The acquisition of air bases in North Africa directly involved the United States in the quarrels between France and her possessions in Tunisia, Morocco, and Algeria. South of the Sahara the United States was not directly involved. During 1953 most of the French troubles were in Tunisia and Morocco. In 1954 Mendès-France promised to offer concessions, but the native leaders wanted nothing less than independence. In 1954 terrorism broke out unexpectedly in Algeria where nationalists were aroused and supplied with arms by Egyptian agents.

In our own hemisphere the Republicans blamed the increasing anti-Americanism on Truman's inadequate policies. The Republicans promised to make a fresh start with the Good Neighbor policy. The President's brother, Milton S. Eisenhower, visited ten Central and South American countries in June, 1953, and reported the need for greater economic cooperation, markets, and investments. The Latin and South American states wanted economic assistance most but the United States was more concerned with Communist infiltration. The American delegation brought a strong anti-Communist resolution to the Caracas meeting of the Organization of American States in March, 1954 and compelled its adoption. Presumably, with the consent of our neighbors, we were ready to deal with the Guatemala Communist situation. On June 18 a small liberation force under Colonel Carlos Castillo Armas crossed into Guatemala from Honduras and within a few weeks toppled the Communist regime of Jacobo Arbenz Guzman. This did not solve any of the hemisphere's basic economic problems. At the meeting of the hemisphere finance ministers in Rio de Janeiro in November, 1954 Secretary of the Treasury Humphrey held out little promise of economic assistance, although he spoke of "good partnership" and "good neighborliness." Eisenhower continued to work in close cooperation with Canada. On September 27, 1954, Canada and the United States agreed to build a third great radar line, the Distant Early Warning or DEW line, to supplement the Pinetree chain and Mid-Canada lines. Of more importance was the approval of the Wiley-Dondero Act on May 13, 1954 authorizing the establishment of the St. Lawrence Seaway Development Corporation to finance and construct this waterway in cooperation with Canada. For years the Congress had delayed this project but finally gave in when the Canadians proposed to build the seaway themselves.

The Cold Peace in the Economic Arena.

How successful did the dynamic Republican foreign policy appear from the vantage point of December 1954? The Republicans pointed to their successful conclusion of the Korean War, the unleashing of Chiang, the establishment of SEATO, the inclusion of Germany in NATO, the saving of South Viet-Nam, the destruction of Communism in Guatemala, the settlement of the Trieste, Iranian, and Suez canal zone disputes, the strengthening of our ties with the northern tier Moslem states, and the Atoms-for-Peace campaign. They insisted that, for the first time in years, Communist expansion had been checked.

The Democrats, naturally, offered a different interpretation. The Korean War, they said, had been settled only by partitioning the country. Chiang had been checkreined again by the new security pact. The Southeast Asian alliance was, at best, a weak thing, denounced by India, Burma, and Indonesia. How, asked the Democrats, could the Republicans claim credit for building a strong Asian alliance when the principal Asian powers would have nothing to do with it? Many Democrats agreed with the British that the future of Asia would have to be based on a strong, friendly

India and they criticized policies which had merely antagonized Nehru. Germany was now a member of NATO but the Democrats contended it was a result of Eden's efforts after the Dulles-sponsored EDC had gone down the drain. Viet-Nam had been saved only by surrendering half the country to the enemy. We had stamped out a trouble spot in this hemisphere but had angered many of our sister states by the methods used. Moreover, we had not curbed Juan Perón in Argentina, who was more of a threat to our position than Arbenz. (Perón was finally overthrown as a result of an uprising which began September 16, 1955 after his policies had cost him the support of the intellectuals, military leaders, Roman Catholic church and the proletariat.) If the Republicans had settled the Iranian, Suez, and Trieste disputes, they had failed to cope with the even more serious problems arising out of Israel, Kashmir, Cyprus, and French North Africa.

The Democrats characterized the Eisenhower-Dulles foreign policy as one of dramatic announcements followed by retreats. The grand design for the rollback of the Iron Curtain and the liberation of the satellites had never materialized. At no point had the curtain been rolled back in two years. The slogans "massive retaliation," "united action," and "agonizing reappraisal" had all been modified. No new policies had been framed which took into consideration the new status of atomic stalemate. The Russian possession of the hydrogen bomb had not led to an agonizing reappraisal of our policies. The Russians had been quick to sense the world's fear of atomic oblivion and promptly posed as the harbingers of peace while the United States was made to appear a warmonger. The Russian emphasis on "peaceful coexistence" ushered in a new era in foreign policy; the era of the Cold Peace. War had become less likely, but victory could be achieved by means other than war. The Russians were able to shift the power struggle to non-military areas by stepping up their pledges of economic and technical assistance just at a time when the United States stepped up its military assistance program.

Although the Russians did not have America's industrial machine, its technological knowledge or its skills, they gambled on one advantage. They surmised that the United States would fail to realize that the Cold Peace was being fought in the economic arena and therefore be outclassed by a poorer country as long as it failed to bring its economic superiority into play. By clever propaganda the Russians gobbled up territory while making the United States appear to be the aggressor. The Russian "peace" offensive polluted the atmosphere with a threat to American security as deadly as any radioactive fallout. Negotiations for atomic control still bogged down. Even the Atoms-for-Peace lost its effectiveness despite the fact that in November, 1954 both America and Britain pledged fissionable material as fuel for peaceful uses in atomic reactors. An uneasy world feared that peace might topple over one of Dulles' "brinks."

IV THE EISENHOWER ADMINISTRATION

The Middle Way

. . . No honeymoon for Ike.

The lack of reference to domestic policies in Eisenhower's first inaugural address incited some adverse remarks, but as Richard Rovere wrote in *Affairs of State*, "The President had chosen to address himself more to the world than to his countrymen, and this was perhaps the statesmanlike thing to do." It was not until his first State of the Union message on February 2 that Eisenhower outlined his domestic policies. He borrowed the keynote from a campaign address he delivered in Boise, Idaho, the preceding August. It was his intention, he said, to pursue the "middle way." Eric Goldman in *The Crucial Decade* said the message had a "taftite" tone. But this lack of a bold program seemed to be what the voters wanted. In his book *Revolt of the Moderates*, Samuel Lubell called attention to the "yearning for conservatism" which characterized the American scene. The two-party system returned to America in 1952 but it was not an alignment of liberal *vs.* conservative. Both parties rejected the extremists and catered to a rising group of moderates. The two parties became, Lubell said, like two fat men in a narrow hall, forced to move in the same direction because they could not squeeze by each other. Neither party exercised control because of the close vote. Each party was forced to bid for the support of groups which held the balance. This, in turn, placed a premium on "domestic conciliation over the needs of waging the cold war abroad," which was dangerous because it might force the parties to "shy from the military or economic actions which might be needed to meet new developments in the cold war." The success of the new moderate coalition depended on its ability to cope with the three main postwar problems—"foreign policy, racial and religious toleration and economic status."

Republican strength in Congress was not conclusive. Republicans controlled the Senate by one vote but they were able to proceed with its

43

organization only when independent Wayne Morse of Oregon voted with them. Robert Taft was majority leader until his death when the job devolved upon William Knowland. Lyndon Johnson of Texas was minority leader. Joseph W. Martin of Massachusetts became speaker of the House. Charles Halleck of Indiana was majority leader and Sam Rayburn of Texas was minority leader. Most of the Republican strength in Congress rested with the pro-Taft Old Guard.

Eisenhower was expected to adopt a commanding tone toward Congress, but he regarded himself as a moderator and thought he could win more congressional support through persuasion. His biographer, Pusey, said that the administration promised to be one of partnership with Congress rather than bossism. Under normal conditions any new President can expect a few months of cooperation from Congress but, according to Robert Donovan in *Eisenhower: The Inside Story,* there was no honeymoon for Ike. Perhaps this was because the time had arrived for Congress—subordinated to the chief executive for twenty years—to reassert its prerogatives. The President had trouble with the Old Guard at once. The first controversy arose over price and rent controls, which the President was forced to remove on February 6. He asked Congress to enact a stand-by program for emergency use but gained no support. The OPA was discontinued on April 30 and rent controls expired July 31. In his State of the Union message the President said that the tax burden would have to be eased. However, he ran afoul of the Old Guard when he added that it would be unwise to do this before the budget was balanced (the Republicans had gone to work immediately to cut Truman's budget drastically). Conservative Daniel A. Reed, chairman of the House Ways and Means Committee, introduced the Republicans' first measure, H.R. 1, which, contrary to Eisenhower's wishes, would have advanced the scheduled date for income tax cuts. Reed also opposed Ike's requests to extend excess profits taxes for six months. In spite of many violent attacks from the conservatives, including Taft, Eisenhower carried both points against Reed: the income tax remained unchanged and a six-month extension was voted for the excess profits tax. In alluding to his Korean War and tax cut problems, reporters jokingly said that Eisenhower's chief antagonist during the first months of his administration was "Syngman Reed."

On February 9 Eisenhower met with congressional leaders and prepared eleven items which he considered "musts" to be brought through Congress. Only on the tideland oil question did they reverse the previous administration, but had it not been for Truman's vetoes in 1946 and 1952 a tideland oil bill would have passed earlier. On May 22 Eisenhower signed Florida Senator Spessard L. Holland's bill which transferred oil reserve titles to the states. Such states as California, Texas, Louisiana, and Florida were given title to submerged oil lands within their historic boundaries, but the courts were given some latitude in determining what those boundaries were. Title to submerged oil beyond these historic limits was given to the federal government by the Outer Continental Shelf Lands Act.

At the end of the first session of the Eighty-third Congress, the President pointed to twelve achievements. In addition to the oil and tax laws they included the termination of the Reconstruction Finance Corporation, which had acquired an unsavory reputation during Truman's administration; the extension of the Reciprocal Trade Agreements Act; the creation of Mrs. Hobby's new Department of Health, Education, and Welfare; the reorganization of the Defense, Justice, and Agriculture Departments and the agencies connected with foreign aid and overseas propaganda; and the passing of an act to permit admission of 214,000 refugees to the United States during a three-and-one-half year period. On the debit side of Eisenhower's ledger must be included general failures: failure to induce Congress to admit Hawaii—he said nothing about Alaska—failures to expand social security, to amend the Taft-Hartley Act, to enact a St. Lawrence Seaway measure, to raise the debt limit of $275,000,000,000 to $290,000,-000,000, to provide for power development at Niagara Falls, to increase postal rates, and to revise the McCarran-Walter Immigration Act.

The reorganization of the Defense Department was aimed at clarifying the powers of the Secretary of Defense. Six new assistant secretaries were added to assume duties previously performed by several boards, and the Joint Chiefs of Staff were relieved of their administrative duties and made advisory to the Secretary of Defense. A new Office of Defense Mobilization, under Arthur S. Flemming, was created to assume the work previously performed by the National Security Resources Board and the Munitions Board, to supervise stockpiling, to determine manpower and production needs, and to determine stabilization policies.

The President had scored some successes during the first session of the Eighty-third Congress, but these had been achieved with Democratic support. The *Congressional Quarterly Almanac* claimed that the Democrats had saved Eisenhower's legislation on fifty-eight occasions. The President, thinking ahead to the election of 1954, hoped to carry a program through Congress which would win support for the Republicans. During the first few months of 1954, when Washington was filled with the furor of the McCarthy-Army battle, the agitation over the Bricker Amendment, and the Indochina crisis, Eisenhower prepared his domestic program. He wished to extend social security, expand public housing, and increase unemployment insurance coverage. He asked for some slight modifications in the Taft-Hartley Act, flexible farm supports, and a program to reinsure voluntary health insurance systems. If he had allowed the first session of the Eighty-third Congress to follow its own devices, Eisenhower was resolved to be more aggressive during the second session. He insisted that the Republican party, if it was worthy of continuing in office, would have to assume more leadership. In spite of high hopes the second session was also a disappointment. The President was at a loss to understand why his followers jeopardized their chances of re-election by failing to cooperate with him. The amount of intra-party bickering was alarming. The Republicans had been out of power for such a long time that they seemed no longer capable of doing anything but oppose. Without a Democrat in the White House, they turned against each other. The President became so discouraged that he toyed with the idea of creating a new personal party of "progressive moderates" to advance his cause of "dynamic conservatism," but he made no serious effort to transform the idea into reality. He knew that American history offers few examples of successful third parties, and he had no desire to become involved in a hopeless cause. What Eisenhower apparently did not realize was that American political parties draw their strength from partisanship rather than from the strength of conservative men of good will who work together in a spirit of complete nonpartisanship.

In his budget message on January 21, 1954 Eisenhower called for tax revisions. Secretary of the Treasury Humphrey argued that industrial taxes would have to be cut to encourage production, but Democrats J. William Fulbright and Paul Douglas argued that it would be more sensible to reduce taxes on lower-income groups to stimulate purchasing power. In line with this, Senator Walter George introduced a bill to increase personal income tax exemptions to $1,000 over a two-year period but this was rejected as too costly. The administration's bill, which passed in July, retained the old income tax rates but granted many important concessions. Businessmen were permitted faster write-offs, more deductions were allowed for medical care, benefits were extended to working wives employing persons for child care, and special concessions were given to parents and persons on pension or in retirement. The date for the payment of income taxes was changed from March 15 to April 15. Other tax measures reduced the excise levies on furs, jewelry, telephone calls, travel and entertainment tickets, luggage, and toilet goods. Congress refused to raise the debt ceiling although the country faced a deficit.

Eisenhower and Secretary of Agriculture Benson had prepared a farm program based on flexible price supports. Actually the Agricultural Act of 1949 had included such provisions, but the supports had not gone into effect. Eisenhower asked for flexible supports ranging from seventy-five to ninety per cent of parity on wheat, corn, cotton, peanuts, and rice. Congress raised supports to 82½ per cent in its final bill. The new laws also included an incentive program for wool production; made a great deal of the surplus agricultural goods in warehouses available for foreign aid, disaster use, and school lunches; and modernized the old parity formula to bring it into line with the current prices farmers paid and received for goods.

In 1954 Congress also revised social security legislation. Benefits were increased. One important provision permitted retired workers between sixty-five and seventy-two to earn up to $1200 annually without sacrificing any benefits. The act also brought an estimated ten million farmers, government employees (both state and local), domestic help, clerics, and others under the provision of the social security system. Eisenhower also signed a new Unemployment Insurance Act which required the participation of all employers hiring four or more workers rather than eight specified in the old act.

One major issue before Congress in 1954 was the control of atomic energy through a federal monopoly or through control shared with private enterprise. Congress passed a law permitting private companies to own reactors for the production of electric power, to own nuclear materials, to sell atomic by-products to the government, and to obtain patents on their own atomic inventions. The Atomic Energy Commission was permitted to sell electricity as long as a priority for its purchase was given to rural electric cooperatives and public power companies. These two groups were also given priority for licenses to build and operate atomic power plants.

In 1954 Eisenhower requested Congress to provide up to one billion in loans for slum clearance and urban renewal and to provide for a maximum of 35,000 low-rental housing units annually for four years. The Housing Act of 1954 made home ownership easier by reducing the down payment requirements and extending the time for payment. The Federal Housing Administration was authorized to insure up to ninety per cent of

47

the value of low cost multi-family projects. Congress limited the construction to 35,000 units only.

Other important administrative and congressional achievements in 1954 included the establishments of an Air Force Academy comparable to the service academies at West Point and Annapolis and the adoption of the St. Lawrence seaway development proposals. But other portions of the President's program did not fare too well. The President's health re-insurance program, amendments to the Taft-Hartley Act, and a Hawaiian statehood bill were all shelved. Senator Clinton Anderson's proposal to admit Alaska was also rejected.

"There must be no second-class citizens."

The explosive issue before the nation in 1953 and 1954 was civil rights. In his first State of the Union message, the President promised to "use whatever authority exists in the office of the President to end segregation in the District of Columbia, including the federal government, and any segregation in the armed services." Eisenhower insisted that desegregation should prevail at all institutions where federal funds were involved. In June, a Negro Congressman, Adam Clayton Powell, Jr., of New York, called the President's attention to the fact that the Department of Health, Education, and Welfare, as well as the Army, Navy, and Veterans' Administration had countermanded his directive and had permitted segregation to exist at some federal schools, hospitals, and navy yards. In an exchange of letters between the two, the President promised that, "There must be no second-class citizens in this country." Powell replied by calling this statement a "Magna Carta for minorities" and "a second Emancipation Proclamation." Desegregation was gradually extended throughout the armed services. On August 13, 1953 Eisenhower replaced Truman's Committee on Government Contract Compliance with a stronger Government Contract Committee. Through its efforts discrimination was ended among Washington telephone company employees and the ban on Negro bus drivers and streetcar operators was dropped. Segregation was gradually eliminated from Washington hotels, restaurants, and theatres. The Veterans' Administration also ended discrimination and segregation as did the schools maintained at army posts. On April 22, 1954, a Presidential order tightened the anti-bias clause in all government contracts.

On November 27, 1953, Attorney General Herbert Brownell filed a brief in which the government maintained that the Fourteenth Amendment prohibited segregation in the schools and that the Supreme Court could decide the issue. On May 17, 1954 the Justices ruled unanimously that "separate educational facilities are inherently unequal." This decision in *Brown* v. *Board of Education* overturned the "separate but equal" doctrine first laid down partially in 1849 by the Massachusetts Supreme Court in *Robert* v. *City of Boston* and restated by the Supreme Court under the Fourteenth Amendment in *Plessy* v. *Ferguson* (1896). Thus the stage was set for a running battle between those states practicing segregation and the judiciary, executive, and legislative branches of the federal government.

... an "inventory recession."

The change in administration and the end of the Korean War apparently had no adverse effect on economic activity. Employment reached 63,408,000 and in August, 1953, the President reported that wages and salaries had risen ten per cent during the preceding year. The one blemish on the shiny surface of the economy was that the farmers had not fared as well as other groups. In the wake of increasing prosperity the Federal Reserve Board tightened its monetary controls in an attempt to forestall inflation, but in September, Arthur F. Burns, chairman of the Council of Economic Advisers, reported unmistakable signs of recession: falling farm and stock market prices, reduced home construction, fewer orders for durable goods, and increased failures in business. As unemployment reached 3,087,000 in January, 1954, the administration was asked to take more positive steps by labor leaders George Meany and Walter Reuther.

Eisenhower refused to be alarmed. He and his advisors were determined to avoid another 1929 crash, but they made it plain that they did not feel the current slump portended a crisis that serious. Eisenhower's advisers assured him that the country was merely undergoing an "inventory recession." He told the public that March, 1954, would be the critical month and that more drastic remedial steps would be taken if there were no improvement by that time. In March unemployment hit 3,750,000, but the crisis seem to have passed. By May signs of recovery were everywhere. The President had relied on American business and labor to get themselves out of their difficulties. Regardless of the economic factors involved, his confidence appeared to have been more than justified. Many safeguards had been built into the American economy to cushion a depression and to pump credit into the stream of business activity. Eisenhower simply eased credit in 1953 and 1954, while the automatic tax cuts that went into effect during the latter year permitted the taxpayers to put another $4,700,000,000 back into the economy.

. . . the richest political ore—Communism.

It is remarkable that Congress found any time for legislative activities at all during 1953 and 1954. Most of the time was consumed by interminable investigations. Some congressmen devoted their attention to such matters as the increase in juvenile delinquency, the rising price of coffee beans, and the preferential treatment of ex-athletes in the armed forces, but the majority continued to mine the richest political ore of all—Communism. Eisenhower was inclined to let the investigations continue and urged department heads to cooperate. Gradually, however, the investigations began to interfere with the normal routines of departmental operation. Moreover, the investigators tended to stir up trouble which might jeopardize the party's chances in the 1954 elections.

One of these problems had been inherited from the previous administration. The traitors, Julius and Ethel Rosenberg, were awaiting execution for espionage. Left-wingers and well-meaning liberals had risen to their defense and an appeal was made for executive clemency which Eisenhower refused to grant on February 11, 1953. This would have ended the matter had not Associate Justice William O. Douglas reopened the case by granting a stay of execution—one of the special powers of members of the Supreme Court. The other Justices ruled against their colleague six to two. On June 19, the prisoners were executed, thus ending a chain of world-wide protest and counter-protest.

Shortly thereafter another public relations crisis developed. In July, J. B. Matthews, Senator McCarthy's staff director of the Senate Permanent Investigations Subcommittee, published an article in the *American Mercury* in which he flatly proclaimed, "The largest single group supporting the Communist apparatus in the United States today is composed of Protestant clergymen." The three national co-chairmen of the Commission on Religious Organizations of the National Conference of Christians and Jews wired Eisenhower asking him to protest. The President's reply did not conceal his displeasure with McCarthy and the senator soon found it expedient to accept Matthew's resignation.

On November 6, in a speech before the Executive Club of Chicago,

Attorney General Brownell insisted that Truman had appointed one Harry Dexter White to the post of executive director of the American delegation to the International Monetary Fund in 1946 at a time when Truman had been given FBI reports indicating that White was a Red spy. Harold H. Velde, chairman of the House Un-American Activities Committee, subpoenaed Truman to testify. This move to call a former President as a witness and "try him for treason before a luncheon club" was denounced by leaders in both parties, and even Eisenhower was alarmed. Truman needed no defenders. He did not testify before the committee but in Kansas City he went before a national TV audience to deny the accusation. He made the point that White had been retained in government service so that his suspicions would not be aroused while he was under FBI surveillance. "The course we took protected the public interest and security," explained Truman, "and . . . permitted the intensive FBI investigation to go forward." In later statements Attorney General Brownell and FBI head, J. Edgar Hoover, denied Truman's version of the story.

In his Kansas City address, Truman had accused the administration of "McCarthyism." The Wisconsin senator demanded that he be given equal air time to reply. On November 24 he not only criticized Truman but also accused Eisenhower of failure to rid the country of Reds. The President had been trying to soft-pedal the Communist issue in anticipation of the political campaign the next year, but McCarthy defied Eisenhower when he said, "The raw, harsh, unpleasant fact is that Communism is an issue and will be an issue in 1954." Both Eisenhower and Dulles replied to McCarthy in moderate tones, since, as Eisenhower said, they would not get into the gutter with the Senator. McCarthy returned to the attack on December 3, 1953 by again assailing the administration's foreign policy. This set the stage for the final battle between the Senator and the administration.

In 1954 McCarthy continued his investigations of subversion in the government and concentrated attention on the Army's Signal Corps laboratory at Fort Monmouth, New Jersey. There, he discovered a certain dentist, Major Irving Peress, who had refused to answer questions before an investigation committee or sign the Army loyalty certificate. While McCarthy thundered and demanded a court martial, Peress quietly slipped out of the Army on February 2 at Camp Kilmer with his scheduled promotion and an honorable discharge. Secretary of the Army Robert Stevens admitted that the Army's discharge and promotion procedure needed

51

some overhauling, but McCarthy was not satisfied. On February 18 he called Brigadier General Ralph Zwicker, commandant of Camp Kilmer, before his committee and accused him of not being fit to wear the American uniform. Stevens refused to permit Zwicker to testify further and swore that he would withhold, if requested, the names of the men responsible for Peress's discharge. On February 24 Stevens completely reversed himself and in a "memorandum of understanding" agreed to let the committee have full information on Peress's case and permit the committee to call Zwicker and other officers. On March 11 the Army struck back at McCarthy. A report was presented to each member of McCarthy's committee purporting to show that the Senator and his counsel, Roy Cohn, and the subcommittee's staff director, Francis Carr, had sought preferential Army treatment for private G. David Schine. (Cohen and Schine made up the 1953 McCarthy team that had conducted a whirlwind tour of overseas libraries, and McCarthy then launched his book-burning campaign based on their report.) McCarthy replied with a forty-six point indictment against the Army. Since both sides were reduced to name calling, another investigation was in order. On April 22, 1954, a series of hearings began before McCarthy's committee with Senator Karl Mundt of South Dakota presiding. The principals of the thirty-six day hearing were McCarthy, Cohn, and Carr, opposed by Secretary Stevens, and John G. Adams and Joseph N. Welch, the counsels for the Army. Between them stood Ray H. Jenkins, counsel for the subcommittee. During the proceedings the reckless McCarthy raised points of order and sought to obstruct the investigation. He relied so heavily upon Cohn, who poured a steady stream of advice into his ear, that Cohn seemed to be an unelected Senator from Wisconsin. The evidence presented seemed to show that McCarthy had sought preferential treatment for Schine and that the Army had tried to hamper McCarthy's investigation at Fort Monmouth. The non-partisan Kleig lights of the TV marathon exposed McCarthy's personality to complete public view for the first time. Following the investigation his influence declined rapidly. But the hearing was not the final blow to McCarthy. In December 1954, on the recommendation of a committee headed by Senator Arthur V. Watkins, McCarthy was censured for conduct unbecoming a member of the United States Senate. Eisenhower publicly thanked Watkins for a job well-done; McCarthy replied that he was sorry he had supported Eisenhower in 1952.

The decline of McCarthy did not end the hunt for subversives although it went a long way toward eliminating the hysteria. Under Eisenhower's new executive order the dismissal of security risks continued. In some instances the government vascillated between the guilt and innocence of a suspect. One celebrated case was that of Wolf I. Ladejinsky, who had worked in Japan as an agricultural attaché and who had been cleared by the State Department only to be rejected as a security risk by Ezra Benson. Although the government finally found a place for him in the Mutual Security Program, Ladejinsky found it difficult to live down the adverse publicity. But the most celebrated case began in November 1953 when William L. Borden, formerly executive secretary of the Joint Congressional Committee on Atomic Energy offered an opinion that J. Robert Oppenheimer, the man who had done so much to develop the atomic bomb, was in reality a Soviet agent. On the basis of material accumulated patiently by the FBI, the President decided in December to place a "blank wall" between Oppenheimer and further atomic secrets. A series of investigations followed which culminated in an AEC ruling against reinstating his clearance. Oppenheimer, the report read, had "fundamental defects in his character" and his association with former Communists was "far beyond the tolerate limits." Many Americans were incensed that such treatment should be meted out to the man who had done so much to assure our military ascendancy, but others argued that the situation was too grave to take a chance. Oppenheimer accepted the judgment with an equanimity that raised his stature not only as a man but also as a loyal and devoted American.

"They could afford to vote Republican."

Even before the 1952 election, Samuel Lubell had developed the thesis in his *Future of American Politics* that in American history there has been a major and a minor party and that the issues of each period have been fought out *within* the former coalition. This was the role of the Democrats before 1952. During that time the Republicans remained "a party of nostalgia," although they were in a strategic position; they now attracted the dissident groups that had deserted the Democrats because of Korea, corruption, and Communism and because increased prosperity and an advance in social position lead many to identify themselves with the party of wealth. His aide, Clayton Fritchey, jokingly told Truman after the election, "You did it. It's all your fault. You just made it too good for the people. They could afford to vote Republican."

History may well record that the Republican victory of 1952 was an absolute necessity. Only a new administration could conclude a peace in Korea on a stalemate basis without expanding the fighting, only a new administration would permit the domestic Communist issue to be settled, and it would also provide a two-party sanction for the gains of the New and Fair Deals. After the election, the big question, according to Lubell was, "Can the Republicans come to grips with the problems of our times?" Eisenhower had approached them gingerly in 1953. Clearly, a majority of Americans wanted a moderate Republican party in power in 1953. In his book, *Is There a Republican Majority?*, Louis Harris pointed out that in the senatorial campaign the Old Guard Republicans did not run as well as the moderate Republican candidates. All but one of the thirteen Old Guard candidates ran far behind Eisenhower. On the other hand, five of the nine moderate candidates ran ahead of him. There was an unmistakable swing to moderation and the Republican vote would have been impressive even without the added magic of the Eisenhower name. Harris contended that it was not true that the Republican party had ridden to victory on Eisenhower's coattails. Admittedly, Eisenhower had taken 54.9 per cent of the popular vote as compared with Republican congressional candidates who had taken 49.4 per cent. But the statistics were deceptive. The Republicans did not run candidates in seventy-three southern districts. In the northern states Eisenhower captured 56.4 per cent of the votes, and Republican congressional candidates captured 54.8 per cent which indicated that in this area the President and his party's candidates polled approximately equal percentages.

By 1953 Republican strength began to decline. In 1952 Eisenhower captured fifty-seven per cent of New Jersey's votes but in 1953 a relatively obscure Democrat, Robert Meyner, was elected governor by taking fifty-four per cent of the votes. The Republicans lost the gubernatorial election in Virginia where Eisenhower had captured the electoral votes in 1952. By-elections in three Republican congressional districts in 1953 led to two Democratic victories. It is an axiom that since 1900 the party in power looses an average of forty seats in the House and four in the Senate during the midterm elections. Based on 1953 results it seemed that history would repeat itself in 1954. However, the Republicans' losses in 1954 were only sixteen seats in the House and two in the Senate. The coalition which had given Eisenhower his 1952 victory was still intact. In 1955 the composition of the House was 232 Democrats and 203 Republicans, and the division in the Senate was forty-eight Democrats, forty-seven Republicans, and one Independent. Nixon called the results "really a dead heat." On the state level the Democrats scored more impressive results. They captured nineteen of the thirty-four gubernatorial contests. The Republicans' control of governorships dropped from twenty-nine to twenty-one, and the Democrats boosted their's from nineteen to twenty-seven. The Democrats were so closely identified with much of Eisenhower's program that his party's defeat did not suggest any additional opposition from Congress. Richard Rovere noted in *Affairs of State* that the problem might be one of Democratic over-enthusiasm when he wrote that the new Congress might "approach . . . 'that splendid Eisenhower program' with a measure of zeal that its promoters will regard as excessive."

From the Summit to Suez

...the New Look continued.

While the Russians pursued their coexistence policies during 1955, the United States refused to be deterred from its principal aims of building new alliances, solidifying old ones, and rearming the West. Eisenhower and Dulles maintained that peace could be won only from a position of armed strength. They continued to emphasize the New Look and the doctrine of mass retaliation. Research was pushed to add to our arsenal of atomic weapons. On January 17, the first atomic submarine was launched and in June the first B-52 bomber was delivered to combat units. Selective Service was continued for another four years. In spite of continued emphasis on massive retaliation the United States did not neglect the cause of peace. In August she joined seventy-two other states at the Geneva meeting of the UN Conference on Peaceful Uses of Atomic Energy. Eisenhower also pressed for disarmament, and Congress made additional appropriations to the Voice of America and the United States Information Agency to counter Soviet propaganda.

During 1955 the foreign aid policies followed the general lines laid down in 1953 and 1954 which meant increasing emphasis on military aid and more funds for those countries which had not been included in the original Marshall Plan. During the ten years since 1946 the United States had disbursed $51,336,000,000 in foreign aid of which only $11,000,000,-000 were considered as loans. At the end of fiscal 1955 the Foreign Operations Administration ceased to function, but on May 9, Eisenhower had replaced it with a new agency, the International Cooperation Administration (ICA), directed by John B. Hollister.

". . . we shall forget about Marx . . . when shrimps learn to whistle."

At the Supreme Soviet meeting on February 8, 1955 Georgi Malenkov astounded the Free World by publicly declaring his unworthiness to continue as Premier. Nikolai Bulganin became Premier, but much of the power passed to Nikita Khrushchev. The first task confronting these two leaders was to deal with the new Western European Union (WEU) which was being formed in 1955. They threatened to form a NATO-type alliance of the Communist states if the Paris agreements of 1954 were ratified. The West ignored the threat and completed ratification on May 5, 1955. This was the signal for the restoration of full-sovereignty to West Germany, and on May 6 she was welcomed as a member of NATO. On the following day the council of WEU met in Paris for the purpose of electing its first officers. The Russians then signed a treaty at Warsaw on May 14 with Poland, Czechoslovakia, East Germany, Hungary, Rumania, Bulgaria, and Albania in which they pledged friendship, collaboration, and mutual assistance in the event of aggression. A joint military command was established in Moscow and efforts were made to coordinate the Five Year Plans of the satellites with Moscow's.

After the Warsaw Pact Russia set the stage for an intensive "peace campaign." They revived Churchill's earlier proposal for a "summit conference." At first the United States had opposed such a proposal, but eventually Dulles and foreign ministers Harold Macmillan of England and Antoine Pinay of France, agreed to invite the Russians to a top-level meeting. Suddenly on May 15 the Soviet startled the West by signing the long-delayed Austrian State Treaty. Apparently Russia was willing to clear the air of some tension as a preliminary to the meeting. The stage was ready for the first top-level meeting since Potsdam. Geneva was chosen as the site of the meeting as a compromise between Lausanne and Vienna.

At the first session on July 18 Eisenhower, Anthony Eden (who replaced Churchill as Prime Minister on April 5), Bulganin, and Edgar Fauré simply issued policy statements, but on the next day they prepared a four-point agenda: German unification, European security, disarmament, and improved communication among the powers. During the meetings which followed no agreements were reached and on July 23 when the meetings adjourned the delegates simply referred the same agenda to their foreign ministers who were to resume negotiations in October. The major issue at the conference was disarmament. After the other three leaders had made their proposals Eisenhower offered a novel plan that had been devised by Nelson Rockefeller and a committee of government experts. The President's proposal called for the inter-power exchange of all blueprints of military installations. Each country would also be given unlimited facilities for aerial inspection of the others' bases. Fauré later remarked how earnest and sincere Eisenhower seemed when he pressed his "Open Sky" proposals upon the delegates. The military hero of World War II emerged as a genuine peacemaker when he assured Bulganin that "the United States will never take part in an aggressive war." Although Bulganin's answer was, "We believe the statement," he made no move to accept the plan.

The Geneva Summit Conference was worthless from the standpoint of positive results, but its psychological effects were amazing. The "Spirit of Geneva" permeated everything for several months after adjournment, and for the first time there seemed to be greater promise of peace. Neither side had retreated one step from its earlier positions, but optimism was stimulated by the fact that the world's four top leaders had met in a conciliatory atmosphere and had spoken against war. The most important result of the conference, according to the President, was the demonstration that America wanted peace and the further realization that war was futile. He was pleased that the four men had met without invective or threats; all seemed serious and desirous of finding some solution to the world's problems. Eisenhower, however, was not duped into thinking that a golden age was about to dawn, and he warned the public not to expect too much from the forthcoming ministers' meeting.

In August Bulganin rejected the Open Sky proposals and the next month Khrushchev let the world know that there was no change in basic Soviet policy when he said, "We are in favor of a détente, but if anybody thinks that for this reason we shall forget about Marx, Engels, and Lenin, he is mistaken. This will happen when shrimps learn to whistle."

On October 27 the four foreign ministers met in Geneva. The Russians still refused to consider German unification on the ground that it would be a threat to their security. Dulles proposed to combine the German unification and European security points on the agenda by offering a pledge that America would join the western European states in a war against Germany if she again attacked Russia. Molotov, however, refused this offer and returned to his old demand for an all-European security pact which would replace NATO, WEU, and the Warsaw Pact. On November 16 the ministers returned home without solving a single one of the four issues; the "Spirit of Geneva" was moribund.

When Bulganin spoke on December 29 he said that "this year will go down in history as a definite turning in the relaxation of world tension." He was partly right, for after Geneva there was a diminution in world tension. Eisenhower and Dulles were proud of their role in the preservation of peace and proud of the fact that America's position in west Europe in 1955 was much stronger. Trade and industry were back at pre-war levels in Europe, and local Communist parties were at a low ebb. The participants in the European Coal and Steel Community began the formation of Euratom in 1955 to pool their nuclear resources. They also considered plans for the creation of a six-nation market area. As the world passed into 1956 these gains in Europe were offset by two serious problems: the continued threat of atomic destruction and the Russians' successful program to win adherents among the neutralist states by personal visits of high dignitaries and a policy of economic and technical assistance liberally interspersed with propaganda.

By the winter of 1955-56 the "balance of terror" was complete; both sides had achieved mutual deterrence. Neither the United States nor Russia showed any signs of decelerating their bomb production even though the capacity for mutual destruction theoretically made the bombs obsolete. The arms race entered a new phase. The objective was, to go back to Confederate General Nathan Bedford Forrest, "To get there fustest with the mostest." The emphasis on intercontinenal bomber and missile research, rockets, and satellites for outer space in both countries was evidence that even though we had achieved mutual deterrence, there was still the possibility that one side could, by superior bomb carriers of some type, obliterate its opponent before massive retaliation could be launched. The age of mutual deterrence worked to Russia's advantage, and she was already shifting the battle front to new arenas. The Eisenhower administration was aware of this, but this changing emphasis in Russian strategy from armaments to propaganda, economic, and technical assistance, was not, in Dulles' judgment, justification for reducing our own military preparedness. He said that the United States would have to redouble its pressure on Russia to roll back the iron curtain. This meant that America would have to keep her retaliatory power at a peak and further strengthen her military alliances.

A spirited controversy broke out in America early in 1956 over the massive retaliation concept. In January Dulles was quoted in a *Life Magazine* article to the effect that the United States had averted a major war on three occasions by going to the brink of war in Korea, Indochina, and

Formosa (described below). "The ability to get to the verge without getting into the war is the necessary art," said Dulles, but Adlai Stevenson countered, "The art of diplomacy, especially in this atomic age, must lead to peace, not war or the brink of war."

Early in 1956 the Russians made a public statement of their new policies aimed at winning adherents among the neutrals. At the Twentieth Party Congress from February 14 to 25, 1956 Khrushchev told the delegates that the world situation was forcing the Reds to alter their traditional attitudes toward the role of Communism. They were not abandoning their devotion to Marx, as Khrushchev said in 1955, but they were simply acknowledging that new conditions made it necessary to achieve the goals of Communism by other means. If new means were to be tried, the old means had to be abandoned. Since the latter were linked with Joseph Stalin, it was necessary first to demote him in public memory. Khrushchev and other Red leaders embarked on a campaign to denigrate Stalin as a megalomaniac, a murderer, and a completely ruthless and irresponsible despot. Having macerated Stalin and his policies, the new leaders exalted themselves and their policies. Freed of the stigma of Stalinism, Khrushchev could bid for the neutrals' support, many of whom had been repelled by Russia's excesses. Khrushchev told the delegates that Russia could coexist and compete with the capitalist states because their inevitable doom through internal contradictions made war unnecessary. Despite their peace talk the Russians did not relax their military vigil.

The Russian "peace offensive" opened a rift between the United States and her allies in 1956. Many leading European spokesmen, who did not share Americans' preoccupation with armaments, believed that the new Russian peace offensive required a different defense strategy. On the other hand, our leaders could not understand the European's refusal to take the need for rearmament more seriously than they did. General Alfred Gruenther of NATO reported that he would be lucky to have fourteen undermanned divisions by the end of 1956. Twelve German divisions were still to be organized, but even when they were ready, Europe would be dangerously short of the thirty divisions which experts deemed necessary to hold the Russians. The inability of the United States to agree with its allies on the true objectives of NATO necessitated a dispassionate reappraisal of the entire alliance. When the NATO foreign ministers met in Paris on May 4, 1956, they appointed a committee of "Three Wise Men"—Lester B. Pearson of Canada, Gaetano Martino of Italy, and Halvard M. Lange of Norway—to consider some of the immediate problems facing the alliance. In December of 1956 they suggested the obvious; a need for greater coordination on political and economic matters and the advisability of more consultation. The Russians were aware of America's difficulties with her allies over the rearmament question and on May 14 they sought to sow more dissention by offering to cut their army by another 1,200,000 beyond their 640,000 cut of the preceding year. It was a gesture of inestimable propaganda value, although it did nothing to reduce Russia's war potential.

While the United States criticized her allies for their complacancy there were similar trends at home. Americans, like Europeans, lost their interest in foreign affairs as the threat of war subsided. Demands for foreign aid and defense-spending cutbacks impeded the necessary adjustments in foreign policy. The situation was further complicated by Presidential illness at a time when foreign affairs were under debate in Washington. The Democrats resisted the administration, partly out of desire to make political issues for the presidential election and partly out of a conviction that the President was wrong. Eisenhower called for increased trade with Europe. He appointed industrialist Benjamin F. Fairless to head a special committee to study means for increasing our trade, but Congress's rejection of the Organization for Trade Co-operation, which had been devised by several European states at Geneva, indicated that there was still strong opposition to a policy of freer trade. By mid-1956 American foreign policy moved to dead center.

. . . to the brink of war for the third time.

In addition to trying to frame a policy to counter the Russian's "peace" offensive, the State Department had to deal with a very serious war scare in the Orient during 1955. In our defense treaty with Chiang, which went into effect on March 3, 1955, the United States had taken an ambiguous stand on the status of Quemoy, Matsu, and the Tachens, a group of islands claimed by the Nationalists. Since September 1954 Quemoy had been under attack from the Red mainland, and in these repeated incidents lay the threat of war. In his memoirs General Ridgway relates that considerable pressure was exerted on Eisenhower by Admiral Radford and others who wanted to force a showdown with the Reds over the islands. Ridgway, who had opposed intervention in Indochina, adopted the same stand in relation to the islands.

The President sent a message to Congress on January 24, 1955 asking for "measures designed to assure the security of Formosa and the Pescadores." In view of the repeated Red threats to Liberate Formosa, Eisenhower said that the United States would have to be ready to take "appropriate military action" against the mainland or Red-held islands. He asked for a resolution enabling him to use American forces if necessary to protect Formosa and the Pescadores. Chairman of the House Foreign Affairs Committee James P. Richards and chairman of the Senate Foreign Relations Committee Walter George, promptly introduced appropriate resolutions in Congress. The next day the House approved by a vote of 409 to three, but a debate developed in the Senate. The President assured the senators that the decision to use force would be his only; no general in the field would be permitted to make the decision. George threw his immense prestige behind the resolution, and it was approved eighty-five to three. On January 29, 1955 the President signed but in spite of all the previous discussion the resolution still left the status of the islands uncertain. Would the United States fight if the Red shelling of Quemoy gave way to a full-scale invasion? No one knew, and the President was still buffeted by conflicting advice from the interventionists and the moderates.

Eisenhower was reluctant to antagonize our allies by promising to defend the islands, but he dared not write them off in the face of pressure from such powerful pro-Chiang Republicans as Senator Knowland and Senator Jenner. In February the Seventh Fleet evacuated the Nationalist garrison from the Tachens, 210 miles from Formosa, and the Reds moved in at once. On February 5 the State Department announced that the United States would "extend assistance to the Republic of China in defending such related positions and territories now in its hands as the United States deems to be essential to the defense of Formosa and the Pescadores." Apparently the administration would fight if an invasion of Quemoy or Matsu appeared to be a preliminary to a full-scale invasion of Formosa. This was the view developed by Dulles in a New York speech on February 16. The United States went to the brink of war for the third time by indicating its willingness to fight in defense of an ally. In late March Admiral Robert B. Carney predicted that the Reds would strike against Formosa after April 15, and the nation faced the worst war scare since Dienbienphu. Eisenhower denied that there was any evidence of a Red threat. April 15 passed without incident; another crisis had been averted.

Following the Formosa war scare a meeting of the African-Asian states at Bandung, Java from April 18 to 24, occupied American diplomatic interest. Delegates attended from twenty-nine countries representing approximately 1,400,000,000 people. The forces of neutralism, anti-colonialism, and nationalism came together to make their feelings known to both the East and the West. The United States had opposed the meeting at first, but eventually she urged her friends to attend, if invited. It was disappointing that Israel, South Korea, and the Nationalist Chinese were not invited, but American diplomats were comforted by the fact that Russia, with legitimate claims to the status of an Asiatic power, and North Korea were similarly disregarded. On April 24 a resolution was adopted which called for the admission of new states to the UN, more African-Asian seats in the Security Council, disarmament, a ban on atomic bomb tests, increased emphasis on peaceful uses of the atom, and an international atomic energy commission. A "Declaration on the Promotion of World Peace and Co-operation" was also adopted which stressed racial and national equality, the rights of self-determination and defense, non-interventionism, and anti colonialism. Actually the conference was by no means as critical of the West or as neutralist as feared originally. The drama was provided by Chou En-lai who announced that Red China was ready for talks with America over Formosa.

Dulles assigned U. Alexis Johnson, ambassador to Czechoslovakia, to open talks in Geneva with the Red's Polish ambassador, Wang Ping-nan. Between August 1 and September 10, 1955 these two discussed many points of friction but the one serious problem was the fifteen American fliers and about forty civilians held as prisoners. It was agreed that some Chinese atomic experts, who had been detained in this country, would be released. In return, the Reds promised to free their American prisoners. Although the Chinese atomic experts were permitted to return home, if they wished; Peiping still detained thirteen Americans at the end of the year.

During 1955 the African-Asian bloc managed to increase its power in the UN. In 1950 UN membership increased from fifty-one to sixty states, but American-Russian rivalry blocked the admission of any new members. By 1955 there were twenty-two states awaiting admission. In that year a compromise paved the way for the admission of Albania, Bulgaria, Hungary, Rumania, Austria, Cambodia, Ceylon, Finland, Italy, Ireland, Jordan, Laos, Libya, Nepal, Portugal, and Spain. The effect was noticeable at once. The Communist bloc was increased to nine members and the African-Asian bloc was increased to twenty members. The Western European-British Commonwealth bloc and the Latin American bloc: were about twenty members each. Before 1955 the United States exerted great influence in the General Assembly, but after that date Russian and neutralist strength increased materially. The addition, in 1956, of Morocco, Tunisia, Japan, and the Sudan further strengthened the African-Asian bloc.

The United States faced critical tests in many eastern areas during 1955, but the most serious were results of Bulganin's and Khrushchev's flying visits abroad with promises of economic aid, technical assistance, and good will. To counter this Eisenhower requested a special President's Asian Development Fund of two hundred million dollars, but Congress doomed the program by paring the grant to one hundred million spread over a three-year period. Neutralism continued to make headway in Asia during 1956, but this apparently no longer alarmed Dulles. When he returned from a journey through the Orient he made a report to the American public on March 24. Asia was in flux, he said—no country was either wholly neutral or wholly committed. No country was either completely pro-Soviet or anti-West. Under these circumstances Dulles maintained that the United States had an excellent opportunity to strengthen its position by offering the Asians a broad appeal based on peace and democracy. In spite of this optimism, neutralism, and in some cases even Communism, seemed to be increasing in India, Pakistan, Burma, Thailand, Ceylon, Malaya, Indonesia, and even in the Philippines. It was only in South Viet-Nam, South Korea, Taiwan (Formosa), and Japan, all exposed to direct Red attack, that the United States continued to wield undiminished influence in the governments of Ngo Dinh Diem, Syngman Rhee, Chiang Kai-shek, and Ichiro Hatoyama.

" . . . to hasten a process which could not be accelerated"

The shift from the Cold War to the Cold Peace was not only economic, political, social, and psychological; it was also geographical. In 1955 and 1956 Bulganin and Khrushchev revived the century-old Russian drive into the Middle East thus taking advantage of the respite gained at the Geneva summit conference. The United States had already found it difficult to devise a successful Middle Eastern policy. In *Middle East Dilemmas* Jacob Hurewitz pointed out that America's difficulties arose from being forced to seek immediate solutions to problems which could be solved only by time and patience. The Russian menace forced America to "hasten a process which could not be accelerated" and to assume more responsibilities from 1947 to 1952 than the British had assumed in 150 years of Middle East experience. Dulles sought to bring to the Middle East the stability the Truman administration had been unable to secure. This quest for stability forced us to support the status quo at a time when the revolutionary ferment in the Middle East made political, economic, and social reforms inevitable and necessary. Dulles tried to find a solution for the two problems of Middle East defense and Arab-Jewish rivalry.

After Egypt rebuffed Dulles' plans for a Midde East Defense Organization in 1953 and 1954 the Secretary of State concentrated on strengthening the northern tier composed of those countries which, by reason of proximity, were fearful of Russia. Turkey had taken the initiative and attempted to conclude pacts with her neighbors. The 1953 treaty with Greece and Yugoslavia was weakened by the growth of Tito's neutralism and the Greek-Turkish argument over Cyprus. On April 2, 1954 Turkey restrengthened her position by concluding a mutual assistance pact with Pakistan. Dulles gave the project his blessing.

According to George Lenczowski in *The Middle East in World Affairs* Iraq had to choose between joining the northern tier and abandoning her 1930 treaty with Britain. Iraqui Premier Nuri as-Said reasoned that he could rid his country of the unpopular bilateral treaty with Britain by joining a regional pact which included Britain as a member. Iraq would still be assured of protection and Britain would then be only one of many states involved. The only drawback was opposition from the Arab League. A series of negotiations followed between Turkey and Iraq which led to a treaty of security and defense signed at Baghdad on February 24, 1955. At the invitation of the signatories, the United Kingdom, Pakistan, and Iran also joined this alliance between April 5 and October 25. Britain's membership was important because it brought a major power into an alliance otherwise composed of second class powers. The Middle East Treaty Organization (METO) was established with a permanent secretariat at Baghdad. The alliance was very weak. With the exception of Britain and Turkey none of the signatories possessed enough arms to meet the military needs of the alliance. Since Egypt and Iraq were rivals for Arab leadership, the treaty drove Egypt into greater western opposition. The treaty was not designed to meet the Russian challenge in the economic, social, and psychological spheres. Since Iraq was the only Arab state to join (although Iran and Turkey were Moslem states their people were not Arabs), the treaty was, as Emil Lengyel wrote in *Egypt's Role in World Affairs,* "one-twelfth of a solution because only one of a dozen Arab coun-

Chronology

tries used it." The United States refused to sign in order to keep on good terms with Egypt and Israel. This angered the Iraqui who felt that Britain would "leave by the door but come back by the window" and still dominate the new alliance. Britain also tried during 1955 and 1956 to get the United States and Jordan to join the alliance. King Hussein of Jordan refused and in 1956 he seemed to move closer to Egypt when he ousted John Bagot Glubb, the British commander of his Arab Legion.

Both Molotov and Nasser warned against the Baghdad pact as a guise for the continuation of imperialism. The Russian strategists vaulted over the northern tier and found a ready ally in Nasser. On September 27, 1955 Nasser plunged the Middle East into an arms race by concluding a barter deal with Czechosloyakia to exchange cotton for guns. Other Arab states appealed to Russia for arms, and the Israeli turned to the United States. The Washington administration wished to avoid an arms race in the Middle East. Dulles was sure it would ultimately work to the disadvantage of Israel, since the Israeli were so badly outnumbered by the Arabs and worked desperately to find a solution for the Arab-Jewish problem.

In an attempt to preserve the 1949 settlement between the Arabs and the Israeli the United States joined Britain and France in 1950 in a Tripartite Declaration "to promote the establishment and maintenance of peace and stability in the Middle East." The three agreed to maintain existing Israel-Arab boundaries and prevent either side from securing additional arms. On August 26, 1955 Dulles offered a program based on compensating Arab refugees who had fled Israel and guaranteeing existing boundaries. The United States was willing, he said, to make a loan to provide the compensation and to negotiate a formal treaty to maintain the boundaries. Neither the Arabs nor the Israeli looked upon the proposals with favor; Dulles found the role of "honest broker" exasperating and unrewarding. America also held out the possibility of economic aid, and Eisenhower had sent film magnate Eric Johnston to the Middle East to try to interest the Jews and Arabs in a joint project to develop the Jordan valley. This offer was also refused.

After the Arabs rejected METO and the Johnston plan, the State department was left without an alternative policy. The Tripartite Declaration was undermined by Nasser's arms deal, and the situation was further complicated when Syria and Egypt signed a military pact on October 20, 1955. One week later Nasser concluded a pact with Saudi Arabia. On December 26 these three states announced a joint military command under

67

Major General Abdel Hakim Amer of Egypt. The Israeli did not add to the stability of the Middle East in 1955. David Ben-Gurion returned as Premier on November 3 in place of the more moderate Moshe Sharett. Soon after the conclusion of the Egyptian-Syrian pact, the Israeli tested the alliance by launching a military strike into the Lake Tiberias region along the Syrian border. This brought strong threats from the Arab League states: Egypt, Iraq, Jordan, Lebanon, Libya, Saudi Arabia, Yemen, Syria, and the Sudan. In 1956 Russia offered arms to Syria and Yemen, extended economic aid to the Arabs, and denounced the Baghdad pact. Nasser continued to behave in a most Hitler-like manner. During the 1930's Neville Chamberlain had made concessions to Hitler on the supposition that it would make him more reasonable but this, as the world learned, proved to be a tragic mistake. Similarly the West offered concessions to Nasser but, like Hitler, he had only become more rapacious.

Unfortunately the British, French, and Americans were poorly prepared to meet these problems in 1956. Each had a particular field of major interest. The United States, through Dag Hammarskjold of the UN, hoped to obtain Nasser's and Ben-Gurion's agreement to respect a cease-fire. In 1956 the British were faced with full-scale riots on Cyprus. In March they deported the nationalist leader, Archbishop Makarios, but this action intensified rather than reduced Cypriot resistance. France was necessarily more interested in North Africa. She was forced to grant concessions in both Tunisia and Morocco. Early in 1956 the Tunisian Habib Bourguiba set up a new government, and on March 20, 1956 the French recognized Tunisian independence. On March 2 the French recognized the sultan's full authority over the government of Morocco. The Algerians continued to resist the French with aid from Nasser and Bourguiba.

In an attempt to encourage an eastern settlement, the United States had supported Nasser's plan for the construction of a high dam at Aswan, a project which would require at least $1,300,000,000 and sixteen years to complete. The United States, Britain, and the International Bank offered financial assistance. Nasser, however, hinted that the Russians were also interested in making a loan—he was holding out for the best deal. Some persons in Washington wished to embark upon a dollar-matching battle with Russia for Nasser's allegiance, but others were aware that this would merely induce Russia to outbid the United States and thereby score propaganda victories without spending a ruble. Other Americans were angered at Nasser's obvious boldness in trying to encourage the

West and East to bid for his favor. At last, on July 17, 1956, the Egyptian government accepted the West's original offer. Two days later Dulles replied that the United States had lost interest in the project and explained that "the ability of Egypt to devote adequate resources to assure the project's success has become more uncertain than at the time the offer was made." After London and the International Bank withdrew their offers, Russia also seemed to lose interest.

On July 26 Nasser announced that he was nationalizing the Suez canal which he characterized as a "state within a state." The hundred million dollars collected annually as tolls would be used by the government to defray expenses and to construct the dam. Nasser pledged that he would compensate the stockholders and not interfere with the right of transit. Although many Americans thought that this move was motivated by our decision to withdraw the loan, this was not true. Nasser had made up his mind to nationalize the canal under any circumstance.

The reaction was immediate. While the Moslem states and Russia approved there were protests from Britain and France. They did not consider Nasser's pledge trustworthy because he had already discriminated against the Israeli in the use of the canal. They also doubted that Egyptian technicians were capable of keeping the canal open. Undersecretary of State Robert Murphy, sent to Europe by the United States, reported to Washington on July 30 that London and Paris were seething with war talk. Dulles visited with representatives from both countries on August 1 and 2, and the three powers issued an invitation to the sixteen most important canal users as well as to the eight remaining signatories of the Constantinople Agreement of 1888, which had provided for free navigation on the canal.

Dulles hoped that the conference would bring some solution, but Nasser's refusal to attend made agreement unlikely. From August 16 to 23 twenty-two states met in London and prepared two reports. The minority report, representing the views of Russia, Ceylon, Indonesia, and India, provided for Egyptian management of the canal. The majority report, in which the United States joined, asked for an international organization to manage the canal. Prime Minister Robert Gordon Menzies of Australia headed a five-man committee which visited Cairo from September 3 to 10 in a vain attempt to sell Nasser on the majority plan.

At this point the United States and her two principal allies drifted apart. Britain and France pushed war preparations and ordered their

Suez pilots to quit work as a means of bringing Nasser to terms. But the resourceful Egyptian kept the canal open by recruiting pilots from other countries. While Britain and France prepared for war, Dulles held to his faith in diplomacy. He proposed that a Suez Canal Users' Association hire the pilots, maintain the canal, and collect the tolls until such time as a permanent settlement could be found. Between September 19 and 21 eighteen states met in London and approved the users' association which was put into operation by October 1. Once again Nasser refused to accept a compromise. There was nothing left to do but place the problem before the UN, but discussions in October bogged down because of a Soviet veto. Dag Hammarskjold also visited with the foreign ministers of France, Britain, and Egypt—Christian Pineau, Selwyn Lloyd, and Mahmoud Fawzi. Although the British and French were ready to make concessions, they held out for some kind of international supervision of the canal. On this point Nasser refused to yield and future negotiations seemed useless.

In the midst of the Suez crisis attention suddenly shifted to East Europe where the United States had kept alive the spirit of independence by its propaganda. Dulles' rollback theory suddenly seemed to be taking effect as some cracks appeared on the surface of the Russian monolith. On June 1 Molotov was replaced by Dmitri T. Shepilov who had not been associated with Stalinism. Tito soon visited Moscow where he joined the Russians in a public statement that all countries had the right to follow their own paths to socialism. This had been Tito's contention during his struggle with Stalin. The next indication that all was not well beneath the Russian surface was a series of riots in Poznań, Poland. Although America's propaganda seemed to be bearing some fruit, the results (if these were results) were not triumphs for democracy; they were Communist nationalist-regimes replacing Communist Russian-oriented regimes. The unrest in Poland resulted in the election of a powerful nationalist Communist leader, Wladyslaw Gomulka, as first secretary of the party.

Tension within the Kremlin mounted with the appearance of the next surface blemish. On October 23 some demonstrations occurred in Budapest, Hungary, centering around a demand for the removal of Russian troops and the appointment of Imre Nagy as prime minister. The Russians allowed Nagy to become prime minister on October 24. Small successes led to larger hopes. Violence flared in Budapest as the citizens demanded freedom from Russian control. On October 30 the Russians indicated that they were prepared to negotiate a settlement but this was suddenly cancelled when the Suez canal crisis flared into open warfare.

. . . "Soviet threats . . . very strongly phrased"

Following the Budapest demonstrations there was a rush of related events. On Monday October 29 came the news of Israeli mobilization. In Washington, Ambassador Abba Eban assured Assistant Secretary of State William Rountree and Fraser Wilkins, in charge of Arab-Jewish affairs, that the mobilization was purely defensive. But in the midst of these talks news arrived that Israel had launched a preventive war against Egypt. Jewish mechanized units were pouring into the Sinai peninsula and the Gaza Strip.

On Tuesday, October 30, Britain and France issued an ultimatum demanding a cessation of hostilities and the withdrawal of the Egyptian and Israeli armies from the Suez area. Egypt was asked to submit to a temporary occupation of Port Said, Ismailia Suez, and certain points along the canal. Eden warned that military intervention would follow within twelve hours if Egypt did not comply. She rejected the ultimatum. On October 31 Britain and France intervened. The next day this was excused by the United Kingdom's representative to the UN, Sir Pierson Dixon, as intervention made inevitable by Egypt's defiance of the UN. In an emergency session, the UN General Assembly demanded an immediate cease fire and the withdrawal of all troops behind the armistice lines. But this demand was ignored. The United States was taken completely by surprise by British and French intervention. Actually, some weeks before the fateful ultimatum, the Israeli and French had hatched the plot for intervention, and on October 16 Prime Minister Guy Mollet and Foreign Minister Pineau of France persuaded Eden and Lloyd of England to join. Both Britain and France were dissatisfied with Dulles' handling of the entire Suez problem.

While the invaders humbled Nasser's vaunted military machine, demonstrations continued in Budapest. On November 1 Nagy defied Moscow by denouncing the Warsaw Pact and calling upon the UN to help the Hungarians defend their neutral status. This was too much; Nagy had gone beyond the Russians' idea of reasonable limits. On November 4 Russian troops poured into Budapest to support János Kádár's new pro-Russian regime.

Events moved suddenly with kaleidoscopic variety. Americans were preparing to go to the polls on November 6 for the presidential election. Eisenhower was still not fully recovered from his illness when Dulles was stricken with a malignant intestinal disorder requiring immediate surgery.

While Herbert Hoover, Jr. carried on in the State Department, the war began to go badly for the British and French. The time lost destroying Nasser's air force and transporting troops from Malta gave the Egyptians an opportunity to block the canal with sunken vessels.

Eisenhower hoped the UN could end the fighting. Although any action in the Security Council could be blocked by a veto, the General Assembly was free to act under the "Uniting for Peace Resolution" of Korean War days. The General Assembly met in emergency session from November 1 to 10. A total of six resolutions was adopted calling for a cessation of hostilities, the withdrawal of all armed forces, and the creation of a special United Nations Emergency Force. The British and French were forty-eight hours short of their military objectives when they yielded and agreed to a cease fire at midnight November 6. It had been impossible to crush Nasser who emerged a greater hero to the Moslems than before. British and French forces were withdrawn in 1956 but the Israeli did not leave until early in 1957.

The American public was scarcely aware of the major role played by Russia in bringing the seven-day war to an abrupt halt. On November 5 Bulganin sent messages to Eden, Mollet, and Ben-Gurion warning that Russia was "fully determined to apply force in order to crush the aggressors and restore peace in the East." The Russians hinted they might send "volunteers." Bulganin was both provocative and self-confident when he asserted that "there are countries now which need not have sent a navy or air force to the coasts of Britain but could have used another means, such as rocket technique." In the face of possible atomic annihilation, Britain and France consented to a cease fire twenty-four hours later. Did the British and French back down in the face of these threats? In discussing the reasons for the cease fire, American Ambassador to France, C. Douglas Dillon, remarked, "The only new element that had come in was those Soviet threats, which were very, very strongly phrased." He discounted completely the influence of moral suasion, fear of antagonizing America, or adverse public opinion in France and Britain. In his *Egypt's Role in World Affairs*, Lengyel cited an article in the January 1957 issue of *Bulletin of the Atomic Scientists* in which its editor, Eugene Rabinowitch, said:

> Britain and France were presented with a virtual ultimatum threatening, by clear implication, the air-atomic destruction of both countries if they failed to call off the Suez expedition. This demonstration of the power of air-atomic deterrence is a turning

point in history, and we should not be distracted from recognizing its significance by incidental events, such as the diplomatic pressure of the United States . . . or the speeches given, and the resolutions passed in the United Nations. . . . What England and France did *not* anticipate was a readiness of the Soviet leaders to unleash all-out atomic war in response to a local conflict so far from their own borders.

It was impossible to tell whether the Russians' threat was real or whether they were simply borrowing a card from Dulles' deck and outplaying him at the game of "brinksmanship." However, their callous indifference toward world public opinion—they ignored ten UN resolutions on Hungary—the ruthless manner in which, at that moment, they were crushing the helpless Hungarians, and the "very, very strongly phrased" note of Bulganin would lead one to conclude that they were not bluffing.

The Suez war left a dismal heritage. The bitterness between Arab and Jew was intensified. The British financial position was weakened, the western alliance was badly undermined, an oil shortage loomed in Europe. British and French good will in the Middle East was non-existent, and the Suez canal was closed for months—littered with sunken hulks and debris. Eden soon resigned and was replaced by Harold Macmillan. Oddly enough Mollet's ministry survived for a short time. The UN gained no new prestige as a result of this flash war. Its ability to win a cease fire was due to a combination of circumstances. The UN had been effective in 1950 during the Korean crisis because Russia was absent from the Security Council and it took action in 1956 only because Russian and American interests coincided. World peace depended less on what the UN did than upon the relationship of the bipolar powers. As 1956 drew to a close there was nothing to suggest that Russia and America were any closer to an understanding than they had been during the Truman Era.

The Russian equivalent of "The public be damned."

The second two-year period of Eisenhower's dynamic foreign policy ended on a sour note. The United States faced a long, hard job of rebuilding. American leaders were unaware that the alliance with Britain and France had been deteriorating for several years. Nor did the public realize the extent of the deterioration until Britain and France joined Israel against Egypt. Reestablishing rapport became one of Dulles' major jobs. Credits and oil were supplied during the financial and fuel crises after the war, but this gesture did nothing to stem the rising tide of anti-Americanism. It remained to be seen whether Dulles could use peaceful means—since he had rejected military intervention—to assure access to eastern oil, guarantee that the canal would remain open to all nations, protect Israeli shipping against Egyptian attack, and curb the troublesome Nasser, who was bent upon becoming the Moslem world's leader. Dulles' long range hope was that our stand on the Egyptian crisis would eventually reestablish American prestige in the Middle and the Far East.

The closing weeks of 1956, however, had vindicated one aspect of the Eisenhower-Dulles foreign policy. In spite of the subtle shift from "cold war" to "cold peace" they had insisted upon the need for maintaining adequate military force. They were denounced at home and abroad for not taking adequate precaution to meet the new Soviet challenge in the economic, social, political, and psychological spheres. After all, it was within these spheres that the "cold peace" was being fought. They refused to abandon the conviction that Russia's threat was still essentially a military one. If world public opinion was shocked by the invasion of Egypt it was even more shocked by the merciless suppression of the Hungarian patriots and the callous indifference of Russia toward international censure. As the West drew back in Egypt, the Russians pushed ahead in Hungary. The Russians had merely applied Commodore Vanderbilt's famous phrase "The public be damned" to a wider audience. The Russians apparently wished to "coexist" on their own terms. The West's protest against the rape of Hungary was met with complete indifference because the Russians knew that the West *would not* resort to war. The West drew back in Egypt because it knew that the Russians *would* resort to war. The Russian threats were taken seriously.

Eisenhower and Dulles had been right. The Russians understood force only, and they would yield only to a position of strength. This was just as true in 1956 as it had been in 1945 when Stalin at Potsdam asked his famous question, "But how many divisions has the Pope?" But if this was true an even more terrifying question had to be answered: Did the West still hold a position of strength from which to compel negotiation or had it been ended by mutual deterrence? The atomic gap had been closed. The balance may have even been thrown the other way. Perhaps Russia's indifference toward Western opinion was prompted not only by a feeling that the West would keep the peace but also by an even stronger conviction that, if war came, Russia's superior firepower would win it. There can be no doubt that, had a war come in November 1956, it would have been an atomic war. General Gruenther of NATO, when asked if a war started by the West would be an atomic war, replied, "That is right . . . We do not have the capability to defend ourselves against this type of dictatorship by purely conventional means."

After November 6 Eisenhower faced another difficult four-year control over foreign policy. In the past the United States had tragically misjudged the Russian and Chinese revolutions; it remained to be seen whether it would cope any better with the Moslem revolution, which in 1956 had led the world to the brink of atomic annihilation.

Dynamic Conservatism and a Democratic Congress

. . . a greater share . . . of increasing wealth.

The Democrats' victory in 1954 strengthened the President. McCarthy, already clipped by the censure vote in 1954, lost his chairmanship of the investigation subcommittee. The Old Guard Republicans were weakened, and the pro-Eisenhower Republicans asserted themselves. During 1955 and 1956 the President sought to advance his dynamic conservatism which, he explained, was based on two principles: "first, the federal government should perform an essential task only when it cannot otherwise be adequately performed; and second, in performing that task our government must not impair the self-respect, freedom, and incentive of the individual."

In the Eighty-fourth Congress power passed to two Texans, Senate majority leader Lyndon B. Johnson and House Speaker Sam Rayburn. Knowland and Martin were minority leaders. The Democrats gave Eisenhower's program considerable support. In many cases they were willing to go beyond what the President requested as in the case of legislation for tax reductions, farm parities, labor, federal aid to education, immigration, housing, and social security. Nevertheless, the accomplishments of 1955 and 1956 were negligible. The urgency of foreign affairs, Eisenhower's illness in 1955, and the impending presidential election kept domestic matters on dead center.

After the tax act of 1954 Eisenhower made further tax cuts contingent upon a balanced budget, but even while the budget remained unbalanced the Democrats offered plans for raising personal income tax exemptions by one hundred dollars or granting each taxpayer a twenty dollar reduction in taxes for himself and each dependent. In January 1956 the President submitted a budget for the fiscal year 1957 with an estimated surplus of $435,000,000. At the same time he revised the figures for the fiscal year 1956 to show that instead of a deficit there would be a surplus of $230,000,000. This was the fourth time since 1930 that the budget had been balanced—the other years were 1947, 1948, and 1951. In spite of the balanced budget no changes were made in the tax structure.

In 1955 gross national production averaged $387,000,000,000 or six per cent more than the peak year 1953. Prosperity had returned. In 1956 gross national production soared to $414,000,000,000 but the farmers complained that they were not getting their share. The administration tried to meet the demands of agriculture. Democratic Senator Hubert Humphrey of Minnesota dredged up an old idea to pay farmers for taking land out of cultivation. This "soil bank" plan was rejected by the administration in October 1955, but Eisenhower and Secretary of Agriculture Benson were forced to change their minds in the face of Democratic and farm pressure. On January 9, 1956 Eisenhower offered the administration's plan which called for an Acreage Reserve Program designed to meet the immediate problem of rice, cotton, corn, and wheat surpluses, and a Conservation Reserve, a long-term soil-saving plan as the name implies. Under the first plan farmers were to reduce crop acreage voluntarily in return for certificates redeemable by the Commodity Credit Corporation in cash or produce. Payment in produce, Eisenhower explained, would reduce the surpluses. Under the second plan the government agreed to defray part of the cost of placing cultivatable land in timber, forage, or water storage. Eisenhower also approved flexible supports and the distribution of the surplus. Congress passed a measure, vetoed by Eisenhower on April 15, which accepted the two-part soil bank plan but reimposed ninety per cent parity prices for wheat, corn, peanuts, cotton, and rice. Eisenhower asked Congress to reconsider the measure and the Department of Agriculture raised minimum parity prices on the five basic commodities from seventy-five to 82½ per cent. Congress accepted the department's change in parity prices and passed a new soil bank plan which the President signed May 28, 1958.

Labor also demanded a greater share of the nation's increasing wealth and its bargaining position was greatly strengthened after December 1955 by the formation of the AFL-CIO Union which represented a fusion of 109 AFL and thirty-two CIO unions under the presidency of George

Meany and the vice presidency of Walter Reuther. During 1955 the United Automobile Workers negotiated a new contract with the automobile industry in which the latter accepted without too much resistance the union's new concept of a "guaranteed annual wage" under which workers would be assured of a steady annual income. Union leaders hailed this as a major victory and said it would act as a cushion against recession. Another main target of the unions in 1955 and 1956 was the increasing number of "right-to-work" laws being enacted in the states. This term was a misnomer, for these laws did not guarantee anyone the right to work or protect anyone against unemployment; such laws merely guaranteed a right to work without compelling the worker to join a union. Apparently Eisenhower was not hostile to right-to-work laws, for when Secretary of Labor Mitchell spoke against them in 1954, the President told reporters that his remarks did not reflect the views of the administration. The President had, however, supported amendments to the Taft-Hartley Act but action was blocked during 1955 and 1956 because several labor bills were tied down by Graham Barden of North Carolina, Chairman of the House Labor Committee. Although he failed to secure any amendments to Taft-Hartley, Eisenhower was successful in his efforts to raise the minimum wage. Leon H. Keyserling, who headed a Conference on Economic Progress, suggested in February 1955 that the minimum wage should be raised from seventy-five cents to $1.25. This proposal was given wide support but the President asked for an increase to ninety cents. Senator Paul Douglas led the fight to boost the minimum to one dollar; this figure was finally accepted in a compromise bill signed by Eisenhower on August 12, 1955.

During the years since World War II the status of American education had become a national scandal. With enrollments soaring each year schools became hopelessly overcrowded. At least 75,000 teachers had been leaving the profession each year because of low salaries. The construction of new facilities lagged badly. In 1955 the White House Conference on Education revealed that by 1960 the nation would need at least fifteen billion dollars worth of new buildings. The resources of many states were clearly inadequate. On February 8, 1955 Eisenhower asked Congress for a three-year program to make approximately $1,100,000,000 available for loans and grants to stimulate school construction. Many Democrats criticized the program as inadequate and claimed that at least six billion dollars would be needed within six years. In 1956 Eisenhower offered a new program calling for $2,020,000,000 in federal funds to be used over a five-year period. His argument was that such a program would solve the classroom shortage, and that at the end of five years it would be possible to terminate federal aid and permit the state and local governments to assume full responsibility. These funds were to be "distributed according to relative need." Republican Senator H. Alexander Smith of New Jersey brought in a bill on January 12 which embodied the President's program, but the Democrats had previously introduced a bill sponsored by Augustine B. Kelley of Pennsylvania which called for $1,600,000,000 for a four-year period to be distributed on an annual basis of $11.30 per child, if matched by the state. The Kelley bill eventually foundered when an amendment was added to prohibit grants to segregated schools. No school aid bills were passed in 1955 or 1956. The Republicans claimed a bill would have passed had the Democrats not substituted a per capita principle of distribution. The Democrats in turn accused the Republicans of wrecking a school-aid bill by supporting the anti-segregation amendment.

In 1956 Eisenhower tackled the immigration question. He proposed that the unused quotas of several nations should be transferred to those nations having long waiting lists and that the 1950 census rather than the 1920 census should be used for determining the number of eligible immigrants. He estimated that this change would increase the annual quota from 154,657 to about 220,000. Republicans Arthur Watkins and Kenneth Keating brought in bills for the administration but Democrats Herbert Lehman and Emanuel Celler sponsored bills which would have abolished the national-origins feature of the immigration system and would have increased the annual quota to at least 250,000. Congress deadlocked and nothing was done.

The President renewed his request in 1955 and 1956 for low-cost public housing. He proposed 35,000 units per year for a two-year period, but in 1955 a compromise bill was adopted for 45,000 units in one year. The Democrats tried to substitute a measure for a four-year program for the construction of a maximum of 135,000 units. In 1956 the National Housing Act was liberalized to permit the FHA to insure long-term mortgages for homes damaged in disasters and to subsidize seventy thousand low-rental units for two years in slum-clearance programs.

In 1955 the House Democrats tried to liberalize social security legislation only to run into opposition from the administration and the Senate. In 1956, however, the social security program was broadened to include another 750,000 farmers and self-employed professional workers, and benefits were made available for women at the age of sixty-two.

During 1955 and 1956 all efforts to gain statehood for Alaska and Hawaii were blocked and so was the President's health insurance plan. On the other hand, the President's highway program was successful. In 1955 Eisenhower proposed a ten-year, multi-billion, federal-state road construction program, but the Senate rejected it in favor of a Democratic substitute measure, which was lost in the House. Finally in 1956 a law was passed which provided for the eventual construction of 42,000 miles of four-lane and six-lane highways costing $33,800,000,000 over a thirteen-year period.

On the foregoing points the Democrats sought to outbid the administration. The result was frequently a deadlock in which no legislation was possible. These issues, however, were all minor points on the legislative agenda for 1955 and 1956. The major issues arose over civil rights, natural resource conservation, and national security. These were the explosive issues out of which election issues could be made.

"null, void and no effect" (Georgia 1956).

After the Supreme Court civil rights decision of 1954, the administration moved to assure the nation that segregation would be ended as speedily as feasible. On May 31, 1955 another unanimous Supreme Court decision charged that segregation must end with all speed. Local school authorities were instructed to decide how desegregation could be effected but no time limit was set. Federal courts could "consider whether the action of school authorities constitutes good-faith implementation" of the decision. The states were to "make a prompt and reasonable start toward full compliance." But when the start had been made the courts might "find that additional time is necessary to carry out the ruling in an effective manner." During 1955 and 1956 segregationists gained strength in the South. State legislatures either declared the decision to be "null, void and of no effect" (Georgia in 1956) or followed the Virginia legislature which took steps to transform the public school system into a "private" system to circumvent the court. The southern legislatures went back to the days of the Founding Fathers and revived the "interposition" theory of the Virginia and Kentucky Resolutions. According to this theory the states had the right to interpose their authority between their citizens and the federal government if the states considered that the federal government was guilty of unconstitutional action. Gallup polls in February 1956 indicated that the southern whites opposed desegregation by an overwhelming eight to sixteen per cent. In March the *New York Times* reported that only

Delaware, Kentucky, Maryland, Missouri, Oklahoma, West Virginia, and the District of Columbia were actively cooperating to achieve intergration.

Segregationists were just as active in Washington. On February 8, 1956 several southern senators met in Senator Walter George's office to prepare their protest. A document was carefully drawn, and the final draft was shaped by J. Strom Thurmond of South Carolina, Richard B. Russell of Georgia, J. William Fullbright of Arkansas, Price Daniel of Texas, and John Stennis of Mississippi. On March 11, 1956 a "Southern Manifesto" was issued which charged the justices of the Supreme Court in upsetting the 1896 ruling "with no legal basis for such action, undertook to exercise their naked judicial power and substituted their political and social ideas for the established law of the land." The manifesto was signed by ninety-six southern Democratic senators and representatives as well as four southern Republican representatives. It was rejected by twenty-four southern Democratic senators and representatives and three republican representatives.

The desegregation question was closely tied to the federal school aid proposals. In 1955 congressman Adam Clayton Powell of New York suggested that federal funds should not be made available to school systems which failed to comply with the court decision, but Eisenhower replied that there was no use "muddying the water" because "we need the schools." In spite of presidential disapproval Powell introduced a segregation amendment in the House, and New York Senator Lehman offered to support a similar amendment in the Senate. The issue was not decided on its merits. Politics played a hand in the entire affair as Republican congressman often voted for the amendment not through genuine conviction but because they wished to attract Negro votes and to embarrass the Democrats, who had been plagued by a party split on this question since 1948

Although the President would not endorse the Powell amendment, he did try in 1956 to advance the cause of civil rights. During the preceding year he created a five-man Committee on Government Employment Policy to stop discrimination in federal employment. At the same time he requested federal department heads to adopt fair employment practices. The administration's civil rights program, which called for a Civil Rights Division in the Department of Justice, was introduced in Congress on April 9, 1956. The plan also called for laws to protect voting rights and to give the Department of Justice civil remedies for enforcing civil rights laws. This bill died in Senator James Eastland's judiciary committee. A belated effort by the civil rights group to get the bill to the floor was blocked by Lyndon Johnson and William Knowland, who argued that it was too late in the session to delay other important legislation by lengthy debate.

The power controversies.

In spite of his efforts to advance "dynamic conservation" and to sell the Republican party to the public as the friend of the little man, Eisenhower could not remove the stigma, whether true or false, that his administration was too pro-business. The President was not helped by his maladroit subordinates. Upon one occasion the able but often too talkative Secretary of Defense Wilson raised a minor tempest with a re- mark about unemployment. In an attempt to stress the importance of self-reliance, Wilson drew an interesting parallel: "I've always liked bird dogs better than kennel-fed dogs myself—you know, one who'll get out and hunt for food rather than sit on his fanny and yell." The Democrats had a field day selling the public the notion that "Engine Charlie" equated laboring men with dogs. On another occasion an administrative spokes- man remarked that the right to suffer through unemployment was "one of the joys of a free economy." It was equally difficult to justify this state- ment.

The exploitation of natural resources by private business was one point where the Republicans were unusually vulnerable. In addition to the tideland oil measure there was an equally important plan—also sup- ported by the President—to remove federal rate-control over natural-gas producers. The major controversies, however, involved water-power pro- jects, particularly TVA and the Hells Canyon site. Eisenhower main- tained that the difference between his party and the opposition was one of degree. He intended to support river and power developments but not at the expense of creating overawing federal agencies. In his State of the Union message in 1954 he promised that the federal government would "continue to construct and operate economically sound flood control, power, irrigation and water supply projects wherever these projects are beyond the capacity of local initiative and consistent with the needs of the whole nation." This promise was supported by Secretary of the In- terior McKay and his successor after June 1956, Senator Fred A. Seaton of Nebraska. The President's pledges, however, were not taken at face val- ue. He was thought to be hostile to TVA because on one occasion he called it an example of "creeping socialism" while ex-President Herbert Hoover, chairman of the reconstituted Commission on Organization of the Executive Branch of the Government and Clarence E. Manion, chairman of the Intergovernmental Relations Commission, suggested in 1953 that it might be a good idea to sell TVA to private investors. Although the President considered such a recommendation unacceptable, it did indicate the climate of opinion which existed among those close to the administration.

The Hells Canyon controversy arose when the Federal Power Commission in 1955 permitted a private company, the Idaho Power Company, to construct three low dams on the Snake River along the Idaho-Oregon boundary. The commission rejected a plan for a federal government high dam, although public power advocates insisted that a single federal high dam would yield more power potential than the three to be built by private capital. Final efforts to get approval for a federal dam went down to defeat in July, 1956. Of even greater importance was the TVA controversy. In 1953, TVA asked for funds to build a steam plant at Fulton, Tennessee, but the President opposed it on the ground that the government could not be expected to supply all the power needs of the valley. Governor Frank Clement of Tennessee received a similar rebuff when he asked for aid in providing more TVA power for Memphis.

TVA was asked to supply 600,000 kilowatts of power for the atomic energy plant at Paducah, Kentucky and Budget Director Joseph M. Dodge proposed that the AEC should contract with private companies to construct new generating plants to sell power to TVA to make up the difference. In this manner TVA would meet its local and governmental power commitments without building any new plants. Negotiations began for a $107,250,000 private power plant at West Memphis, Tennessee on Presidential order on July 16, 1954. These negotiations involved the Middle South Utilities, Inc., and the Southern Company headed respectively by Edgar H. Dixon and Eugene A. Yates. When they joined forces it became known as the Dixon-Yates combine. Eisenhower was accused of trying to wreck TVA, and the Democrats, sensing an election issue, began probing. It was discovered that the famous golfer, Bobby Jones, was a director of the Southern Company, and the Democrats alleged that Jones stood to benefit financially because of his friendship with the President. In November, 1954, the Democrats requested that the AEC refrain from signing the contract until the newly elected Eighty-fourth Congress would have an opportunity to study the matter. This proposal was rejected and the contract was signed November 11.

The Republican-controlled Joint Congressional Atomic Energy Committee also waived, at Eisenhower's request, the thirty-day period required between the signing and effective dates of the contract. After January, 1955, when the committee was in Democratic hands, the matter was reopened. Other complications arose. In 1954 the President had made "all" of the Dixon-Yates records available, but in February 1955 Senator Lister Hill announced that important facts had been withheld. Adolphe H. Wenzell, Bureau of the Budget Consultant, had participated in the Dixon-Yates negotiations, but he was also vice president of the First Boston Corporation which became Dixon-Yates' financial agent. This raised a conflict of interest problem. In June, 1955, Sherman Adams asked J. Sinclair Armstrong, chairman of the Securities Exchange Commission to postpone a hearing on the day the House debated some aspects of the Dixon-Yates affair. The Democrats accused Adams of trying to hush up Wenzell's connection with the company. The controversy continued for six months until Mayor Frank Tobey of Memphis took the administration off the griddle by announcing that the city would build its own power plant. On July 11, 1955, the Dixon-Yates contract was cancelled, but the suspicion of chicanery and the widespread belief continued that the administration was hostile to public power.

... The Maginot line of industrial potential.

No problem struck closer to the hearts of the American people than national security. There was consistent opposition to stand-by mobilization legislation and to the controls needed if defense costs were to be held down. In *Revolt of the Moderates* Samuel Lubell called attention to the contradictory position of American businessmen who, by keeping defense costs high through their opposition to controls, helped prevent the tax cuts which they desired. The defense budget provoked a sharp conflict between those who wanted just enough defense to keep from cutting into civilian production and those who wanted defense even if it meant curtailing civilian demands.

Could the United States have both guns and butter? The people insisted upon answering this question with a thunderous affirmative, relying on the known or imagined nuclear superiority over the Reds. The President went along with this prevailing sentiment in his long-haul concept of defense. American strategy was based on the Maginot line of industrial potential. The theory was that Russia would be rocked on her heels by massive retaliation, allowing ample time to switch the economy to full military production for the *coup de grace*. Science, however, seems to have reduced modern war to one gigantic "Sunday punch" for each side. Those who visualized war in these terms insisted that the nation needed greater force-in-being, and that such a force would have to be maintained even if it meant curtailing civilian production. It was conceivable, they argued, that the next war would be fought only with the forces and weapons at hand and there would be no time to mobilize or rearm. There would be no repetition of our 1914-17 and 1939-41 experiences when America prepared its defenses while Britain and France held the line. With the political balance so delicately poised between Republican and Democrats neither party was willing to demand an all-out defense program when the public obviously did not want it.

By 1955 existing plans called for the reduction of American armed forces to 2,850,000 men with an army of 1,027,000. General Ridgway had advocated an army of 1,300,000. After his retirement in June 1955 he precipitated a national-defense debate by publishing a series of articles in January in *the Saturday Evening Post*. He explained that he had not approved the drastic cuts recommended by the administration. He deplored "civilian secretaries making military decisions on the basis of political expediency," which was the sort of thing that had "brought us to the brink of disaster in Korea." He did not believe that it was advisable to depend entirely on nuclear weapons or strategic bombing since this type of weapon was designed to destroy industrial developments—which neither China nor Russia had. There was still room for the foot-slogging G. I.

The defense program continued to emphasize air power, but during the May Day review in Moscow in 1955 American observers were dismayed by the sight of so much Russian power. Although Secretary Wilson had announced that the Russian air force was primarily one of defense, a flight of ten Bison bombers participated in the air show. These were long-range intercontinental bombers similar to our own vaunted B-52. At once, critics insisted that Eisenhower had permitted the Russians to forge ahead in aircraft production. The administration denied this, but persistent reports continued that the Soviet air force was at least comparable to ours; others maintained that it was superior. No less a personage than General Curtis E. LeMay of the Strategic Air Command said in April 1956 that "we believe we now have the capability of winning any war the Soviets might start." But this encouraging news was blunted when he added, "We are not capable of winning it without this country receiving very serious damage." In June 1956 General Nathan F. Twining, Air Force Chief of Staff, returned from a visit to Moscow with a report that the Soviets were catching up both quantitatively and qualitatively with the American Air Force. He warned Congress that it would be wise to consider "the possibility of their achieving a scientific breakthrough and consequent technological surprise in new weapons." Both Eisenhower and Wilson pointed out that the Strategic Air Command was not our only line of defense. It was backed by the Tactical Air Force as well as by carrier task forces on constant alert around the Russian periphery. Our many bases and refueling techniques greatly added to the efficiency and effective range of our medium B-47 bombers. Wilson promised every effort would be made to hasten the development of guided ballistic missiles.

Both the United States and Russia devoted much attention to developing ground-to-air and air-to-air missiles. The rapid advance in electronics enabled both countries to perfect missiles capable of seeking out their targets. More attention was paid to the intercontinental ballistic missile (ICBM) with a range of thousands of miles at supersonic speeds to a predetermined target. Since the design problems involved would take much time, the United States also worked to develop the presumably less intricate intermediate range ballistic missile (IRBM). These could be fired from overseas bases at Russian targets. In spite of the administration's assurances that the United States was maintaining its lead over the Russians, the alarming reports continued. In 1956, Trevor Gardner, Assistant Secretary of the Air Force for Research and Development, resigned because he felt that the administration was not devoting enough attention to research. He predicted that by 1957 the United States would have only the "second best air force in the world."

. . . a remarkable victory for Eisenhower.

On the evening of September 24, 1955, the President retired early at his mother-in-law's home in Denver, Colorado. During the night he complained of severe chest pains, Mrs. Eisenhower summond General Howard Snyder, who diagnosed the President's illness as a coronary thrombosis. The President was rushed to Fitzsimons General Hospital for treatment and remained there until November 11. While the President was recuperating Nixon, Sherman Adams, James Hagerty and a small group of aides kept the government functioning smoothly. The illness, which cardiac expert Dr. Paul Dudley White described as "neither mild nor serious", came at a time when official duties were light and thanks to the efficient routine introduced by Sherman Adams, work at the White House went on without interruption. While the governmental machine worked well, the political mechanism began to sputter. Eisenhower was apparently out of the presidential race and politicians began to examine Nixon, Dewey, Earl Warren, Harold Stassen, Henry Cabot Lodge, William Knowland, and Sherman Adams as possible candidates. Some attention was also given to Milton Eisenhower and the governor of Massachusetts, Christian Herter. When the President returned to Washington he kept his political thoughts to himself, but in January 1956 some of his friends suggested, as biographer Robert Donovan wrote, that "The President had a God-given ability for reconciling differences among men and nations and, if his health permitted, he should go on using his talent." On February 29 the President announced that he was a candidate after several physicians had assured him of complete recovery.

On March 7 the President spoke about the vice presidency. He said that he had discussed the election with Nixon and recommended that he "chart his own course and tell me what he would like to do." This seemed to leave the Vice President's status uncertain, but when Nixon announced on April 26 that he would like to stand for re-election the President replied that he was delighted to have the Californian on the ticket. The matter was not entirely settled, however, for as the Republican convention approached, it became apparent that an anti-Nixon rebellion was brewing. Harold Stassen indicated to the President that he wished to campaign against Nixon. Nixon had been a controversial figure since the fund episode in 1952. He was like McCarthy inasmuch as he made thousands of devoted friends and many bitter enemies. In *Revolt of the Moderates* Samuel Lubell indicated that he found that these strong feelings arose because of Nixon's connection with the Red issue, an explosive one because it revived "all the animosities and loyalties of the 1935-40 period" when America debated the New Deal and decided between Stalin and Hitler as her enemy. The Red issue was closely tied with opposition to the New Deal as well as with isolationism and interventionism. Lubell found the strongest opposition to Red hunting in those areas which had favored our entry into World War II and the strongest supported in those areas which had been isolationist. Nixon became a symbol of these animosities. The appellation of "Tricky Dick" had been fastened upon him by his enemies. During Eisenhower's first term Nixon worked to rid himself of the stigma of opportunism. But even with all of his efforts Nixon could not convince his critics, who still accused him of furthering his ambitions by trying to appear all things to all men—ambassador-at-large, party mediator, able administrator, defender of minority rights, defense planner, and nemesis of traitors. Stassen insisted that Nixon's name on the ballot might defeat Eisenhower.

The situation was complicated when the President was forced to undergo an emergency operation for ileitis on June 9, 1956. Under normal conditions the life expectancy of a man who had both a heart condition and an intestinal disorder would be less than a four-year presidential term. It seemed a possibility that Nixon would be President before 1961. This new situation served to intensify the anti-Nixon movement and it brought the President's health into the campaign as an issue. Both sides quoted cardiac experts to prove that Eisenhower would or would not survive another term. Republican orators maintained that the President was actually in better physical condition after his illness than before. Columnist Raymond Moley had such confidence in Eisenhower's future that he suggested that it might be a good idea to amend the constitution again so that he could stand for re-election in 1960. Stassen fought a futile fight to prevent Nixon's re-nomination; at the San Francisco national convention both Eisenhower and Nixon were triumphantly re-nominated without opposition.

The leading Democratic contenders were Adlai Stevenson and Estes Kefauver. Early in 1956 political battles shaped up in the Minnesota, Florida, and California primaries. Estes Kefauver captured twenty-six of the thirty Minnesota delegates because many Republicans, wishing to embarrass Stevenson, had voted for Kefauver in the Democratic primaries. Stevenson decided it was time to run "like a singed cat." The brilliant intellectualism of 1952 was replaced by a traditional campaign. Stevenson adopted Kefauver's coonskin tactics. He shook hands with thousands and permitted himself to be photographed in picturesque circumstances and in countless samples of local and native regalia. In Florida he lugged around a stuffed alligator and downed Kefauver in the primary. When Stevenson carried California by nearly 500,000 votes, Kefauver closed up shop. This did not clear the way for Stevenson. Two days before the national convention in Chicago, Truman announced his support of W. Averell Harriman. Many delegates were angry because of Stevenson's support of desegregation. Nevertheless Stevenson was nominated on the first ballot, and Kefauver was picked for the vice presidency.

According to Stevenson's biographer, Kenneth Davis, the campaign went through three stages. During the first two stages Stevenson held his own, but during the final stage he committed some strategic errors. On

September 5 he told the American Legions national convention that it was time to end the draft. He made a second grave error when he announced that as President he would seek to end A-bomb testing. When Bulganin took time to write a letter stating that he endorsed Stevenson's bomb-test stand, the Democrats' defeat was assured. Stevenson's words were distorted to appear as if he favored unilateral disarmament for America. The Democrats again appeared as appeasers. Stevenson's attempts to capitalize on the President's health also worked to his disadvantage. Eisenhower was a greater hero than ever after his two bouts with death and he had aroused much sympathy. Even the tragic failure of his foreign policy in the Near East did not hurt him. Thousands voted for him because they thought his military experiences would be invaluable in the event the Egyptian crisis flared into World War III.

On November 6, 1956 Eisenhower carried forty-one states (Truman had said earlier that Stevenson would not carry more than nine states) and 457 electoral votes to Stevenson's seventy-four. The popular vote was 62,118,936 of which Eisenhower captured 35,582,236 and Stevenson polled 26,028,887. Eisenhower took the Northeast, the Pacific region, all of the Midwest except Missouri, and even broke the Solid South by taking Texas, Florida, Virginia, Kentucky, West Virginia, Tennessee, and Louisiana. Stevenson carried only Missouri, Arkansas, Mississippi, Alabama, Georgia, and the Carolinas. Stevenson had based his hope of victory on the South, the dissident farmers, labor, and religious, racial, and ethic minorities. But Eisenhower cut across all these groups. Experts erred in predicting that the South, with the exception of Florida, would vote Democratic. The predicted farm revolt did not occur. The President piled up huge majorities in the cities and among Negroes and other racial and religious groups. Labor voted for Eisenhower in spite of the opposition of its leaders. The Republican slogan of "Peace, Progress, and Prosperity" was unbeatable. Eisenhower had concluded the Korean War. The Republicans, despite Democratic predictions of depression, had kept the nation prosperous and Eisenhower's philosophy of dynamic conservatism demonstrated that he was interested in public welfare. It was impossible in 1956 to find any sizeable group with strong objections to what the administration had done.

The election was a remarkable victory for Eisenhower. He polled approximately ten million more votes than his rival and captured fifty-eight per cent of the total. Party leaders had prayer for such a landslide as a means of carrying other Republicans into office. They hoped to regain control of the Senate, but when the votes were tallied, the Democrats still held that body forty-nine to forty-seven. Independent Wayne Morse of Oregon had been re-elected despite the fact that Secretary of the Interior Douglas McKay had resigned to campaign against him. The Democrats also retained control of the House 235 to two hundred. In the House elections some changes occurred in the century-old voting patterns inasmuch as the Republicans made some gains in the cities but lost seats in the country. At the state level there were twenty-nine Democratic governors, although the Democrats had captured only fifteen of the thirty posts which were up for election in 1956.

In 1956 the public still wavered between the two parties. There was no clear desire to commit the nation's care to the Republicans. Even the magic of Eisenhower's name had not given the Republicans control. Eisenhower faced the problem of rebuilding the Republican party during his second term; its future depended on it. Eisenhower praised as the clearest statement of dynamic conservatism, a 1956 book by Under-Secretary of Labor Arthur Larson entitled *A Republican Looks at His Party*. The genius of Eisenhower, Larson said, was that he "merged and brought into balance all the positive forces in our country." Eisenhower had established the "Authentic American Center," which was a "common meeting-ground of the great majority of our people." Larson reduced Eisenhower's new Republicanism to an eight-point creed. The first five points were a belief in a God of order, justice, and love, the all-importance of the individual, the localization of government, reliance on private initiative whenever possible, and political philosophy based on American tradition. In his explanation of the last three points Larson said the government should maintain prosperity, enable workers to improve their condition through collective bargaining, and advance the general welfare. But all three, he was careful to point out, would be accomplished with a minimum of interference with private initiative. It was for the future to say if Eisenhower was to remake the Republican party into a reasonable facsimile of Larson's description. Eisenhower's victory should have enhanced his power and prestige within the party but his unwillingness to be an aggressive leader, his weakened physical condition, and the twenty-second amendment, placed him in a disadvantageous position. With the amendment in effect, party leaders were no longer bound to follow the President's lead, not even out of gratitude for having saved them in 1956. After January 1961 his only future was to be that of a country squire of Gettysburg.

The Dawn of the Space Age

The Eisenhower Doctrine and the Middle East

Early in 1957 conferences were undertaken in Washington and Bermuda to rebuild the western alliance. Khrushchev also faced a task of rebuilding. His soft line was challenged by powerful Russian leaders and he was forced to trim sail. "When it comes to fighting imperialists we are all Stalinists," he said as he signaled a return to a stronger policy. It was felt in Washington that there would be no serious Soviet threats until Khrushchev ironed out the difficulties within the Communist empire and dealt with a rival clique headed by Molotov, Kaganovich, Malenkov, and others. This respite gave Eisenhower time to frame a new Middle Eastern policy, which was sharply tested during 1957 and 1958. At the same time Communist pressure was being applied relentlessly in Asia and Europe.

The Middle Eastern situation was the first foreign policy consideration of Eisenhower's new administration, but as John Campbell wrote in *Defense of the Middle East* the "problem was one of a new public posture rather than of new policies." The "Eisenhower Doctrine", proposed to Congress on January 5, 1957, was an attempt to inaugurate a comprehensive Middle Eastern policy. In effect it warned the Reds that America would permit no further Communist conquests in the Middle East and implied to the American people that, as Hanson Baldwin wrote in *Middle East in Turmoil,* "in still another area of the world the American GI and the United States dollar have replaced the British Tommy Atkins and the British pound as instruments of diplomacy."

A resolution was introduced by Representative Thomas A. Gordon of Illinois on January 5 which embodied the President's request for authority to undertake "programs of military assistance and cooperation with any nation or group of nations which desires such aid," and this was to include "the employment of the armed forces of the United States to secure and protect the territorial integrity and political independence of such nations requesting such aid against overt armed aggression from any nation controlled by international communism." The President explained that the Russians might attack if they felt the Middle East was inadequately protected. He was "convinced that the best insurance against this dangerous contingency is to make clear now our readiness to cooperate fully and freely with our friends of the Middle East in ways consonant with the purposes and principles of the United Nations.

Congressional debate began January 7 and there were many objections to Eisenhower's request. The doctrine was challenged on constitutional grounds, while others objected to the fact that it was unilateral, gave Eisenhower a "blank check", did not protect against subversion, had not been cleared by the National Security Council or America's allies, was confined only to Communist aggression, and met only the Red military threat. Eisenhower asked for $200,000,000, but he was unable to tell precisely how they were to be spent. Congress was reluctant to appropriate funds for indefinite use. Some congressmen complained that the boundaries of the Middle East were not defined in the resolution and that it did not come to grips with such basic questions as the Suez canal and Jewish-Arab rivalry. After considerable debate in the Senate, a modified version of the resolution was passed on March 7 and signed two days later. Eisenhower was authorized to assist any nation or group of nations in the Middle East in developing economic strength or military power. For this purpose $200,000,000 was made available. The main portion of the resolution provided that the United States regarded the independence of the Middle Eastern states as vital and "if the President determines the necessity thereof, the United States is prepared to use armed forces to assist any such nation or group of nations requesting assistance against armed aggression from any country controlled by international communism; *Provided,* that such employment shall be consonant with the treaty obligations of the United States and with the Constitution of the United States." The doctrine could be terminated at any time by concurrent resolution.

Eisenhower admitted that his doctrine was incomplete but claimed that it set the stage for the gradual development of a comprehensive policy. He knew that the United States would have to tread carefully through a maze of conflicting interests. America was fortunate that the Communists had made little headway in the two powerful Moslem, non-Arab, northern tier states Turkey and Iraq, but the British insisted that the METO alliance would soon dissolve without American participation. The only man of sufficient stature to counter Nasser was Nuri As-Said of Iraq but his position was insecure as long as America remained outside the Baghdad pact. Even more overshadowing was the problem of raising the Middle Eastern economy. Early in 1957 the administration thought of a great Middle Eastern Marshall plan but these demands for additional funds came in the midst of an economy wave. America's offer of military assistance in the Middle East came at a time when the Sixth Fleet in the Mediterranean had one Marine battalion landing-team of 1,800 men. The fleet relied mainly on atomic power. It was fortunate that the Russians had no military bases in the Middle East; any attack they might launch would have to be mounted from Russia herself. The likelihood of war was thereby reduced but nevertheless the Russians would probably try to accomplish their goals by subversion. Early in 1957 Eisenhower worked to settle the two immediate Middle Eastern problems: the reopening of the Suez canal and the withdrawal of Israeli troops from Egyptian territory.

When the Eisenhower doctrine was promulgated, Egypt, Syria, and India joined Russia's Khrushchev in consigning it to the "garbage heap of history," but this reaction was anticipated. Turkey, Iraq, Iran, and Pakistan supported the doctrine, but as allies this was also anticipated. Of more concern was the situation in the uncommitted states. To explain America's position and to offer aid, Eisenhower sent James P. Richards on a lengthy tour of the Middle East and he also invited King Saud of Saudi Arabia to Washington in January. King Saud was impressed by his visit and returned home with a better understanding of America's position. He also visited Nasser and Syrian and Jordanian leaders and relayed to them his favorable impressions.

During 1957 the Eisenhower Doctrine was submitted to two tests which revealed its weakness in dealing with anything less than an attack by Communist forces. On April 10 King Hussein of Jordan requested the resignation of Premier Sulayman al-Nabulsi and this led to rioting. Jordan seemed on the verge of collapse as greedy neighbors stood by for a share of her territory. Eisenhower sent the Sixth Fleet to the eastern Mediterranean but Hussein did not request its aid. Eventually, order was restored. During August the Communists moved into key governmental jobs in Syria as they scored successes against the moderates. In both instances the upheavals were internal and the United States was unable to intervene. Communist power continued to increase in Syria. In October Khrushchev accused the United States of trying to provoke a war between Syria and Turkey. Andrei Gromyko, the Russian foreign minister, reported that the attack would occur shortly after the Turkish elections on October 27. Dulles predicted there would be no war. The general feeling in Washington was that the Reds were trying to cover a domestic crisis by sabre-rattling in the Middle East. The crisis abated when Gromyko's danger-date passed without incident. Under the guise of the crisis, the Russians concluded new economic and technical assistance pacts with Syria and Egypt.

The major test of the Eisenhower Doctrine came in 1958. In a move to counter increasing Communist strength President Shukri al-Kuwatly of Syria joined Nasser on February 1 in proclaiming the formation of the United Arab Republic (UAR). Nasser became the republic's first president, and Abdel Hakim Amer became commander of combined forces. Yemen joined the UAR in March. This increase in Nasser's power provoked a reaction among Moslem states. King Faisal II of Iraq and King Hussein of Jordan linked their Haashemite kingdoms in the Arab Federal State. General Nuri as-Said became premier of Iraq in an attempt to strengthen the new federation against the UAR. King Saud of Saudi Arabia was accused of trying to have Nasser assassinated and of stirring up a military coup in Syria. However, on March 24 the Nasserites claimed a victory when King Saud gave more power to his brother Faisal who was known to be hostile to METO.

After some minor disturbances in April, an armed rebellion broke out in Lebanon on May 9. This rebellion, supported by the UAR, grew out of religious rivalries between Moslem and Christian Lebanese and out of opposition to the pro-western policies of Premier Sami es-Solh and Foreign Minister Charles Malik. President Camille Chamoun was also accused of trying to amend the constitution so he could hold a second term. Chamoun denied this charge and insisted the rebellion was caused by those who wanted to bring Lebanon into line with the UAR. While Khrushchev assured Nasser that Russia favored a union of all Arab peoples under the UAR, the United States moved its Sixth Fleet to the eastern Mediterranean. On June 25 Premier Sami es-Solh appealed to the UN for assistance in preventing the flow of arms from the UAR to Lebanese rebels, and on July 15 American marines landed in response to requests from Chamoun for assistance under the Eisenhower Doctrine. More than 14,000 marines were eventually landed at strategic points in Lebanon.

While the first marine contingents were preparing to debark in Lebanon, violence flared in Iraq. On July 14 a group of pro-Nasser army officers staged a coup under Brigadier General Abdul Karim el-Kassem. Faisal II, crown prince Abdul Illah, and Nuri as-Said were murdered. When a similar fater threatened King Hussein, Britain rushed troops to Jordan. Eisenhower sent Under Secretary of State Robert Murphy to Beirut, Lebanon on July 17; Later after visiting Egypt, Jordan, and Iraq he returned to America on August 12 with a hopeful report. Dag Hammarskjold also went to the Middle East as a UN representative. General Fuad Chehab became president of Lebanon, but since he, like Chamoun, was a Christian, religious strife with the Moslem continued. It was finally halted in October by the appointment of a coalition cabinet under Premier Rashid Karami. As order was restored in Lebanon and Jordan, American and British troops were gradually withdrawn.

The settlement of the Jordanian and Lebanese problems left the United States and Britain free to consider METO and Cyprus. Premier Kassem of Iraq told Murphy that his government would reconsider the METO alliance. On July 19 Iraq signed a mutual defense treaty with Nasser and five days later set up several joint committees with the UAR. Iraq drifted away from METO. The United States negotiated closer economic ties with the remaining METO states before the end of 1958, and in February 1959 Britain, Greece, and Turkey negotiated a settlement of the Cyprus question by turning that island into a republic.

Nasser's position was strengthened further when King Hussein dissolved the Arab Federal State of Jordan and Iraq after the Iraqui military coup, and the President of the UAR also met with crown prince Faisal of Saudi Arabia during August 1958 to settle the long-standing disputes between Egypt and Saudi Arabia. American intervention in Lebanon had again raised Nasser's prestige as the leader of Arab nationalism but before the end of 1958 he realized that he had won a Phyrric victory. The rapid growth of pro-Communist (not necessarily pro-Russian) strength in Iraq's government alarmed him. On February 7, 1959 the anti-Communist members of Kassem's cabinet resigned and were replaced by a socialist group. At the same time Russia offered greater economic assistance to Iraq. Nasser feared Communist infiltration in Iraq and Syria. He discovered, as did the man in the Arabian story

97

who permitted his camel to poke its nose under the tent flap—it was impossible to keep the beast from taking over the whole tent. As the Russians gained footholds in Iraq, they were able to use the precedents established by the Eisenhower Doctrine and the Lebanon intervention to justify armed assistance to Kassem.

Quemoy and Matsu ... a desultory kind of Warfare ...

During 1957 the threat of an Asian war lessened as China became less belligerent. However, this did not diminish the possibility of increased subversion and propaganda and, at the Canberra meeting of SEATO foreign ministers, various methods were discussed for meeting this problem. China's passive attitude throughout most of 1957 was probably due to an internal problem. By 1957 popular discontent against the First Five Year Plan to revolutionize China's economy had increased. Mao Tse-tung was unable to put the second plan into effect as scheduled but adopted an interim plan. While China reconsolidated its position at home it was less belligerent abroad. However, Mao did not neglect subtle means of flanking America's Pacific alliances. China echoed the "Five Principles of Peaceful Coexistence," called for an all-Asian defense treaty, and sought to conclude favorable trade pacts with her neighbors. By the end of 1957 there seemed to be no noticeable gain of Communist influence in Thailand, Malaya, Pakistan, and the Philippines, nor did there seem to be an immediate Red menace in South Viet-Nam, Burma, Ceylon, or Indonesia. The only danger came from increased Communist pressure in Laos, Cambodia, and Nepal. The accession of Premier Nobosuke Kishi in Japan marked the beginning of a period when Japan reclaimed her independence. Kishi was neither a neutralist nor a pro-Communist, but he wished to reach an accomodation which would benefit Japan. After he visited Eisenhower in June, the United States began to cut its ground forces in Japan but would not yield on the question of Chinese trade or give the Japanese a role in administering the occupied islands. Kishi acted unilaterally on the trade question. America's European allies had ruled, in spite of protest, that Chinese trade would be placed on the same basis as western trade with Russia's European satellites, and Kishi adopted this position on Japanese-Chinese trade. The Washington talks led also to the formation of the Japanese-American Committee on Security to discuss all problems arising out of the security pact between the two countries.

There had been some anti-American demonstrations on Formosa in

1957. In August, 1958 the Red Chinese suddenly intensified their shelling of Nationalist-held islands while Foreign Minister Chen Yi announced that this was a preliminary to a liberation of Quemoy and Matsu. Both Eisenhower and Dulles announced that any attempt to seize the islands would be a breach of peace. The Seventh Fleet was alerted and reinforced and on August 29 the State Department explained that the offshore islands were an intimate part of Formosa. America warned Peiping that any fighting in that area would not be contained. On September 4 Dulles explained the administration's position. He called attention to the terms of the American-Formosan mutual defense treaty and the resolution adopted by Congress defining America's position on Quemoy and Matsu. Eisenhower was prepared, Dulles said, to order military measures if the attack on Quemoy menaced Formosa. On September 11 the President reaffirmed his Secretary of State's explanation and blamed Peiping for having caused the new crisis. A series of conferences between the American and Chinese amabassadors to Poland, Jacob Dyneley Beam and Wang Ping-nan, failed to find a solution.

The Seventh Fleet convoyed Nationalist supplies to Quemoy during the Communist bombardment. Suddenly on October 6, after daily bombardment since August 23, the Chinese announced they would suspend hostilities for seven days and on October 13 they extended the truce for two weeks. During the truce the Nationalists reinforced the islands and rejected a Red offer for direct negotiations. The American convoy had been discontinued as soon as the truce went into effect. Eisenhower said it would not be resumed unless the Reds reopened the attack, while Peiping announced that the bombardment would not be resumed unless American ships resumed convoy duty. Suddenly on October 20 the shelling of Quemoy and other islands began again. The Communists claimed that American ships had entered Quemoy waters, an allegation which Dulles denied. On October 25, the intensive shelling of Quemoy gave way to a bombardment limited to the odd-numbered days of the month. Gradually it settled down to a desultory kind of warfare in which the Communist and Nationalist batteries exchanged occasional salvos. By the end of October 1958 Dulles reported that the threat of an imminent attack on either Quemoy or the other islands had passed.

Europe moves closer to cooperation

The recession and the economy wave which swept America in 1957 had repercussions on foreign policy. Eisenhower's mutual security program was drastically cut. He also asked for a Development Loan Fund with an appropriation of $500,000,000 for the first year and $750,000,000 for each of the two following years. Congress passed the measure but reduced the funds. The reappearance of a dollar-gap among the western allies during the winter of 1956-57 added to the economic problems. In his book, *Tides of Crisis,* Adolphe Berle pointed out that in the long run America's western alliance would crumble unless the United States integrated the economies of all participants. A military alliance could not stand without a strong economic and political basis, since no nation would stay in a military alliance just to save somebody else. Eisenhower was aware of that fact. He called for increased foreign trade, overseas investments, tariff adjustments, and a revision of America's immigration laws. In 1957 he made a second unsuccessful attempt to persuade Congress to join the Organization for Trade Cooperation. However, he did persuade Congress to approve the International Atomic Energy Agency which had been established in Europe in October 1956. Congress also cut State Department and United States Information Agency funds in 1957 and precipitated a long debate over the revision of the status of forces agreements with the allies which gave them the right to try American personnel for certain offenses committed while overseas. The debate was sparked by a highly publicized case involving a young soldier, William S. Girard, who was placed on trial before a Japanese court for killing a woman. The Defense Department finally permitted the trial to proceed, and on July 11 the Supreme Court upheld this decision.

The decision to cast a protective mantle over the Middle East placed additional strains on American military forces and raised the question of whether the United States should rely on massive retaliation or be prepared to fight local wars. If the United States committed itself to fighing local wars it then had to face the additional question of conventional or atomic weapons. In *Nuclear Weapons and Foreign Policy and Limited War: The Challenge to American Strategy* the authors, Henry A. Kissinger and Robert Endicott Osgood, were persuaded that tactical atomic weapons would be used. The notion of massive retaliation had been sold to the public as an economy move, but by 1957 this had become illusory. Defense costs rose constantly. Each new scientific advance meant costlier weapons. It was equally true that the increased national wealth and a rising standard of living made increased defense costs bearable but it did not mean any reduction in the amount of money spent. While Eisenhower asked for more defense funds for the fiscal year 1958, Secretary of the

Treasury Humphrey warned of a recession unless taxes were cut. Congress appropriated thirty-four billions for defense. In the meantime, the Defense Department was spending at a rate to exceed forty billions in fiscal 1958. Drastic cuts were initiated at once. Contracts were cancelled, research on new weapons was suspended, naval vessels were "mothballed," and the Air Force was reduced to 123 wings. When the budget was first presented, Eisenhower and Secretary of Defense Wilson insisted that any reductions in defense outlays would leave the nation unprotected but when they began to reduce the armed forces the propaganda line was altered. The administration revived the "more bangs for a buck" philosophy of previous years as it explained that the nation would actually be better defended through consolidation and increased efficiency.

The reduction of ground forces did not meet with the approval of NATO commander Lauris Norstad. Ground forces were necessary, he maintained, to protect American bases in Europe and to save the continent from being overrun while massive retaliation was being launched. NATO was ill-prepared in 1957 to meet a Soviet attack but talk of reductions continued under British leadership. Driven by economic exigencies, Britain began to restudy her defense posture early in 1957. On April 4 an official report made it clear that Britain intended to cut her manpower, create an atomic striking force, and to maintain in Britain a highly mobile reserve which could be quickly transported to threatened areas. By 1962 British armed forces were to be cut from 690,000 to 375,000. France was worried that a British and American reduction in NATO forces would enhance the importance of Germany. Other NATO states also proposed arms reductions. On April 12 the United States announced that it would soon be ready to supply several NATO states with Honest John, Matador, and Nike missiles but Norstad insisted that even these, plus the growing supply of tactical atomic weapons, were insufficient reasons for cutting western arms programs. Little could be done to halt the arms reduction.

The European states had come to feel insignificant in 1957. The threat of Russian rocketry had exposed Europe's vulnerability. Moreover, America's reaction to the Suez venture convinced Britain and France they could not always count on their ally. It was partly for this reason that Britain was seeking to free herself of complete reliance on the Strategic Air Command by building her own atomic arsenal. Premiers Guy Mollet of France and Paul-Henri Spaak of Belgium took the lead in a movement to unite Europe as a third force. On February 8, 1957 the former spoke his thoughts on the subject:

For each of our countries, Europe offers the only opportunity for real independence. Besides those colossi, which the Soviet Union and the United States are, what European country can claim to make its own views prevail? Before an America sometimes too impulsive, sometimes too slow to understand dangers, and a Soviet Union which is the cause of disquietude and at times is still menacing, a united Europe will become a world force, not neutral but independent, will have a great part to play and will enable our peoples to make their contribution to the peace.

Widespread discussion of plans to create common agencies for markets atomic energy, communication, transportation, and agriculture, bore fruit in the signing of two treaties at Rome on March 25, 1957 by France, Western Germany, Italy, and the Benelux states. These treaties established a European Economic Community and a European Atomic Community (Euratom). The agreements provided for commissions to manage these two international agencies, which were destined to take their place with the European Coal and Steel Community as means of integrating western Europe. An assembly composed of parliamentary representatives from each of the participating states administered the three communities.

Russia thundered against the Rome treaties and the decision to supply NATO with American missiles but she could do little about them until her domestic difficulties were settled. On February 15, 1957 a change in Soviet foreign policy was heralded by the replacement of Shepilov by Andrei Gromyko. Within a few weeks Khrushchev seemed to be returning to his 1956 soft-line. In June the ground suddenly began to slip from beneath his feet. Once again he showed himself a worthy successor to Lenin and Stalin as he outmaneuvered his enemies in the presidium. The party and the army stood behind Khrushchev; Malenkov, Kaganovich, Molotov, and Shepilov were sent to minor posts in distant provinces. Khrushchev felt so certain of his position that he was able to forego the customary liquidation of his opponents. Even Bulganin lost power, although he remained as premier. Marshall Georgi A Zhukov, who assured Khrushchev of army support, rose to prominence in the new regime. Khrushchev's victory was followed by an official explanation that the culprits had opposed vital domestic policies and had "attempted in effect to oppose the Leninist policy of peaceful coexistence between states with different social systems, of relaxing international tension and establishing friendly relations between the USSR and all the peoples of the world."

The Russians were given an opportunity to show their interest in coexistence at the conference of the UN Subcommittee on Disarmament which went on in London throughout most of 1957. The United States insisted that disarmament had to be preceded by the settlement of outstanding political problems. The major stumbling block was again the atomic bomb. There were two areas of dispute: the control of the bomb and the end of testing. The United States wanted some form of open sky inspection but the Russian delegate, Valerian A. Zorin, favored only a renunciation of atomic weapons. Neither Dulles nor disarmament representative Harold Stassen found this acceptable. At one point the Russians seemed on the verge of accepting some form of aerial inspection but on August 27 they rejected it. From that moment until the conference adjourned on September 6 they concentrated on their demand to end bomb testing. This had a wide propaganda appeal. America was not in favor of ending tests without first reaching some general disarmament agreement but eventually Stassen indicated a willingness to accept some suspension of testing provided the Reds accepted other phases of America's program. Throughout the entire negotiation not one of the disarmament questions was handled individually. Both the American and Russian delegations presented omnibus proposals to end testing, control the production of fissionable material, renounce the use of atomic energy for war, limit convential armaments, and inspect military installations. Although it was occasionally possible to agree on one of the points neither government would buy the other's "package deal."

Sputnik and the control of atomic weapons

In the midst of the London talks the Russians announced on August 26 that they had successfully completed tests of intercontinental ballistic missiles. America greeted this announcement with skepticism despite the corroborating evidence of overseas observers. The United States did not expect to be able to supply its allies with intermediate range missiles for at least another year. It seemed impossible that Russia could be ahead on missile development. The United States was caught flatfooted when Russia launched a satellite, *Sputnik I,* on October 4. They proved the first experiment was not a fluke when they sent *Sputnik II* into orbit on

November 3. It contained no explosive warhead; only the first space explorer and martyr, a dog. The Russians had scored a major victory and it was not diminished by American efforts to ridicule the satellite as a "silly bauble" or a "global basketball." America's missile program had lagged badly through a lack of direction and funds, and there were too few leaders in Washington who understood the psychological advantage of getting the first satellite into orbit. The Russians knew this could mean a victory in the Cold Peace and they bent every effort toward success.

The administration added that although the Russians might have secured a temporary advantage in one area of research, they had not upset the power balance. The United States still possessed enough conventional aircraft to flatten Russia if a war began, and in the meantime she could close the gap in missile research. The public awaited America's first satellite experiment. On December 6 the prestige of the United States suffered severe damage when the Vanguard rocket, which was to catapult a satellite into outer space, exploded on the ground after an elaborate, suspense-building countdown of many hours duration. The United States suddenly became the object of ridicule. Russian science had given the world the first satellite in 1957, said the joksters, while American genius had given the world the Edsel, undoubtedly a fine car but not to be compared with *Sputnik*.

The remaining months of 1957 were filled with drama. The Russians knew they had scored a major victory. Khrushchev exploited it to the full. On October 7 he told the American public through a *New York Times* interview, "I think I will not be revealing any military secret if I tell you that we now have all the rockets we need." The world learned the obvious lesson. Confidence in American leadership was shaken. Khrushchev rattled the sabre, grew more obstinate, and more reckless. He demanded that the United States alter its foreign policy and drop the notion that socialism was doomed. His position in Russia became even more secure when, on October 26, he ousted his former ally, Zhukov, the Minister of Defense. On November 6 the Supreme Soviet met to celebrate the fortieth anniversary of the revolution. Khrushchev predicted the ultimate victory of socialism and called for the end of colonialism. He also suggested a summit conference. On December 3 the United States replied that such a conference would be unable to solve existing problems and reaffirmed its confidence in the UN as a suitable arena for negotiation.

The General Assembly of the UN was in session when the Russians launched their satellite. Interest immediately revived in disarmament. The United States offered the same proposals that the West had made at the London disarmament meeting. In the West's "working paper", presented in London on August 29, the United States had agreed to consider a maximum bomb-test-suspension of two years, but this was made contingent upon Russian acceptance of the rest of America's proposals. These included provisions for stopping the production of fissionable materials for war purposes, limitations on conventional armaments, and aerial inspection. Once again it proved to be impossible to reach any agreement.

The failure to reach a disarmament agreement enhanced the importance of the NATO council, meeting in December 1957. So grave was the situation that the heads of state, including Prime Minister Macmillan and French Premier Félix Gaillard, attended. Eisenhower suffered a mild stroke on November 25 but he came to the conference on December 16. The Russians kept up a steady clamor for a summit conference. They knew that Eisenhower and Dulles wanted agreements with the western allies for IRBM launching sites similar to the agreement America had made with Britain when Eisenhower and Macmillan met in Bermuda in March. These missiles were not available but they would be in production before the ICBM. It was America's intention to deploy them in Europe to offset Russia's possession of long-range missiles. In the final communique the NATO leaders supported the London disarmament proposals and suggested another foreign ministers' conference to Russia. No definite settlement was reached on the request for missile sites. This was left to negotiation between the United States and individual NATO countries.

In 1958 there was no lightening of spirit in the direct relations among the United States, the West, and Russia. The Lebanese flareup and the Quemoy bombardment were minor crises in comparison with the events in Europe. On January 5 a report was issued by the Rockefeller Brothers' Fund. After fourteen months of study their investigators drew a depressing picture of America's power: "For perhaps the next two years we still possess a superiority in strategic striking power, and any Soviet attack on us would meet a crushing reply. But our position a year or two hence depends on decisions which must be taken immediately. Unless present trends are reversed, the world balance of power still shifts in favor of the Soviet bloc."

This disquieting news spurred more American missile research and kept alive the talk of disarmament and international atomic control. The

United States reclaimed lost prestige on January 31, 1958 when the Army succeeded in placing a small 30.8 pound satellite, *Explorer I*, into orbit by means of a modified Jupiter-C rocket. After repeated failures the Navy's Vanguard project finally bore fruit on March 17 with the successful launching of a 3¼ pound satellite. The Russians dwarfed these achievements on May 15 by launching a 2,925 pound satellite. America and Russia aimed other rockets at the moon. The American public was delighted when an Air Force Thor Able rocket reached an altitude of 79,173 miles in October and when the Air Force fired a one hundred ton Atlas ICBM in November for its full range of over six thousand miles. In January and February 1959 both Russia and the United States fired satellites which went into orbit around the sun, but the Russian achievement was more spectacular. Their payload weighed 3,238 pounds to America's 13.4 pounds and passed within five thousand miles of the moon —a remarkable tribute to Russian instrumentation.

On December 10, 1957 Bulganin set off a chain reaction of proposals and counter proposals when he called for a summit conference to discuss various problems including the control of atomic weapons. He suggested such things as a non-aggression pact, a ban on atomic bomb testing, an agreement among Russia, Britain, and America to control atomic weapons, and the so-called Polish plan (proposed by Foreign Minister Adam Rapacki) which provided for the denuclearization of a wide area in eastern Europe. Eisenhower offered counter proposals including an agreement to control outer space, a permanent ban on atomic testing, reduction of conventional armaments, and controls on the production of nuclear weapons. Premier Bulganin and Khrushchev, who replaced him as Premier on March 27, continued to exchange letters with the western heads of state. America and Russia were as far apart as ever. The United States assented to a summit conference in principle but insisted that preparation would have to be made through a foreign ministers conference or regular diplomatic channels—a sop to her allies. Finally on April 11, 1958 the Russians accepted the West's proposals for ambassadorial talks. These would set the stage for a foreign ministers conference and an ultimate summit meeting. The Russians wanted to limit the foreign ministers meeting to procedural matters only; the United States wished it to discuss substantive matters too. The question soon became academic, however, for when Gromyko began to meet with the American, British, and French ambassadors in Moscow on April 17 the West protested that he should meet them together rather than separately. The Russians refused to do this since they would be outnumbered by the three western powers. The failure of the lower level conference put the quietus on talk for upper level meetings, although during the Lebanese crisis Khrushchev volunteered to come to the United States for a summit talk. This proposal also evaporated when neither side could agree on whether the meeting should be held in conjunction with the UN or as a separate conference.

The diplomatic interchange concerning a summit conference was accompanied by negotiations for a conference to control atomic testing. On March 31, 1958 the Russians suddenly announced the suspension of further tests. Eisenhower, who dismissed the Russian announcement as valueless since they had previously completed their current testing program, indicated that the United States would continue its tests at Eniwetok in April but also said that America was willing to discuss the questions of detection and disarmament. After considerable negotiation the two nations agreed to call a conference of experts at Geneva on July 1 to devise means of detecting bomb tests. The United States made it clear that it would not automatically suspend further tests if the experts agreed on methods of detection. The conference, which remained in session until August 22, made some suggestions on test detection.

In the meantime the United States continued its tests in spite of serious opposition from Nobel prize winner Dr. Linus Pauling and other scientists who said the tests were polluting the atmosphere and would eventually have undesirable effects on the health and eugenics of the race. In August the Russians announced that they would supply nuclear weapons to Red China, although they denounced the United States in February for agreeing to supply Britain with ICBMs. America's decision to supply Germany with nuclear weapons had also been scored by the Russians who said it had changed the entire picture of German unification.

On August 22 Eisenhower announced that the United States would suspend tests for one year if the Russians would do the same and would attend another conference at Geneva on October 31 to find some means of stopping tests and for setting up controls based on the recommendations of the detection experts. Russia joined the United States and Britain in Geneva but no basis for agreement could be found. On September 30, 1958 the Russians also resumed their bomb tests, which they did, Dulles said, because the Geneva conference had revealed they were lagging behind the West in atomic research.

Charles de Gaulle resumes leadership in France.

During 1957 Eisenhower and Dulles were criticized for regarding the French North African revolt as a domestic problem. Early in 1958 America was drawn into the debacle when French planes (American built) bombed a Tunisian village. The State Department sent expert Robert D. Murphy to negotiate between Paris and Tunisian leader Habib Bourguiba but a compromise was impossible. On April 16 Premier Félix Gaillard resigned because of the Tunisian problem. Algeria, however, was still the main French concern. On January 31, 1958 the French drafted a reform measure offering the Algerians a semi-autonomous status in which Christian and Moslem rights would be protected. They refused to concede independence and rebel resistance stiffened. There were many rightists in Algeria who objected to the way the French were handling the entire rebellion and on May 13, as representative of both the military and civilian population, they revolted against the new government of Premier Pierre Pflimlin. They accused it of intending to negotiate with the rebels. General Jacques Massu formed a committee of public safety in Algeria and demanded Charles de Gaulle's return to power. There were similar rightist demonstrations in Paris. Pflimlin denied that he intended to yield to the rebels and he ordered General Raoul Salan to assume full military authority in Algeria. Massu's committee placed itself under Salan's direction and he, in turn, extended recognition to a seventy-one member committee which was established to coordinate all the committees of public safety which had been formed in Algeria. This committee also called for the return of de Gaulle.

On June 1 de Gaulle assumed the premiership with six months of dictatorial power. He alternated his attention between the Algerian revolt and drafting a new constitution for France. He did not offer the Algerian nationalists independence but he did offer conciliation, closer links with metropolitan France, and promises of liberty, well-being, and dignity for each Algerian. An Arab Nationalist Republic of Algeria, set up in Cairo in September, insisted that it would consider nothing but independence. The rightists in Algeria, who had sponsored the uprising against Pflimlin, were not entirely satisfied with de Gaulle's promises. They suspected he intended to make too many concessions to Arab nationalism. De Gaulle acknowledged that the Fourth Republic was moribund and he set out to draft a stronger constitution which was submitted to the electorate on September 2. De Gaulle had promised that any portion of the French empire which did not approve of the new constitution would be granted immediate independence and on September 29 he accorded this privilege to French Guinea. Every other state within the empire—including Algeria —had approved the constitution by handsome majorities. The Algerian nationalists boycotted the election. On October 23 de Gaulle offered to open direct negotiations with Algerian rebel leaders to end a war that had cost the lives of seven thousand French soldiers and nearly eighty thousand rebels but the offer was rejected. As 1959 began it was apparent that Algerians were still strongly opposed to French control although most of the voters had already assented to the new constitution which bound the country close to France.

In November 1958 the French voters elected the conservative candidates in the first election under the newly inaugurated Fifth Republic. In January 1959 de Gaulle became its first President.

The Russians begin their move to force the West from Berlin.

American concern over readjustments in France obscured the deeper problems growing out of German reunion and rearmament. George Kennan, the author of the containment policy, had warned of a new German crisis in his book, *Russia, the Atom and the West,* in 1957. The division of Germany, Kennan maintained, could no longer endure. He suggested that the time had come for a bold policy based on a withdrawal of both western and Russian forces from Germany so that it could be neutralized. He admitted the danger in a policy that would virtually destroy NATO but he felt that it would be no less risky than the West's current policy which would possibly lead to war. In 1958 the Russians began their drive for victory in Germany. In April, Anastas Mikoyan told Konrad Adenauer that German unification was no longer a question to be settled by free elections but only through direct negotiation between the two German states. In November the Russians began their move to force the West from Berlin when they announced a plan for a "Free City" of Berlin. They said that complete control of western military traffic into the city would be turned over to the Communist East German government within six months unless the West accepted their proposal. Eisenhower was just as insistent that the West would not budge from Berlin.

The Russians gave the western power until May 27, 1959 to comply with their request. While Khrushchev hinted that Russia now possessed atomic superiority, western diplomats planned their strategy. Dulles made a hurried trip to Europe while Prime Minister Macmillan visited both Russia and the United States. The western powers were determined to maintain their position in Berlin but they were resolved not to abandon negotiation. The United States had opposed a summit conference and both Eisenhower and Dulles had used every expedient to avoid one since 1955. At last it was announced that the western powers would assent to a summit conference during the summer if proper preparations were made by a foreign ministers' conference on May 11. This was a major concession by the United States. The Russians agreed to attend the foreign ministers' conference in Geneva, and on March 6 Khrushchev indicated that Russia might delay its May 27 deadline for turning over its occupation functions to East Germany. Shortly after his return from Europe, Dulles admitted that he was suffering from a return of cancer. While he was hospitalized, Dulles' duties were assumed by Undersecretary of State Christian Herter. Dulles' illness soon forced his resignation and he was replaced by Herter. The West lost a firm and able negotiator at a very critical time. In April Konrad Adenauer announced that he would soon give up the Chancellorship in Germany. The President was compelled to take a more active role in foreign affairs. For many months Khrushchev had been trying to come face-to-face with Eisenhower. He had proposed a Big-Two summit talk in 1957 and at the time of the Lebanon crisis offered to come to the UN Security Council for a summit talk but this had been overruled by Red China. In his talks with Macmillan, Khrushchev again hinted that he wished to converse directly with Eisenhower and with no one else. Barring unexpected developments such a tete-à-tête would most likely occur late in the summer of 1959.

Human ingenuity . . . faced one of its severest tests.

New Year's Day 1959 arrived under inauspicious circumstances. Faced with a solemn Russian deadline, the West considered the inevitability of World War III. The constant ebb and flow of tension, the proposals and counter proposals, the kaleidoscopic pattern of crises in one area and another, the alternation of threats with honeyed words of coexistence, the interminable negotiation, the mountainous promises laboring to produce mice-like results seemed to have led again to a threat of war. The West was moving back after ten years to another Berlin Blockade. It was most exasperating, and there had been, as Macmillan remarked in 1957, "a kind of wearying of the spirit, because the struggle goes on so long, year after year, and the peoples do not see the end of it." At the last moment another reprieve arrived when the offer of a foreign ministers' conference was made and accepted.

The possibility that the world was moving toward a settlement of Central European affairs in 1959 enabled many to view the foreign policy developments of 1957 and 1958 with greater leniency. There had been both victories and defeats. In the Far East a line had been drawn again at Quemoy and the Red Chinese were compelled to drop their boasts that they would soon liberate Formosa. As 1959 began they suffered a widespread insurrection in Tibet and their ruthless efforts to extirpate the rebels compelled many of the eastern neutralist states to take another look at peaceful coexistence. Even Nehru welcomed the dispossessed Dalai Lama of Tibet in India. Middle East threats had been met successfully by the Eisenhower Doctrine which was the basis for intervention in Lebanon. Although Lebanon was saved, Iraq was lost. On March 24, 1959 Iraq withdrew from the METO alliance and left a dangerous gap in the northern tier, a situation which Washington tried to rectify by concluding bilateral treaties with Turkey, Pakistan, and Iran on March 5. These treaties offered American aid without involving the United States directly in METO. On the other hand, the Eisenhower Doctrine of intervention had provided the Russians with a precedent whereby they could legally intervene in Middle Eastern affairs to aid their friends. In April 1949 when Kassem's pro-Communist regime in Iraq was faced with possible overthrow, it was reported that Russian Kurd "volunteers" crossed the border to sustain him. In the American hemisphere during 1957 and 1958 there were revolts against dictators Marcos Pérez Jiménez of Venezuela and Fulgencio Batista of Cuba. Although the first of these failed after a few days, the second was carried to a successful conclusion early in 1959 by its leader Fidel Castro. During these years there was also an increase of anti-Americanism in South America. Good will ambassador Richard Nixon was subjected to villification and even physical abuse in Peru, Venezuela, Uruguay, Paraguay, and Colombia during an eighteen day tour in May 1958. So serious did the difficulties become that the President rushed marines to Puerto Rico and the Cuban naval base as a precaution.

The threat of a Berlin war kept the defense question alive. The West's defense premises were in need of overhauling. In line with recommendations made at the head-of-state NATO council meeting in December 1957 the foreign ministers of NATO, who met in April 1958, approved, in principle, plans to increase NATO ground forces to a maximum of thirty-two divisions and to speed up arms modernization programs. The Russians and their satellites were reputed to have 150 available divisions. The central theme of the defense debate had remained unchanged as 1959 began. The West still heeded the wisdom of the statement facetiously attributed to movie producer Sam Goldwyn, "Watch the A-bomb. It's dynamite." America had insisted that the West would triumph because of its power and technological know-how, but *Sputnik I* seriously weakened that thesis. Dulles had built a foreign policy on the notion that right would win. He saw history as a drama in which the forces of good would ultimately triumph because of the inexorable working of a universal moral principle. In some respects he sounded almost Marxian in his conviction that the Communist state would "wither away" and be supplanted by democracies. His continued insistence upon conducting foreign policy solely on a moral basis was criticized and so was the notion that a righteous cause would win. European states, with long histories of victories and defeats, were skeptical of both these premises, which had found a receptive audience in America because of an unblemished record of military victory. In America, only a Southerner, with the history of the Confederacy before him, might question the thesis that a "righteous" cause must win. An agonizing reappraisal of defense policy was underway as 1959 began.

The budget for fiscal 1960 called for 40.8 billions for national defense, a sum which Eisenhower said was adequate. His opponents, however, insisted that the President had made a fetish of a balanced budget and that he was sacrificing security by holding down expenditures to unrealistic limits. Arrayed against Eisenhower and Defense Secretary McElroy was an impressive list of critics: Democratic Senators Lyndon Johnson, Stuart Symington, Paul Douglas, and Richard Russell, Army Chief of Staff General Maxwell D. Taylor who wanted an army of 925,000 men rather than 870,000, Naval Chief of Staff Admiral Arleigh Burke who wanted a Marine Corps of 200,000 rather than 175,000 as well as more planes, missiles, and research. In 1959 the United States was reputed to have fourteen combat divisions. The Strategic Air Command had approximately two thousand planes operating from nearly 300 bases. The Sixth and Seventh Fleets consisted of about thirty-six ships and 250 planes each. The United States had 1,800-mile-range Thor missiles and two-hundred-mile-range Redstone missiles in Europe. It was reported that Russia would have a three-to-one advantage in missiles by 1960-61. If such were the case, diplomacy of the highest order was the only answer. It remained to be seen whether Dulles' successor, Christian Herter, would be able to provide the brilliant leadership so necessary to survival. In *Nuclear Weapons and Foreign Policy* Kissinger suggested that "one of the paradoxical lessons of the nuclear age is that at the moment when we have at our disposal an unparalleled degree of power, we are driven to realize that the problems of survival can be solved only in the minds of men." Human ingenuity, which had seldom failed in the past, faced one of its severest tests.

VIII THE EISENHOWER ADMINISTRATION

Beginning the Lame Duck Years

"There were signs of disenchantment. . . ."

On May 15, 1957 Eisenhower told reporters that he had grown more conservative since 1952 but, although believing in "sound fiscal policies", he also felt that "some reasonable solution" would have to be found for meeting the people's needs in the 1950's. Never before had a President been given such a popular mandate to find that reasonable solution. It was logical to expect that the second term would be marked by an aggressive and far-reaching domestic program. There were high hopes that much would be done in 1957. However, little was done, and the failure to produce a significant body of domestic legislation stood out in stark contrast against the mountainous vote of confidence Eisenhower had received in 1956. The twenty-second amendment, which made him a "lame duck" President, ill-health, and a continuation of passive leadership worked against Eisenhower. He only made a strong fight for his defense and foreign aid programs.

During 1957 and 1958 there was a marked increase in criticism of the President. In retrospect, the *New York Times* editorialized, "As 1957 unfolded it was unmistakable that Mr. Eisenhower himself was losing political strength . . . He no longer seemed to have the invulnerability to criticism that characterized his first term. There were signs of disenchantment among important groups of voters." Eisenhower entered his second term with only three changes in his cabinet: Mitchell, Folsom, and Seaton. He made more changes during the first two years of his second term than he did during his entire first term administration; Robert B. Anderson, Neil H. McElroy, and William P. Rogers replaced Humphrey, Wilson, and Brownell in 1957, and in 1958 Arthur S. Flemming replaced Folsom.

The Eighty-fifth Congress met on January 3, 1957. Lyndon Johnson and William Knowland were Senate majority and minority leaders. Sam Rayburn became Speaker of the House and John W. McCormack and Joseph W. Martin were elected the majority and minority leaders. The first session produced few victories for the President. Trouble began on January 16 when the President submitted his budget for the fiscal year 1958. Conservatives in both parties were angered when the President, who had forseen a balanced budget, recommended further delays in tax cuts. The conservatives were shocked by the highest proposed peace-time budget in history, especially at a time when the President was criticizing the Democrats as "spenders." The President no sooner presented his budget, which presumably represented the administration's official view, when Secretary of the Treasury Humphrey insisted there would be a depression which would "curl your hair" unless drastic cuts were made. Congress made drastic cuts of more than five billion dollars. Defense funds and foreign assistance suffered heavy cuts of $2,400,000,000 and one billion respectively.

... "a 'minimum meaningful program.'"

The most controversial issue during the first session was civil rights. On January 10 Eisenhower asked for a four-point civil rights program based on a bipartisan Civil Rights Commission, a Civil Rights Division within the Department of Justice. He also asked for laws to prevent individuals from interfering with voting during federal elections, to permit citizens to take civil rights cases directly to federal courts, to enable the Department of Justice to file civil suits and to seek federal injunctions in civil rights cases. The National Association for the Advancement of Colored People (NAACP) regarded this as a "minimum meaningful program." Civil rights measures were before Congress during the entire session. Finally, a compromise was reached in the Civil Rights Act of 1957— the first such legislation since Reconstruction days.

The battle for civil rights legislation was fought by a bipartisan bloc headed by Senator Knowland of California against stubborn southern resistance. Although there was no filibuster Senator Strom Thurmond held the floor for twenty-four hours and eighteen minutes in an "educational debate" which set a new record. An amendment offered by Senators Clinton P. Anderson and George D. Aiken knocked out Part III of the bill and reduced it to a right-to-vote measure. They proposed to delete those portions of the bill which gave the Attorney General power to seek injunctions in any type of civil rights case either with or without the victim's consent. Opponents of the measure insisted that this provision would have given the government power to use federal troops to enforce school desegregation. Eisenhower denied this allegation on July 17 when he told the South, "I can't imagine any set of circumstances that would ever induce me to send federal troops . . . to enforce the orders of a federal court."

The second controversial portion of the bill provided that any disobedience of a federal injunction would be punished under contempt of court proceedings without a jury trial. A revised amendment offered by Senators Estes Kefauver, Henry M. Jackson, Frank Church, and Joseph C. O'Mahoney guaranteed jury trials in criminal contempt cases arising from more than forty laws (the House later limited this to the right-to-vote law). Attorney General Brownell argued that no southern jury would find a white man guilty of interfering with Negro voting rights and the federal judiciary would be weakened by the law. This amendment, which broke the power of the civil rights law, was said to have been planned by Senators Richard Russell and Lyndon Johnson.

Although enacted, the law was a far cry from the "minimum meaningful program." It provided for the creation of a six-member bipartisan Commission on Civil Rights and a Special Civil Rights Division in the Department of Justice. The Attorney General was authorized to seek federal injunctions or other forms of relief against interference with voting rights. The judges were given power to try offenders for contempt of court without a jury but the defendant was entitled to a second trial, with jury, if his punishment exceeded a fine of three hundred dollars or forty-five days imprisonment. The maximum fine and imprisonment were $1,000 and six months.

. . . the court responds to historical circumstances.

The question of subversion again raised its head in 1957. Francis E. Walter, chairman of the House UN-American Activities Committee, recommended that the government exercise more control over passports, the mail, and devise stricter measures to compel testimony and punish obstructionism at hearings.

On Representative Walter's two final points the Supreme Court took a decidedly different view. It may not be true, as Mr. Dooley once remarked, that the Supreme Court follows the election returns, but the

117

Court does respond to historical circumstances. In the days of McCarthyism the Court had adopted Oliver Wendell Holmes' concept of a "clear and present danger" and upheld the nation's security laws. By 1957 it was evident that the "perilous night" about which Elmer Davis had written three years earlier in his *But We Were Born Free* was drawing to a close. On May 2 McCarthy died and his replacement by Democrat William Proxmire was regarded by the Republicans as a bitter blow.

The country and the Court moved toward moderation. Since 1953 the Court had undergone some personnel changes. In addition to Chief Justice Earl Warren, Eisenhower had appointed John M. Harlan, William J. Brennan, and Charles E. Whittaker to join the justices Hugo L. Black, Felix Frankfurter, William O. Douglas, Thomas C. Clark, and Harold H. Burton. Burton left the court in 1958 and Eisenhower appointed Potter Stewart to replace him.

In 1957 the Court handed down some decisions which, in the words of John Caughey, author of *In Clear and Present Danger,* were "the most encouraging developments for civil liberties of the whole postwar era." In the Yates case the Court ruled that the mere statement of a belief in the overthrow of the government by force, as an abstract doctrine, was not indictable under the Smith Act and acquitted five California Communists and remanded nine others for retrial. In the Jencks case a labor union official was accused of filing false affidavits under the Taft-Hartley Act. The Court ruled that Clinton E. Jencks had not been able to defend himself because he was denied access to FBI files containing statements against him. Various groups were shocked by these decisions. "Well, comrades, you've got what you wanted," said the *Cleveland Plain Dealer,* "The Supreme Court has handed it to you on a platter. Come and get us." J. Edgar Hoover of the FBI complained that the Jencks' decision made it harder to collect evidence. In August 1957 Congress passed a law to the effect that no FBI file would be opened unless the witness testified. If the witness testified and the defendant wished to see the files, they would be turned over to him after the trial judge had first examined them and excised those portions which were not relevant to the witness's testimony.

As congressional adjournment approached in August very little had been accomplished. At a press conference the President was asked if he was satisfied with his relations with Congress and whether or not a more aggressive presidential approach was in order. "I . . . never employ threats," explained the President, "I never try to hold up clubs of any kind. I just say 'This is what I believe to be best for the United States,' and I try to convince people by the logic of my position." After adjournment on August 30 Eisenhower admitted that he was not satisfied with what Congress had done, although he praised it for passing his Middle East resolution, the civil rights and FBI file laws, and the resolution to permit American participation in the International Atomic Energy Agency. He was disappointed that Congress had not passed laws requiring the registration of union welfare and pension funds and the publication of financial statements, flood insurance, and tax relief for small businessmen. He was equally disappointed over the failure to provide for adequate foreign aid, to admit Hawaii and Alaska to statehood, to increase postal rates, or to provide a formal method of presidential succession in the event of an illness that impaired the usefulness of the chief executive. His efforts to foster a succession amendment gave rise to a rumor, widely circulated by editors Louis Seltzer of the *Cleveland Press* and Ralph McGill of the *Atlanta Constitution,* that the President intended to step down in favor of Nixon. Eisenhower called this the "worst rot" he had ever heard but rumors of his impending retirement persisted throughout 1957 and were accentuated when he suffered an illness on June 9, which, fortunately, proved to be no worse than an upset stomach.

Some measures passed which could be considered achievements. The McCarran-Walter Immigration Act was amended to permit the entry of approximately 60,000 more immigrants and made special provision for orphans adopted by Americans overseas as well as fifty diplomats who might break with their own governments and 1,500 specialists and technicians. The act also revalidated more than 18,000 visas which had not been used when the Refugee Relief Act of 1953 expired at the end of 1956. (This act permitted the admission of 214,000 refugees over a three-year period without regard to 1952 quotas.) Another 8,000 persons were permitted to enter from Spain and certain Iron Curtain countries by cancelling the mortgages against their quotas. Congress made no provision for the 25,000 Hungarian refugees who had been admitted temporarily after the abortive revolution against the Russians.

A compromise housing bill was passed which reduced down payments on government insured housing and provided funds for slum clearance, urban renewal, military, collegiate and co-operative housing mortgages. Congress also continued the soil bank plan and expanded the scope of the Agricultural Trade Development and Assistance Act of 1954 which enabled American surpluses to be bartered abroad for strategic goods.

Two facts stood out at the end of the session. The traditional coalition between the conservative southerners and the conservative Republican legislators disintegrated during the civil rights debate. The southerners were forced to change their strategy from trying to prevent any legislation at all to trying to weaken the bill because they knew a bill of some kind would eventually pass. The second highlight was the opposition of the Democrats, who heretofore had made a fetish of internationalism, to Eisenhower's Middle East doctrine and foreign aid program, while the traditionally isolationist Republicans gave it wide support. The session was also characterized by partisanship and revealed some widening fissures in the structure of the Republican party. The Old Guard Republicans were thinking ahead to 1960 leadership. When Secretary Humphrey criticized Eisenhower's budget with impunity, the Old Guard opened a general attack on the President. Ultraconservative Senator Barry Goldwater of Arizona made a speech in April in which he said that the President had been lured by "the siren song of socialism." Goldwater deplored the approach of an age in which every American would be "federally born, federally housed, federally clothed, federally educated, federally supported in their occupations, and die a federal death, thereafter to be buried in a federal box in a federal cemetery." He described the New Republicanism as a "splintered concept of Republican philosophy," but the President replied "In this day and time we cannot use the governmental processes that were applicable in 1890." Goldwater and other Old Guard Republicans insisted that Eisenhower had weakened the party. They pointed out that since 1952 Republican strength had declined in both houses of Congress, that Democrats had replaced Republicans in the statehouses of Arizona, Colorado, Connecticut, Iowa, Kansas, Maine, Massachusetts, Minnesota, New Jersey, New York, Oregon, Pennsylvania, and Washington and that Republican strength in the state legislatures had declined by 141 upper house seats and 308 lower house seats. "Conservatives are going to win the next election," said Goldwater, "and the group which wins the 1958 elections will control the 1960 elections."

The Old Guard fought the President successfully because he permitted it. Eisenhower's insistence upon the role of a detached and impartial observer rather than a battling participant weakened his party leadership. "Ike's detachment is one of the reasons for his popularity," wrote *Time,* "it is also one of the reasons for his party's troubles." The Old Guard continued to be troublesome because the President would not be a practical politician who supported his friends and penalized his opponents.

The adjournment of Congress ushered in a critical period in the Eisenhower administration. Troubles had started with the budget battle and were followed by a series of devastating events which shattered the prestige of the administration. The first of these was the school desegregation issue. Marquis Childs, in his biography of the President, called it the "great divided . . . the first series of cataclysmic events that were to bring to an end an era to which the President had given the color of his hopeful, buoyant temperament." This first major crisis was followed by the growing realization that a recession had begun. Then the Russians destroyed American complacancy by beating us across the threshhold of the space age. The country was then disquieted on November 25 by a report that Eisenhower had suffered a blockage in a small brain artery. He was able to resume his duties in a few days, but the nation wondered what effect this new attack would have on the President's vigor. The grave situation late in 1957 required more than a part-time President.

The Little Rock crisis slowed integration to a standstill.

Despite the fact that 122,000 Negroes had been integrated in formerly all-white schools in the District of Columbia and some of the seventeen segregationist states since 1954, integration was still an explosive issue in 1957. The President appeared to be a disinterested spectator. He seemed to have no genuine conviction on the desirability of integration but like a soldier ordered to assault an enemy position, the President appeared to move solely out of a sense of duty. His hand was forced by events in Little Rock, Arkansas.

Plans had been drawn to begin integration in Little Rock in 1957. On September 2 Governor Orval Faubus ordered that a cordon of national guardsmen be placed around the Little Rock Central High School. Two days later, in defiance of the federal district court's order, these troops turned back nine Negro students who attempted to attend classes. Faubus told a national TV audience that he had had evidence that integration in Little Rock would have led to rioting. He argued that since it was the governor's sworn duty to preserve order, he had called out the National Guard. He hinted broadly at some kind of a conspiracy when he said that the federal judgeship in Arkansas had been deliberately left vacant so that a northerner could be brought in at the opportune time. According to Faubus, Judge Ronald N. Davies, who had come to Arkansas temporarily from Fargo, North Dakota, did not have all the facts when he refused to delay integration.

THE EISENHOWER ADMINISTRATION

On September 14, Faubus and Representative Brooks Hays of Little Rock met in Newport, Rhode Island with President Eisenhower, Attorney General Brownell, and Presidential Assistant Sherman Adams. No solution was reached. On September 20 Faubus's attorneys appeared before Judge Davies to show cause why a temporary injunction should not be issued against the governor. The judge was satisfied that integration was "thwarted by the governor" and issued the injunction. Faubus quickly withdrew the guards and a mob assembled outside the school. The Negroes were undaunted and on September 23 the nine students slipped into the school. Integration in Little Rock laster three hours, but eventually Mayor Woodrow Wilson Mann, who meanwhile had requested federal troops in a wire to the President, and Superintendent of Schools Virgil Blossom, decided to withdraw the Negroes because of the tumultuousness of the crowd.

Eisenhower could ignore the issue no longer. He had previously remarked that when he moved "you can bet one thing. It will be quick, hard and decisive." On September 24 he ordered Secretary of Defense Wilson to federalize the Arkansas National Guard and to send regular troops if needed. On September 25 the nine Negro students returned to school under the protection of 1,000 men of the crack 101 Airborne Division who had been flown to Little Rock from Kentucky. Faubus, who had welcomed the brief rioting in Little Rock as vindication of his position, was shocked by the President's decision. Eisenhower placed the entire guilt on Faubus when he said, "My conviction is that had the police powers of the State of Arkansas been used not to frustrate the orders of the court but to support them, the ensuing violence and open disrespect for the law and for the federal judiciary would never have occurred."

While efforts to find a suitable solution continued, the President withdrew five hundred federal troops on October 14, and removed the Federalized Arkansas National Guard from Central High School on May 29, 1958. In June an effort was made to suspend integration in Little Rock for two-and-one-half years, but this was refused by the Eighth U. S. Circuit Court of Appeals in St. Louis. When the Supreme Court upheld this decision, Faubus closed the Little Rock high schools on September 12. He also scheduled a referendum on integration for September 27. Although professing to believe in integration, Faubus loaded the referendum with a qualification that a majority of Little Rock's more than 40,-000 qualified voters would have to vote for integration before it could be adopted. Since fewer than 10,000 voters had ever turned out for a previous school election it was obvious that the chance of getting a majority of the voters to the polls, much less a majority of all eligible voters to vote for integration was slim to say the least. On September 27 the voters defeated integration 19,470 to 7,561.

The Little Rock crisis slowed integration to a standstill. In May 1958 the *Southern School News* reported that only 764 school districts had been integrated while 2,125 remained segregated. Desegregation had moved rapidly in Kentucky, West Virginia, Maryland, Oklahoma, Delaware, Texas, and Missouri. Only fifteen districts had been integrated in Arkansas, North Carolina, and Tennessee, and in the remaining seven states, Alabama, Florida, Georgia, Louisiana, Mississippi, South Carolina, and Virginia, no progress had been made.

During the later months of 1958 public attention shifted to developments in Virginia, one of the seven states in which no move had been made toward segregation. Virginia seemed to be a test state and, as the months passed, other southern states looked to Virginia for leadership. Governor J. Lindsay Almond closed schools in Norfolk, Charlottesville, and Warren County. By the end of 1958 schools were closed to more than 13,000 white students some of whom were idle and others continuing with a makeshift brand of education in private homes, churches, or night classes. Early in 1959 Governor Almond was forced to yield to the federal government and integration was undertaken in the Virginia schools.

Still another device for continuing segregated schools was found in 1957 by the Alabama legislature. It passed a law directing local school boards to consider seventeen factors when assigning students in schools. These were broad enough so there would be little or no trouble in rejecting Negro student applications for several reasons other than race. The law contained no reference to race. Some Negro parents brought suit to test the act, and on November 24, 1958 the Supreme Court in *Shuttlesworth* v. *Birmingham Board of Education* upheld the law "on its face" but inferred that it might be unconstitutional "in application." Conservatives hailed this decision as a means of maintaining almost exclusively segregated schools while still complying with the court's 1954 order. However, the court's threat was apparent, and it would undoubtedly be invoked if the Alabama act were used as a discriminatory measure.

The effect of the integration fight on America's world position cannot be overestimated. Millions throughout the world asked themselves, "If Americans look upon Negroes as inferior, how do they look upon us?" The whole affair, and particularly the dramatic Arkansas episode, played

123

into the Communists' hands, and they exploited it to the full. Eisenhower, because of his reluctance to act before the crisis had been reached, was placed in an unenviable position. Intervention in Little Rock presented the world with the picture of a great democracy overawing its citizens with bayonets. Non-intervention presented the world with a picture of a great democracy unable to handle a minor public official. Faubus, the minor public official, became a world figure. His opponents called him a demagogue trying to insure his own re-election; his friends attributed only the highest motives to his actions, and he insisted that he had only called out the National Guard to prevent disturbances, not to uphold segregation. As proof of his contention, he pointed to the riots which occurred after the Negroes were admitted to school on September 23, but his critics said there would have been no disturbances had he not encouraged the rabble by calling out troops and by his inflamatory utterances.

During the crisis Harry S. Ashmore, editor of Little Rock's *Arkansas Gazette,* published a book entitled *Epitaph for Dixie* in which he maintained that the Old South was doomed. The segregationists, he said, had no hope of victory but only wished to delay the inevitable. While the diehards fulminated against the North, the NAACP, and the courts, they were faced with the inescapable presence of the southern economic revolution, which was destroying segregation, the sharecropping system, and one-party rule. Ashmore called for patience. To those who said that the Negro had been patient long enough, Ashmore replied that Negro rights were not the only factor involved. The economic revolution was remaking the whole social fabric, the political system, and the intellectual climate of the South, and such momentous changes made patience mandatory. On the other hand, whether world opinion would be patient or whether the exigencies of the Cold Peace would force America to move more rapidly in solving a long neglected problem was a question that could not be limited to the confines of the militantly segregationist states.

. . . *unprecedented in a recession.*

Although some businessmen and economists blamed the tight money policy of the Federal Reserve Board for the 1957 and 1958 recession, this was only a minor factor. When the Defense Department found it was spending far ahead of its budgetary allotment it reduced its orders by six billion dollars. Many European states were compelled to reduce their imports. Exports dropped by two billion. There was also a decline of nearly three billion dollars in capital investment for plant-expansion, and a ten billion dollar reduction in inventory buying. The American economy had cut its rate of spending by $21,000,000,000, and a recession was inevitable.

As in most crises in human affairs, there are warnings that are not easily recognizable, or tend to be ignored. A serious break on the stock exchange in October, 1957, was dismissed by Eisenhower as "a breather after a long surge." Between July and October the Dow-Jones industrial average dropped one hundred points. By January, 1958, unemployment reached 4,494,000, the largest number since 1950. The Department of Labor then designated any area with an unemployment rate above six per cent as a "labor surplus area" and made it eligible for additional defense contracts. The January before (1957) there had been nineteen such areas out of 149. This had risen to twenty-four by November 1957, to forty-five by January 1958, and to eighty-six by May 1958. In his press conference on February 26, 1958 the President used the word "recession" for the first time.

As the recession gained momentum early in 1958, both businessmen and politicians called upon the President to prime the economic pump with heavy tax cuts, public works programs, and federal assistance; however, Eisenhower refused to follow what he believed to be drastic courses. Some action was taken. The Federal Reserve Board eased credit restrictions. The liberalization of home down payments and other changes in FHA and veterans' housing legislation stimulated some home construction. Defense spending was increased in key employment areas as were expenditures for urban renewal, natural resource development projects, hospitals, schools, government building and civil work programs. On April 16 the President signed the Federal Aid Highway Act of 1958 which increased federal spending for all classes of highways.

The President urged all Americans to buy more goods. Under ordinary circumstances a recession is a period of retrenchment but savings were at such an all-time high that consumers were able to draw on more than two-hundred billion dollars. The Dow-Jones industrial average went up in 1958. The cost-of-living index rose from 120.2 in June 1957 to 123.9 in July 1958, an unprecedented development in a recession period. A drop in labor income was taken up by loans to the states for the purpose of extending, by fifty per cent, the period during which an unemployed worker could receive compensation. State, local, and industrial pensions, as well as federal social security, gave old folks an income of seventy-five billions.. Since these funds were usually pumped back into the economy within thirty days they provided a powerful economic stimulant. In 1958 the money the American people had available after taxes and necessities—the money they could spend as they liked—was estimated at 104 billions. Never had there been such a demand for gadgets, luxuries, and labor saving devices. Industry was driven to finding means to satisfy these cravings. Although unemployment zoomed to 5,537,000 in June, wages showed an increase, which was again unprecedented in a recession.

It was therefore with considerable confidence that the President reported signs of recovery in May and businessmen, economists, and politicians were optimistic about complete recovery by the end of 1958. Secretary of Labor Mitchell, however, reported that unemployment would remain high during 1959. The upturn of business activity had been solid enough, based as it was on increased spending by business, government and consumers, but increased productivity per man per hour and the entry of more than 800,000 new workers into the labor market annually, created a problem of absorbtion. Economic Sylvia Porter wrote in January 1959 that "unemployment . . . [would be] one of the great challenges of the new year." It was a problem which transcended party lines and it was the major one the Russians insisted we could not solve.

Historian David Potter had sought the key to American character in *People of Plenty* and was sure he had found it in economic abundance. Rising productivity, the goal of America for generations, was the secret of the high living standard that made us the envy of the world. This article of faith was challenged in 1958 by economist John Galbraith in his best-selling book *The Affluent Society*. The author suggested the novel approach of cutting our productive pace to avoid the extremes of economic booms and busts. Increasing production caused inflation and more spiraling of prices and wages thus creating more problems than it solved. Money and energy in America were diverted to the production of too many unnecessary goods and not enough attention was paid to public services. There seemed to be no point in making more cars unless there were roads to accomodate them, or in selling homes to Americans in suburban communities unless we provided them with adequate hospitals, schools, sewers, utilities, fire and police protection. While the Russians concentrated their efforts, we dissipated ours. We were a nation threatened with suffocation in our own trivia and burial under a surfeit of chrome hub caps and plastic seat covers.

The largest budget in peace time history.

The sudden emergence of Russia as a scientific nation compelled the President to present a "space age" budget to the second session of the Eighty-fifth Congress in January 1958. He asked for $73,934,000,000—the largest sum in peace-time history. Unfortunately, Congress had to wrestle with this budget just at a time when the full-force of the recession had hit. It was difficult to stave off tax cuts in spite of an estimated twelve billion dollar deficit. Only a few minor tax changes were finally allowed. Congress voted to spend $76,256,000,000 and an additional $4,194,000,000 in supplemental appropriations for the fiscal year 1958.

On June 6 the President told Republican leaders that he hoped for only four things from Congress: the extension of the Reciprocal Trade Agreements Act, the enactment of his foreign aid and Defense Department reorganization plan, and a "reasonable attitude" on anti-recession legislation. The President scored an impressive victory on all of these points. He was given much cooperation by majority leader Johnson of the Senate and Speaker Rayburn of the House. The *Congressional Quarterly Almanac* reported that forty-seven per cent of the President's program had been passed, which was the highest percentage since the Democrats gained control of Congress. It was a victory for the moderates on most points. The left-wing was beaten on such things as aid to education, high farm supports, a vigorous anti-recession program, and drastic tax cuts, while the right-wing failed to score on bills to restrict the Supreme Court and the labor unions.

The Reciprocal Trade Agreements Act encountered some of the stubbornest opposition since it was originally passed in 1934. The recession made tariff cuts unpopular. The final compromise bill extended the act for four years until June 30, 1962. The new act was a major victory for the President inasmuch as it was the longest time-extension ever voted. Foreign nations could thus be assured of several years of a continuous American trade policy, which was important if the President was going to arrange suitable mutual trade agreements with the newly organized European Economic Community. On other points of his foreign program the President scored victories and suffered defeats. His Mutual Security funds were cut, but this was balanced by congressional approval of a loan of $135,000,000 on May 29 to the European Atomic Community for the construction of six atomic reactors. Congress did not change the naturalization legislation but it finally provided a means for naturalizing the Hungarian refugees who had been admitted in 1956. The United States

Information Agency, which had been badly penalized in 1957 when its director Arthur Larson quarrelled with the Democrats, was given more funds in 1958. The new director, George V. Allen, was more skillful in his public relations with Congress.

On April 3 the President submitted his recommendations for strengthening the Department of Defense. He emphasized that separate land, sea, and air operations were past history. He was careful to avoid congressional hostility to the appointment of a single chief of staff for the entire armed forces or fear that the Navy and Marines might be weakened. A compromise measure emerged on July 24 and was signed by the President on August 6. The three departments of the Army, Navy, and Air Force were to "function under the direction, authority, and control of the Secretary of Defense." The Secretary of Defense was to report, for congressional approval, any transfer, abolition, reassignment or consolidation of service functions that he might propose. However, during war times the President was given the right to transfer existing functions without congressional approval. The service secretaries and service chiefs of staff retained their right of appeal to Congress on their own initiative, a fact which Eisenhower called "legalized insubordination" and which he had tried to prevent in his original recommendation. The Secretary of Defense could consolidate supply and service functions but only the President, through the secretary and with the advice of the Joint Chiefs of Staff, could establish unified commands for combatant missions which would be responsible to him and the Secretary of Defense. The Joint Chiefs of Staff became the Secretary of Defense's assistants in conducting unified command operations and the Joint Staff was expanded from 210 to 400 officers. Officers could be transferred between services if they consented and a Director of Defense Research and Engineering was to coordinate all research activities. The act also included a statement that the Marines, Naval Air Force and National Guard were to remain permanent institutions. The task of implementing this law still confronted Secretary McElroy. Congress also gave the President most of his other defense requests. The Atomic Energy Act of 1954 was amended to make it possible to cooperate more fully in atomic and other scientific research with our allies. Congress also provided for a National Aeronautics and Space Administration to develop a coordinated space program. For national defense the legislators gave Eisenhower $39,602,000,000 or $836,000,000 more than he requested.

The second session of the Eighty-fifth Congress passed other important measures. One of the most significant was an act admitting Alaska to statehood. Statehood bills for Alaska and Hawaii had been repeatedly introduced, and a bill for the former territory was bogged down in the House Rules Committee for several months in 1957. Its supporters eventually bypassed the committee and the bill was accepted on May 28, 1958 by a 208 to 166 vote. Senate Republicans resisted the temptation to combine it with a Hawaiian statehood bill, since, now that this one was approved, they did not wish to send it back to the House. But Democrat Senator A. S. Mike Monroney of Oklahoma delayed the proceedings slightly in a futile attempt to give Alaska a "commonwealth" status. The statehood bill was finally approved on June 30 by a sixty-four to twenty vote. Alaska became the forty-ninth state on January 3, 1959.

Other acts granted a seven per cent increase in social security payments and raised postal rates. A school aid act became a must when the report of the President's Committee on Scientists and Engineers on November 30, 1957 exposed the widening gap between American and Russian scientific education. After Senators James E. Murray of Montana, Pat McNamara of Michigan and Representative Lee Metcalf of Montana tried to introduce bills which combined a government scholarship program with a school construction program the legislators finally passed the National Defense Education Act which authorized $887,000,000 for four-years of which $295,000,000 was to be used for loans to bright students planning to attend college and $300,000,000 in matching-grants to assist the teaching of science. The residue was to be used to subsidize language teaching, graduate fellowships, vocational training, research on visual aids, and to train teachers in counseling.

The Agricultural Act of 1958 was a long step away from the time-honored policies of production controls and high price supports. It was also a triumph for Secretary Benson who had long since called for changes in the old parity idea. It was a remarkable recovery inasmuch as several Republicans had tried to force his resignation in February. Congress passed an act which ended acreage controls on corn, provided a price support of sixty-five per cent of parity with the farmer's approval, and allowed cotton producers either eighty per cent of parity with low-controlled acreage or sixty-five per cent of parity with high acreage. The act also cut rice supports to sixty-five per cent by 1962 and repealed the escalator clause in earlier farm legislation which permitted parities to rise as the surplus was reduced. The President insisted that this escalator clause had encouraged the formation of new surpluses. In accord with Eisenhower's request Congress also voted an extension of the Agricultural Trade Development and Assistance Act which permitted the sale of $2,250,000,000 in surplus crops abroad for foreign currency.

Two of the most controversial, but unsuccessful, measures before Congress in 1958 were aimed at curtailing the Supreme Court and organized labor. William Jenner and Senator John Marshall (an ironic name for a man who wished to weaken the Supreme Court) Butler of Maryland proposed a bill which would have made it a crime to advocate the forcible overthrow of the government thereby nullifying the Yates decision. Their act also reversed *Pennsylvania* v. *Nelson* in which the court had nullified forty-two state anti-subversive laws on the ground that the government, through the Smith Act, had preempted legislation in this field. The Senate appointed a Select Committee on Improper Activities in the Labor and Management Field under John McClellan, and during 1957 and 1958 its investigations into union corruption revealed shocking conditions. On March 24, 1958, after one year of investigation, the committee reported that union funds in excess of ten millions had been stolen, embezzled, or misused during a fifteen year period by officials of the union. The major target was the International Brotherhood of Teamsters, whose president, David Beck, was accused of taking more than $320,000 from the union's treasury between 1949 and 1953. Beck invoked the Fifth Amendment during his appearance before McClellan's committee and the AFL-CIO Executive Council, which had adopted an anti-racket code in 1957, suspended him as a council member and as an AFL-CIO vice president. In 1958 Beck was finally sentenced for stealing $1900 from his union on an automobile sale and in 1959 he was found guilty of tax evasion.

Another target was teamster vice president James R. Hoffa who was accused of corruption and racketeering. In spite of an eighty-two point indictment brought by McClellan's committee Hoffa was elected president of the union at its October 1957 convention. The AFL-CIO Executive Council suspended the teamsters and on petition of some union members an injunction was granted by the federal courts against Hoffa assuming office. In January 1958 the judge dissolved his injunction and agreed to let Hoffa assume the presidency if he consented to the appointment of three monitors to represent the court. Throughout 1958 Hoffa insisted he was not bound to follow the monitors' recommendations whereupon he appointed a committee headed by former Ohio Senator George H.

Bender. After a perfunctory investigation the committee reported that there was no evidence of corruption in the union.

At no time since 1945 was the demand for union controls stronger. There had always been a powerful element throughout the country determined to smash the unions but now it was reinforced by groups which normally were pro-union. Most Americans had come to realize that unions perform a salutary function in our society. In his volume on American capitalism, John Galbraith assigned the unions a significant role. It was Galbraith's contention that American big business enterprise inevitably led to monopolies, but that these were no longer to be feared because they were checked by "countervailing powers" which had transformed American business into a public benefactor. Galbraith contended that a strong labor union movement constitutes one of the most effective countervailing powers. The question in 1958 was how far the attack would go. Was it possible to control union corruption without weakening the labor movement itself? Labor controls bogged down in 1958 in Congress caught between the extremes of being too severe or not severe enough. The most important labor bill was introduced by Senators John F. Kennedy and Irving M. Ives, but it died in the House.

The pendulum had begun to swing in 1958.

The Democrats faced the 1958 election with a confident air. All signs pointed to victory. Popular concern over the recession, defense costs, the Russian scientific menace, and the mounting crises in the Far and Middle East offset whatever gains Eisenhower made in his congressional program. He was criticized more than before. He seemed to have lost his ability to meet emergencies. Rumors of resignation persisted and were intensified by his own report in January that he and Vice President Nixon had reached an agreement on how the latter would assume the presidential duties in the event of Ike's disability.

Despite the President's precautions against illness it was not his heart which failed him in 1958 but his strong right arm—Sherman Adams. As presidential assistant Adams had taken over most of the administrative routine of office. He was an indefatigable worker, astute and reliable, but his reputation tumbled when he was accused of accepting gifts in return for favors from industrialist Bernard Goldfine. Republican leaders recognized that since they had risen to power by denouncing Democratic corruption, Adams' conduct left them completely vulnerable in an election year. But the President refused to let him go. "I need him," was the

President's simple explanation. The first fruit of this decision came on September 8 when Democrat Edmund E. Muskie defeated Republican George Payne, who had also been accused of accepting Goldfine's gifts, in the Maine senatorial election. It was the first time that a Democrat had been popularly elected to the Senate from Maine. Nixon and other party leaders prevailed upon Eisenhower to accept Adams' resignation on September 22. He was replaced by General Wilton B. Persons. However it was too late; the damage had been done.

When comedian Bob Hope said that the 1958 election made Alf Landon look good, he was more nearly right than he imagined. The Democrats elected more congressmen and controlled more statehouses than they had since 1936. They elected 282 Representatives to the House and twenty-five Democratic Governors which raised their occupancies of executive mansions to thirty-four. They elected twenty-six Senators to increase their Senate total to sixty-two, the largest number since 1940. Then, on November 25, Alaska capped the climax by electing a Governor, two Senators, and a Representative—all Democrats. The *Congressional Quarterly Almanac* attributed the Democratic victory to four factors: the recession, the farmers, the Negroes, and the weakness of Republican organization in some areas. These findings were borne out by the *U. S. News & World Report's* statistical summary on November 14, 1958. Wage earners gave their greater support to the Democratic party. The Republicans lost forty-nine congressional districts and in twenty-eight of them the "blue collar" workers constituted approximately fifty per cent of the inhabitants. The recession and union agitation accelerated this trend in the labor vote. The unions spared no effort in turning out the labor vote particularly in those six states where right-to-work laws had been submitted to the electorate. Kansas approved such a law but similar ones were rejected in California, Colorado, Idaho, and Washington. Many who turned out to reject right-to-work laws may have also taken time to reject the Republican candidates. In 1952 only three Democrats had been elected to the House in the twenty major farming districts, but in 1958 thirteen Democrats were elected. In nine midwestern states; Indiana, Illinois, Wisconsin, Iowa, Minnesota, Nebraska, Kansas, and the Dakotas, the Democrats replaced nineteen Republican congressmen, while the Republicans replaced but one Democrat. Two of the four Republican senators seeking re-election were replaced by Democrats in Indiana and Minnesota and Democrats also replaced Republican Governors in Wisconsin, South Dakota, Nebraska and re-elected Governors in Kansas, Iowa and Minnesota. There were thirty-five districts outside the South in which Negroes constituted more than ten per cent of the voting population. In 1956 the Republicans elected seven seats in these areas but only three in 1958. The Democratic party seemed to be re-establishing the coalition of labor-farm-Negro voters which had sustained it during the Roosevelt-Truman era.

In 1956 Eisenhower had carried the seventeen states in which the Republicans lost the governorships and the Senate seats in 1958. He also carried forty-nine Congressional districts in which his party candidates lost. His personal victories were not accompanied by the creation of strong Republican machines. There were also thirty-two districts in which Republicans who had been elected with Eisenhower in 1956 did not stand for re-election. The Republicans retained only eighteen of these in 1958. Of the thirteen Republican Senators who had been elected with Eisenhower in 1952 only five survived in 1958.

As 1959 began it did not appear that the Eighty-sixth Congress would find solutions to the civil rights, farm, and labor problems. Powerful, conservative Democrats, well versed in the art of bottling legislation, controlled important committees. The very size of the majority would encourage sniping. Even Roosevelt found it difficult to hold an overwhelming majority in line and in 1959 a Republican President was bound to find the task much greater.

The results of the election left the President bewildered and unhappy. "The United States did give me, after all, a majority of I think well over 9,000,000 votes. Now here, only two years later, there is a complete reversal; yet I do not see where there is anything that these people consciously want the administration to do differently," he told reporters. Yet the administration had been rebuked and it was not without reason. Columnist Walter Lippman wrote that in 1958 the people really wanted the government "to come alive and to be alert and to show vigor, and not to keep mouthing the same old slogans, and not to dawdle along in the same old ruts . . . the President has lost touch with them, and with their problems, and is living in the past" Lippman further explained that usually, approximately fifteen years after a major war, "there occurs a big political change marked by the passing of the war generation and the advent of the generation which had no responsibility for, even though it participated in, the war." The pendulum had begun to swing in 1958.

The Old Guard Republican Senators took a heavy pounding. The

133

conservatives could take comfort only in the victory of Barry Goldwater in Arizona, a victory which he achieved in spite of an all-out labor campaign against him. The elections seemed to signalize a victory for the liberal forces in both parties although liberals were unable to defeat Faubus for a third term in Arkansas and that state's moderate Representative Brooks Hays was displaced by a write-in vote for the outspoken segregationist Dale Alford. Perhaps the most significant campaign occurred in New York where Republican millionaire Nelson A. Rockefeller ruined Democratic Governor Averell Harriman's presidential hopes by defeating him in the gubernatorial race. Rockefeller raised his own presidential prospects. Up to that moment Nixon had been the heir-apparent but Rockefeller's victory, coupled with the defeat of Californias Knowland and Goodwin J. Knight for the governorship and Senate seat, weakened Nixon's chances. This delighted the Democrats who emerged from the campaign with a number of presidential candidates of their own. Nixon's position was further complicated by a strange political anachronism. He was a young man grown old before his time. In years he belonged to the generation now striding decisively to the political stage, but his career had actually begun earlier with the men who were now being repudiated. With which group were the voters to identify him?

To Eisenhower the repudiation meant that the "spenders" were in power and they would have to be kept down. He promised to fight for economy. With each move to the left, Eisenhower moved to the right. Rockefeller's victory indicated support for any candidate identified with a forward-looking policy. In the midst of a Republican catastrophe, he and other like-minded Republicans had floated into office on, of all things, a Democratic wave. This seemed to prove that the wave cut across party lines. It was not a party the voters wanted to support but men with acceptable ideas. To cry out against the "spenders' was to deny the crushing needs of mid-century America. Roads, slum clearance, urban renewal, schools, medical care, power for the growing West, conservation, housing, and peaceful application of atomic energy were only some of those needs and the public seemed intent on having them. It was up to the party in power to find the means for a high level of national defense and at the same time stimulate the production of enough goods and services to meet those needs. The President could no longer be a disinterested spectator nor continue to pose as a liberal in human matters and a conservative in economic matters. These two elements were being driven closer together and the barrier that heretofore had separated them was crumbling.

Bibliography

This bibliography suggests a few titles available from the abundance of excellent volumes written since 1945. I am particularly indebted to these authors. The student can find additional works listed in the *Harvard Guide to American History*. The student's particular attention is called to the following works: *Documents on American Foreign Relations* (Boston and Princeton, 1938—), *U. S. in World Affairs* (New York, 1932—). The *Headline Series* contains many excellent studies on international problems written by experts. The *Annual Volume* of the *Americana* encyclopedia, the *Britannica Book of the Year,* and the *New International Yearbook* are mines of valuable information as are *Facts on File, Keesing's Contemporary Archives,* the *World Almanac, Information Please Almanac,* and *Congressional Quarterly Almanac.* The following works, which are part of my regular reading fare, will be of invaluable assistance to students in keeping abreast of current developments: *The Annals of the American Academy of Political and Social Science, The Atlantic Monthly, Current History, Foreign Affairs, Foreign Policy Bulletin, Harper's Magazine, The Nation, New Republic, Newsweek, New York Times, The Reporter, Time, U. S. News & World Report.* In my courses in contemporary history and twentieth century America I have used Oscar T. Barck and Nelson Blake, *Since 1900. A History of the United States in Our Times,* (New York, 1952), Arthur Link, *American Epoch. A History of the United States since the 1890's,* (New York, 1955), Harvey Wish, *Contemporary America. The National Scene since 1900,* (New York, 1955), and J. Hampden Jackson, *The World in the Postwar Decade, 1945-1955,* (Boston, 1956).

Agar, Herbert. *The Price of Power: America since 1945* (Chicago, 1957).

Allen, Frederick L. *The Big Chance* (New York, 1952).

Anderson, Jack and Ronald W. May. *McCarthy: the Man, the Senator, The Ism* (Boston, 1952).

Barth, Alan. *Government by Investigation* (New York, 1955).

——. *The Loyalty of Free Men* (New York, 1951).

Beal, John Robinson. *John Foster Dulles: A Biography* (New York, 1957).

Berle, Adolf A. *Tides of Crisis: A Primer of Foreign Relations* (New York, 1957).

Bingham, J. B. *Shirt-Sleeve Diplomacy: Point 4 in Action* (New York, 1954).

Bolles, Blair. *The Big Change in Europe* (New York, 1958).

Brown, John Mason. *Through These Men: Some Aspects of Our Passing History* (New York, 1956).

Byrnes, James F. *All in One Lifetime* (New York, 1958).

——. *Speaking Frankly* (New York, 1947).

Campbell, John C. *Defense of the Middle East* (New York, 1958).

Carleton, W. G. *Revolution in American Foreign Policy* (New York, 1957).

Castle, Eugene W. *The Great Giveaway* (Chicago, 1957).

Caughey, John W. *In Clear and Present Danger. The Crucial State of Our Freedoms*. (Chicago, 1958).

Chambers, Whittaker. *Witness* (New York, 1952).

Cheever, Daniel S. and H. Field Haviland. *Organizing for Peace: International Organization in World Affairs* (Boston, 1954).

Childs, Marquis. *Eisenhower: Captive Hero. A Critical Study of the General and the President* (New York, 1958).

Commager, Henry Steele. *Freedom, Loyalty, Dissent* (New York, 1954).

Cooke, Allistair. *A Generation on Trial: U. S. A. v. Alger Hiss.* (New York, 1950).

Daniels, Jonathan. *The Man of Independence* (Philadelphia, 1950).

Davis, Elmer. *But We Were Born Free* (Indianapolis, 1954).

Davis, Kenneth S. *A Prophet in His Own Country: The Triumphs and Defeats of Adlai E. Stevenson* (Garden City, 1957).

——. *Soldier of Democracy: A Biography of Dwight Eisenhower* (Garden City, 1952).

Davison, W. Philip. *The Berlin Blockade: A Study of Cold war Politics* (Princeton, 1958).

de Toledano, Ralph. *Nixon* (New York, 1956).

Divine, R. A. *American Immigration Policy 1924-1957* (New Haven, 1957).

Donovan, Robert J. *Eisenhower: The Inside Story* (New York, 1956).

Drucker, Peter F. *America's Next Twenty Years* (New York, 1957).

Ellis, Harry B. *Israel and the Middle East* (New York, 1957).

Feis, Herbert. *The China Tangle: The American Effort in China from Pearl Harbor to the Marshall Mission* (Princeton, 1953).

Fifield, Russell H. *The Diplomacy of Southeast Asia, 1945-1958* (New York, 1958).

Finletter, Thomas K. *Foreign Policy: The Next Phase.* (New York, 1958).

——. *U.S. Foreign Policy and Military Power in the Hydrogen Age* (New York, 1954).

Franklin, Jay. *Republicans on the Potomac. The New Republicans in Action* (New York, 1953).

Galbraith, John Kenneth. *The Affluent Society.* (Boston, 1958).

——. *American Capitalism, the Concept of Countervailing Power* (Boston, 1952).

Gavin, James M. *War and Peace in the Space Age* (New York, 1958).

Gervasi, Frank. *Big Government: The Meaning and Purpose of the Hoover Commission Report* (New York, 1949).

Goldman, Eric F. *The Crucial Decade. America, 1945-1955* (New York, 1956).

Graebner, Norman A. *The New Isolationism: A Study in Politics and Foreign Policy since 1950* (New York, 1956).

Gunther, John and Bernard Quint. *Days to Remember, America, 1945-1955.* (New York, 1955).

——. *The Riddle of MacArthur* (New York, 1951).

Harris, Louis. *Is There a Republican Majority? Political Trends, 1952-1956* (New York, 1954).

Hillman, William. *Mr. President. The First Publication from the Personal Diaries, Private Letters, Papers, and Revealing Interviews of Harry S. Truman* (New York, 1952).

Hurewitz, Jacob C. *Middle Eastern Dilemmas: The Background of United States Policy* (New York, 1953).

Jones, Joseph M. *The Fifteen Weeks, February 21-June 5, 1947* New York, 1955).

Jowett, William A. *The Strange Case of Alger Hiss* (Garden City, 1953).

Kennan, George F. *Realities of American Foreign Policy* (Princeton, 1954).

——. *Russia, the Atom and the West* (New York, 1957).

Kintner, W. R. *Forging a New Sword: A Study of the Department of Defense* (New York, 1958).

Kissinger, Henry A. *Nuclear Weapons and Foreign Policy* (New York, 1957).

Knappen, Marshall. *An Introduction to American Foreign Policy* (New York, 1956).

Koenig, Louis W. (ed.) *The Truman Administration. Its Principles and Practice.* (New York, 1956).

Larson, Arthur. *A Republican Looks at His Party* (New York, 1956).

Lerner, Max. *Actions and Passions. Notes on the Multiple Revolution of Our Time* (New York, 1949).

Lubbell, Samuel. *The Future of American Politics* (New York, 1952).

——. *Revolt of the Moderates* (New York, 1956).

Lattimore, Owen. *Ordeal by Slander.* (Boston, 1950).

Lohbeck, Don. *Patrick J. Hurley* (Chicago, 1956).

Major Problems of United States Foreign Policy, 1949-1954 (4 vols. Washington, 1949-1954).

Ridgway, Matthew B. *Soldier: The Memoirs of Matthew B. Ridgway* as told to Harold H. Martin (New York, 1956).

Millis, Harry A. and E. C. Brown. *From the Wagner Act to Taft-Hartley* (Chicago, 1950).

Millis, Walter and E. S. Duffield (eds.) *The Forrestal Diaries* (New York, 1951).

Moore, Ben T. *NATO and the Future of Europe* (New York, 1958).

Osgood, Robert E. *Ideals and Self-Interest in America's Foreign Relations: The Great Transformation of the Twentieth Century* (Chicago, 1958).

——. *Limited War. The Challenge to American Strategy* (Chicago, 1957).

Payne, Robert. *The Marshall Story* (New York, 1951).

Poats, Rutherford M. *Decision in Korea.* (New York, 1954).

Potter, David M. *People of Plenty: Economic Abundance and the American Character* (Chicago, 1954).

Price, Harry B. *The Marshall Plan and Its Meaning* (Ithaca, 1955).

Pusey, Merlo J. *Eisenhower the President* (New York, 1956).

Reischauer, Edwin O. *Wanted: An Asian Policy* (New York, 1953).

——. *The United States and Japan* (Cambridge, 1957).

Reitzel, William, Morton A. Kaplan and Constance G. Coblenz. *United States Foreign Policy, 1945-1955* (Washington, 1956).

Roberts, Henry L. *Russia and America, Dangers and Prospects* (New York, 1956).

Rorty, James and Moshe Decter. *McCarthy and the Communists* (Boston, 1954).

Rovere, Richard. *Affairs of State. The Eisenhower Years* (New York, 1956).

———. and Arthur M. Schlesinger Jr. *The General and the President* New York, 1951).

Smith, Merriman. *Meet Mister Eisenhower* (New York, 1955).

Sobel, Lester A. *National Issues: A Facts on File Handbook* (New York, 1956).

Strausz-Hupé, Robert, Alvin J. Cottrell and James E. Dougherty (eds.) *American-Asian Tensions* (New York, 1956).

Truman, Harry S. *Memoirs* (2 vols. Garden City, 1955-1956).

Vandenberg Jr., Arthur H. *The Private Papers of Senator Vandenberg* (Boston, 1952).

Vinacke, Harold M. *Far Eastern Politics in the Postwar Period* (New York, 1956).

———. *The United States and the Far East, 1945 - 1951* (Stanford, 1952).

Wade, William W. *U.S. Policy in Asia* (New York, 1955).

Weyl, Nathaniel. *Battle Against Disloyalty* (New York, 1951).

White, Theodore. *Fire in the Ashes: Europe in Mid-Century* (New York, 1953).

White, William S. *The Taft Story* (New York, 1954).

Willoughby, Charles A. and John Chamberlain. *MacArthur: 1941-1951* (New York, 1954).

The Author

William Frank Zornow was born in Cleveland and resides in Mentor, Ohio. He has taught at Western Reserve University, where he received his A.B., A.M., and Ph. D., degrees, Case Institute of Technology, The University of Akron, Washburn University of Topeka, and Kansas State College. He is currently a member of the history department of The Kent State University.

Mr. Zornow's published works include *Lincoln and the Party Divided,* (The University of Oklahoma Press, 1954). This book is on the authoritative list of basic Lincolniana compiled in 1957 by Lincoln scholar Ralph G. Newman for *Civil War History*. He is the author of *Kansas: A History of the Jayhawk State,* (The University of Oklahoma Press, 1957), which was cited as a 1958 Award of Merit winner by the American Association of State and Local History. He has contributed chapters to *Kansas: The First Century,* (4 vols., Lewis Historical Publishing Company, 1956) and *Abraham Lincoln A New Portrait,* (G. P. Putnam's Sons, 1959), and is the author of many articles for various historical journals.

Guide to Abbreviations

A *Reader's Guide to Abbreviated Nomenclature,*
Alphabetical Agencies and Organizations
Cited in this Book

AFL	American Federation of Labor
ADA	Americans for Democratic Action
AEC	Atomic Energy Commission
ANZUS	Australia, New Zealand, United States Security Treaty
CIA	Central Intelligence Agency
CEEC	Committee of European Economic Cooperation
CIO	Congress of Industrial Organizations
DEW	Distant Early Warning
ECA	Economic Cooperation Administration
Euratom	European Atomic Community
ECSC	European Coal and Steel Community
EEC	European Economic Community
EDC	European Defense Community
ERP	European Recovery Program
FEPC	Fair Employment Practices Commission or Committee
FBI	Federal Bureau of Investigation
FHA	Federal Housing Administration
FOA	Foreign Operations Administration
ICBM	Intercontinental Ballistic Missile
IRBM	Intermediate Range Ballistic Missile
ICA	International Cooperation Administration
IIA	International Information Administration
JCS	Joint Chiefs of Staff
METO	Middle Eastern Treaty Organization
MRP	Mouvement Républicaine Populaire
MSA	Mutual Security Agency
NAM	National Association of Manufacturers
NAACP	National Association for the Advancement of Colored People

NSC	National Security Council
NATO	North Atlantic Treaty Organization
ODM	Office of Defense Mobilization
ODT	Office of Defense Transportation
OMGUS	Office of the Military Government of the United States
OPA	Office of Price Administration
OWMR	Office of War Mobilization and Reconversion
OAS	Organization of American States
OEEC	Organization of European Economic Cooperation
RFC	Reconstruction Finance Corporation
ROK	Republic of Korea
RPF	Rassemblement du Peuple Français
SEATO	Southeast Asian Treaty Organization
SAC	Strategic Air Command
SCAP	Supreme Commander for Allied Powers
SHAPE	Supreme Headquarters for Allied Powers Europe
TCA	Technical Cooperation Administration
TVA	Tennessee Valley Authority
USSR	Union of Soviet Socialist Republics
UAR	United Arab Republic
UAW	United Automobile Workers
UMW	United Mine Workers
UN	United Nations
USIA	United States Information Agency
UMT	Universal Military Training
WPB	War Production Board
WEU	Western European Union
WU	Western Union

Index

145

Minimum Wage Law: 18, 79
Missiles: 60, 87, 101, 103, 105-107, 112
Mitchell, James P.: 15, 79, 115, 126
Mollet, Guy: 71, 72, 101
Molotov, Vyacheslav: 24, 28, 59, 67, 70, 93, 102
Morocco: 38, 65, 68
Morse, Wayne: 9, 44, 91
Murphy, Robert: 69, 97, 108
Nasser, Gamal Abdel: 37, 38, 67-70, 72, 74, 95-97
National Defense: 23, 26-28, 45, 57, 62, 85, 86, 87, 100, 101, 111, 116, 128
National Defense Education Act: 129
Nehru, Jawaharlal: 31, 38, 40, 111
Nepal: 64, 98
The Netherlands: 25, 102
New Deal: 1, 11, 54, 88
New Zealand: 33, 35
Nixon, Richard M.: 3, 5, 6, 8, 33, 54, 87-89, 111, 119, 131, 134
Norstad, Lauris: 101
North Atlantic Treaty Organization: 1, 2, 15, 21, 26, 28, 29, 39, 40, 58, 59, 61, 101, 102, 105, 109, 112
Norway: 61
Offshore Islands: 36, 62, 63, 98, 99, 105, 111
Open Sky Plan: 59, 103, 105
Organization for Trade Co-operation: 62
Organization of American States: 38, 39
Outer Continental Shelf Lands Act: 45
Pacific Charter: 35, 36
Pakistan: 35, 37, 38, 65, 66, 95, 98, 111
Philippine Islands: 15, 32, 35, 65, 98
Pinay, Antoine: 58
Pineau, Christian: 70, 71
Pleven, René: 25
Poland: 58, 64, 70
Portugal: 64
Powell, Adams Clayton: 48, 82
Presidential Succession: 119
President's Asian Development Fund: 65
Price Controls: 44
Public Health: 48
Public Housing: 46
Public Power, 14, 18, 45, 83, 84
Radford, Arthur W.: 27, 33, 62
Randall, Clarence B.: 23, 28
Rayburn, Sam: 44, 77, 116, 127
Recession: 49, 50, 124-127
Reciprocal Trade Agreements Act: 23, 45, 127
Reconstruction Finance Corporation: 45

34